Rik Dovey/Sally Samins

12-METRE
THE NEW BREED

The Battle For The 26th America's Cup

©
R·P·Y·C
AMERICA'S
CUP 1987

Rik Dovey/Sally Samins

12-METRE
THE NEW BREED

The Battle For The 26th America's Cup

Ellsyd Press – Sydney

Sally Samins' worldwide travel during 1985/1986 to take these photographs was funded by the Honeywell Corporation.

First published 1986 by Ellsyd Press Pty Ltd,
an imprint of David Ell Press,
137-139 Regent Street, Chippendale 2008, Australia

Designed by Patrick Coyle & Associates
Art Direction by John Byrne
Typeset by Computer Integrated Art, Sydney
Printed by Walter Alteri Printing, Melbourne, Australia

National Library of Australia
Cataloguing-in-Publication Data
Dovey, Rik.
12-metre, the new breed: the battle for the 26th America's Cup.
ISBN 0 949290 03 3.
1. America's Cup races. 2. Yachts and yachting – Australia. I. Samins, Sally. II. Title. III. Title: Twelve-metre, the new breed: the battle for the 26th America's Cup.
797.1'4

FOREWORD

Ben Lexcen

The 12-Metre is an amazing yacht. These dinosaurs of yachting are built to a rule that is so out of date that if it were not for the America's Cup they would have been long extinct. Instead, they represent the ultimate in yachting technology and the end result is more sophisticated than even a Formula One racing car. In fact, the only products more sophisticated today are those used by the Russians and the Americans to probe space.

I first became interested in 12-Metre design in 1967, when I saw Australia's second 12-Metre yacht *Dame Pattie* thrashed by that era's superboat, *Intrepid*. Thanks to the generosity of Alan Bond, since 1972 I've done little else except design 12-Metre yachts.

We started with *Southern Cross*, which was also thrashed in 1974. From that time we kept our little group alive so that we would keep learning what it took to succeed. Sometimes we knew we had no chance of winning, but it was important to "hang in" to keep our America's Cup culture developing.

Australia II's success in 1983 was the culmination of getting it all together over those long and often frustrating years. Part of our success was due to our attitude: we did not just have to copy the successful defenders.

Developing the revolutionary *Australia II* was made possible by Alan Bond's approach to the Cup which, in its own way, is quite revolutionary. Unlike other designers, I was given a free hand to explore new avenues of development within the Rule. Too often, America's Cup yachts were the work of designers who had their hands tied by unimaginative syndicates insisting on a conservative approach. The results inevitably yielded little development.

Australia II has provided a marvellous service to all yacht designers who have the ability to add imagination to creativity. She opened a Pandora's Box – and who knows where that will lead. I know I am exploring the ramifications of *Australia II* even further with my new boats for Australia's first defence of the America's Cup. All other yacht designers also face the challenge of exploring that Pandora's Box. If the result of their work and their massive research programs is a string of conservative versions of *Australia II* in Perth in 1987 then I will be disappointed.

The freedom of the 12-Metre Rule, with its minimum restrictions, gives designers the opportunity to explore new ideas and different answers to age-old problems. With the big budgets supporting us, this is our best opportunity to break barriers of design tradition resulting not just in better 12-Metre yachts but better yachts of all sizes and classes.

Examining the growth of the 12-Metre class gives designers and yachtsmen many insights into possible developments. Always we must study history because it puts us on the right track and shows us the pitfalls.

12-Metre – The New Breed is a clear, concise account of the history of this fascinating class and a comprehensive guide to the players in the 26th America's Cup.

Sally Samins is the best pictorial chronicler of the America's Cup that I know; her photographs never cease to amaze me. And Rik Dovey succeeds in putting a highly complicated and technical subject into terms that bring it within the grasp of all, not just yachtsmen.

Australia's first defence of the America's Cup is going to be a momentous occasion in the history of international sport. *12-Metre – The New Breed* is an invaluable guide to this, the latest battle in the war that is the America's Cup.

Seaforth, New South Wales
September 1986

N308

CONTENTS

INTRODUCTION

12-Metres: Yachting's Ultimate Weapons

Today's 12-Metre yacht is without doubt the most sophisticated and expensive piece of sporting equipment in the world. Thanks to *Australia II* winning the America's Cup in 1983, yacht, rig and sail designers have unprecedented and, in some instances, unlimited budgets at call to try to come up with an edge in speed so that their yachts' professional crews have a better chance of victory in what has become the world's most prestigious ''sporting'' event, even eclipsing the Olympic Games.

When Australia ended sport's longest winning streak to win the America's Cup in 1983, the sport of yachting was revolutionised. In seven countries around the globe, more than 30 yacht designers began to labour feverishly to come up with Twelves which they now hope will be just that fraction faster and more manoeuvrable than those of their rivals.

In their search for success they have harnessed the resources of the world's best research and engineering bodies, within both government and private sectors. Names such as Aerospatiele, NASA, Boeing, Grumman Airspace and Macchi have become commonplace in yacht club bars everywhere.

The world's leading computer companies have vied with each other to put their powerful resources in the hands of the designers. The world's finest mathematical brains have developed new software programs enabling them to test theories and thousands of variations before committing themselves to thorough tests in the most sophisticated tanks, normally used for military and civilian shipping.

More than $200 million has been spent on the 12-Metre yachts endeavouring to be the first to win four races in the 26th America's Cup, beginning 31 January 1986. Similar amounts have been donated in the form of goods and expertise.

All this for a class of yacht born in 1907 in an overall effort to get some order into what was then a totally disorganised sport. The 12-Metre yacht is an old fashioned design that has never been popular worldwide and which would be extinct by now if it were not for the America's Cup.

In that year representatives of yacht clubs from 13 nations met in London to form the International Yacht Racing Union, which still controls the sport today. At the same time they developed an International Rule which laid down metric formulas for boats that would measure 5, 6, 7, 8, 9, 10, 12, 15, 19 and 23 metres. This measurement does not relate to the yacht's length; rather, it is a complex series of calculations aimed at allowing different yachts to compete with each other and be fairly handicapped. The Metre Rule also encourages strength, seaworthiness and longevity in construction. Yacht owners made up the IYRU and it was in their own interests to develop a rule which would not allow dramatic developments making their expensive craft obsolete overnight. So, while they framed the Rule to allow development, they made sure they included sufficient provisions to keep the hands of designers tied reasonably tightly. They were very successful. In the entire history of the class only two yachts have succeeded in ''breaking'' the Rule: *Intrepid* (1967) and *Australia II* (1983).

In the interests of seaworthiness, the IYRU also stipulated that yachts built to the Rule had to comply with Lloyds scantling standards which define minimum construction strengths in the hull and rig. There were other requirements, too, such as the size of bulkheads and fittings for accommodation. The result was strongly built, heavy displacement yachts.

Inherent in the Rule were provisions that encouraged multi-purpose 12-Metre boats. The Twelves were racer/cruisers with full accommodation below in their sleek hulls so their crews could live aboard as they sailed the busy summer regatta circuit.

Before the Metre Rule was introduced, various handicap systems, usually involving waterline length, sail area and displacement, estimated the difference in yachts' speeds. Handicap corrections were applied to finishing times and races decided by these corrected times. With the Metre Rule, its inventors planned to reduce the differences between yachts and have them race against each other equally, with the first yacht to cross the finish line declared the winner.

The Rule established a formula in which the yacht would finish up "measuring" 12 metres which was updated constantly (see current Rule, p. 158).

$$\text{Rating (12 metres)} = \frac{L \div B + \tfrac{1}{2}G + 3d + \tfrac{1}{3}\sqrt{SA} - F}{2}$$

L = Waterline length corrected by penalties for excessive overhangs out of the water in the bow and the stern.
B = Maximum beam.
G = Skin girth, measured around the hull's surface, waterline to waterline, at a point 60 per cent of the waterline length aft.
D = Difference between the skin girth and the chain girth measured at the same point of the hull. (Skin girth follows the line of the hull, whereas chain girth takes a straight line from the bottom of the keel to the turn of the bilge.)
SA = Area of the mainsail plus topsail plus 100 per cent of the foretriangle.
F = Freeboard.

Length overall, draft and displacement were not included in the formula; instead they were subjected to certain restrictions.

Displacement and seaworthiness were encouraged in two ways. Greater freeboard implied a drier and safer platform for the crew, and by including it as a subtraction in the formula, designers would have a lower rating. Similarly, the smallest measurement between the two girths encouraged displacement and gave the designer a lower rating, which meant that to have his yacht measure 12 metres and be legal, he could then increase waterline length or sail area, his principal factors in increasing speed.

Caledonia, designed to this Rule by successful Englishman David Boyd, measured:

Length overall..... 72 ft 6 in (22.098 m)
Length waterline.. 46 ft 0 in (14.021 m)
Beam............... 11 ft 10 in (3.606 m)
Draft............... 9 ft 0 in (2.743 m)
Displacement...... 25.25 tons (26,670 kg)
Sail area........... 1,800 sq ft (167.23 sq m)

The International Rule was developed by 13 European and Scandinavian nations, and after they revised it in 1919 to discourage gaff-rigged yachts, the 6, 8 and 12-Metre yachts began to grow in popularity. By 1920 nearly forty 12-Metres were racing regularly.

Yachtsmen from the United States remained unimpressed by the European formula, preferring to draw up their own Universal Rule five years later. Unlike the International Rule which designated its classes by linear metre ratings (6, 12, etc), America's Universal boats were designated alphabetically (J, M, R). The American Rule met with success in its first years but as it contained considerably fewer restrictions, the Americans were forced into continued amendments as the designers found loopholes.

As they watched the development of particularly the 6 and 12-Metre classes across the Atlantic, American yachtsmen realised they were "missing" the boat and rectified the situation with typical style.

In 1928 the New York design firm of Burgess, Rigg and Morgan designed a 12-Metre and had six boats built to the plan in Germany for American owners. The well-known German boatbuilders Abeking and Rasmussen built the boats from timber but added steel frames.

Measuring in at 69 ft 2 in (21.05 m) overall in length, 42 ft 11 in (13.1 m) on the waterline and with a sail area of 1,970 sq ft (183 sq m), these yachts were somewhat smaller than their average European counterparts. Their successful debut prompted further interest, with three more being ordered from Scandinavia and Great Britain by American owners eager to join this new class of racing. Encouraged by the success of the 12-Metre formula in the USA, the IYRU further modified the Rule in 1936. Seaworthiness and longevity were increased, while sail area was reduced to around 1,800 sq ft (167.22 sq m). This effectively eliminated masthead rigs (where the headsail is rigged from the masthead) and led to the large overlapping genoas later adopted by all modern high-aspect racing yachts.

American owners were quickly recognising the attributes of the 12-Metres which had appealed to their counterparts in Europe. The yachts were fast (capable of 7 knots to windward and more under spinnaker), roomy below with ample, comfortable accommodation, and sufficiently seaworthy for offshore cruising. Unlike many of the boats developed under their Universal Rule, the Twelves were more than day racers requiring big crews to handle their big rigs. Until the 1960s the Rule required that Twelves be fitted out with stoves, a head and accommodation. Some were also fitted with motors.

In addition, the fact that they were built to strict Lloyds guidelines meant that they lasted for years. Yachts from the original fleets are still sailing today in all countries where the class developed. The initial interest in foreign-built Twelves in the US began to attract the attention of the country's best yacht designers. One of two local yachts launched in 1935 was designed by L. Francis Herreshoff, son of the legendary Nat Herreshoff who had designed six successful J Class defenders of the America's Cup between 1893 and 1920.

Three years later Olin Stephens of the leading design company Sparkman & Stephens was commissioned to design three Twelves for new owners. One was Harold Vanderbilt, who had twice successfully defended the America's Cup. His new yacht *Vim* was to become the benchmark for 12-Metre design until the 1970s.

After her launch *Vim* was taken to England in 1939 where she thrashed the cream of the European fleet of Twelves, winning 21 of her 27 starts. However, World War II broke out and the yacht was laid up. It was not until 1958 that she was restored to her prime for the first America's Cup to be contested in 12-Metres. Although the yacht was almost 20 years old she went very close to defending the Cup, being beaten in the final elimination races by an average margin of just half a miunte. The yacht that went on to successfully defend the Cup, *Columbia,* had been designed by none other than Olin Stephens.

Vim's career subsequently included an important role in Australia's entry into the America's Cup in 1962. She was purchased by Sir Frank Packer as trial horse for his first Twelve, *Gretel*, designed by Alan Payne.

The clear superiority of *Vim* is believed by many to have played a role in the decision by the holders of the America's Cup to revive the Cup after World War II.

The America's Cup had begun in England in 1851, when the New York Yacht Club schooner *America* beat the cream of the British racing fleet to depart with the 100 Guinea Cup. Renamed the America's Cup, the New York Yacht Club later invited other nations to challenge and mounted its first defence campaign against England in 1870. Before the Second World War, America successfully defended the Cup against the English, Scottish and Canadians 16 times, first in schooners and then in the mighty J Class boats.

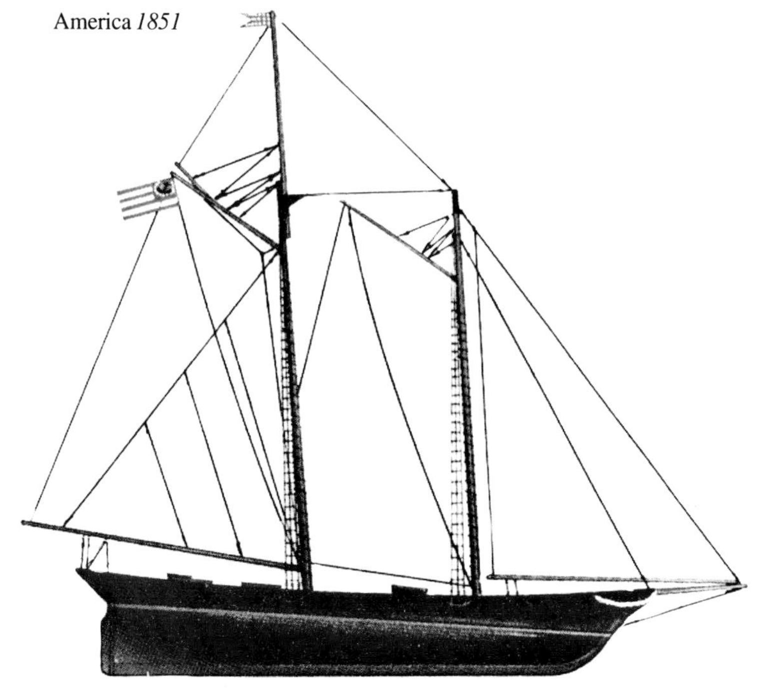

America *1851*

Olin Stephens in Perth in 1986 – retired but still actively interested.

The first yachts were huge floating platforms for monstrous spreads of sail area. The biggest was *Reliance*, which successfully defended against Sir Thomas Lipton's *Shamrock III* in 1903. From the tip of her bowsprit to the end of her main boom measured 202 ft (61.56 m). An astonishing 40 per cent of that was in her long overhangs, which gave her an effective waterline length of 130 ft (39.6 m) when she was heeled, and a theoretical hull speed of 12 knots to windward. Aloft she spread 16,159 sq ft (1501.17 sq m) of sail. Her crew of 64 were not just there to handle the huge rig; their weight was also needed to help keep the yacht upright.

Finally accepting that America's Cup yachts had become dangerous (one crewman was killed when a mast broke on a British yacht during a training sail), the New York Yacht Club agreed that the Cup should be contested in J Class boats under the Universal Rule. These were undoubtedly the finest looking craft ever created, with long, lean hulls supporting towering cutter rigs. Sadly, their reign was cut short by the Second World War. The Js were expensive, costing well over $1 million, and almost all were cut up to become fighter planes and weapons of war. As the world recovered from the War, it became obvious that the Big Boat era was dead. In the 1940s, no-one could afford a J Boat.

In 1948 Britain and America decided to revive the America's Cup with yachts that should be ocean racers with lives after the Cup. However, under the Deed of Gift, the Cup had to be contested in yachts with a waterline length of at least 65 ft (19.81 m). That meant a yacht more expensive than anyone involved was prepared to build, so the Cup languished for a further decade.

Advised by Britain's Royal Yacht Squadron that it would be prepared to challenge in 12-Metres, the NYYC eventually changed the Deed of Gift and Britain challenged in 1958. The decision gave the 12-Metre class a new lease of life. With renewed interest and quickly growing popularity in ocean and small boat racing, the old-fashioned 12-Metres were in danger of becoming relics of a bygone metre boat era.

Happy in the knowledge that it had the fastest 12-Metre in the world with *Vim*, the New York Yacht Club also had the advantage of other owners commissioning new yachts. Finally it was Olin Stephens' newest design *Columbia* that only narrowly edged out *Vim* to face the latest 12-Metre from England. Looking for an edge over *Vim*, Stephens had designed a Twelve that was slightly better in the heavier weather that is typical in Newport in September.

Sceptre, the British challenger, was the work of a man who had never designed a 12-Metre before, David Boyd. He had been invited, along with three other designers, to submit two models for tank testing. His final selection was not surprising as he had designed the 6-Metre *Circe* which had won the Sewanakawa Cup from America. Boyd fully understood the 12-Metre rule as it was exactly double the rating of the Six.

When his new Twelve went public for the first time it shocked many. They saw that he had given it a cockpit arrangement and deck layout exactly the same as a 6-Metre, with the boat only half decked and most of the crew below the gunwale. The rule insisting on accommodation below had been dropped and Boyd exploited it. This made a lot of sense. Weight eliminated from the deck could be put into the keel to increase stability, and by having most of the crew and their heavy winch equipment lower, stability could be further improved.

Good boats alone do not win yacht races, it also takes good sails, tactics and crew work. Most experienced yachtsmen agree that the three share equal responsibility for success. When the untested *Sceptre* with her untried crew arrived in Newport they ran smack into *Columbia* which had won the right to defend after a rigorous elimination series of 40 close races against three other yachts. Her crew work and tactics were honed to near perfection, and she had the choice of the best synthetic Dacron sails from the wardrobes of all four yachts.

Columbia *1958*

American yachtsmen raised their eyebrows when they first set eyes on the hull of *Sceptre*. Used to the fine entry of their hulls, they noted that Boyd had given his yacht full, almost bulbous sections for'ard. At the stern the yachts were also opposites with *Sceptre* having a fine run aft while Columbia displayed comparatively full lines. Many recalled the lessons of the first "Cup" in 1851 when the schooner *America* thrashed the beamy British yachts, their full entries causing massive water resistance.

As it turned out, the British failed badly in all three areas needed to win a yacht race. The Americans, with better sails, crew work and tactics, and a faster yacht, thrashed the English 4-0. *Sceptre* never showed the speed of *Columbia*, and the British showed themselves to be well behind in the technology race. It was an embarrassing setback for the British, from which they have never really recovered.

The subtleties of 12-Metre design are graphically illustrated when you compare the specifications of each yacht.

COLUMBIA

Length overall ..... 69 ft 4 in (21.12 m)
Length waterline .. 46 ft 2 in (14.06 m)
Beam............... 11 ft 9 in (3.58 m)
Draft .... 9 ft 0 in (2.74 m)
Sail area .... 1817 sq ft (168.97 sq m)

SCEPTRE

Length overall ..... 68 ft 10 in (28.97 m)
Length waterline .. 46 ft 6 in (14.17 m)
Beam............... 11 ft 9 in (3.58 m)
Draft .... 9 ft 1 in (2.77 m)
Sail area .... 1819 sq ft (168.18 sq m)

For two yachts to have such differing performances there was obviously a considerable difference in their lines, despite the closeness of the quoted dimensions. Most observers believed *Sceptre* hobbyhorsed in the Newport slop due to her full sections for'ard. By comparison, *Columbia* sliced through the water with less fuss.

The humiliation of the British spurred interest in another part of the world, interest that very well may have saved the America's Cup from extinction if the British had been allowed to keep challenging without any hope of success. The newcomer to the scene was Australian press tycoon, Sir Frank Packer, a keen yachtsman and an irascible dominating bear of a man with a strong will which fitted in neatly with the tradition of the America's Cup. That was about all that did fit. No 12-Metre yacht had ever sailed in Australian waters and the country was better known for her flying dinghy classes such as the outrageous 18-Foot Skiffs. Australian ocean racing yachts had never raced in international events, and in the Olympic Games the country had only two medals to show for its efforts, a bronze medal to Jock Sturrock and a silver to Rolly Tasker in 1956 on their home waters in Melbourne.

Australia's first challenger Gretel. *Single steering wheel with helmsman's own cockpit; fully enclosed deck. Courtesy Australian Consolidated Press.*

Undoubtedly it was *Sceptre's* dismal performance that prompted the New York Yacht Club to hastily accept the challenge from the Southern Hemisphere. But with the challengers' lack of international impact in sailing it was little wonder that the Americans refused to take the challenge seriously.

Not so the British who had been planning another challenge and were outraged by the cheek of yachtsmen in their former Dominion. When it became obvious that Sir Frank Packer would not back down they suggested to the Australians that it should be a joint Commonwealth effort. In an uncharacteristic bout of diplomacy, Sir Frank advised them that the kangaroo effort was designed merely to soften the Americans up for the next British effort. While this ploy succeeded, Packer also convinced the members of the New York Yacht Club that he was more interested in using the challenge to encourage better understanding between both countries.

Consequently the Americans promised all their support to the Australian challenge. First they gave Packer *Vim* to use as a trial horse and to provide a benchmark for Australia's sole qualified naval architect Alan Payne to study before drawing up his own yacht. In addition they agreed that Payne could use their own yacht model test tanks as there were no comparable facilities in Australia. The use of American hardware and sailcloth was also permitted.

While Australia's leading yachtsmen rallied around the flag and began learning the art of 12-Metre sailing on *Vim*, Payne was learning all he could about 12-Metre design. He had been responsible for several successful craft, including ocean racers,

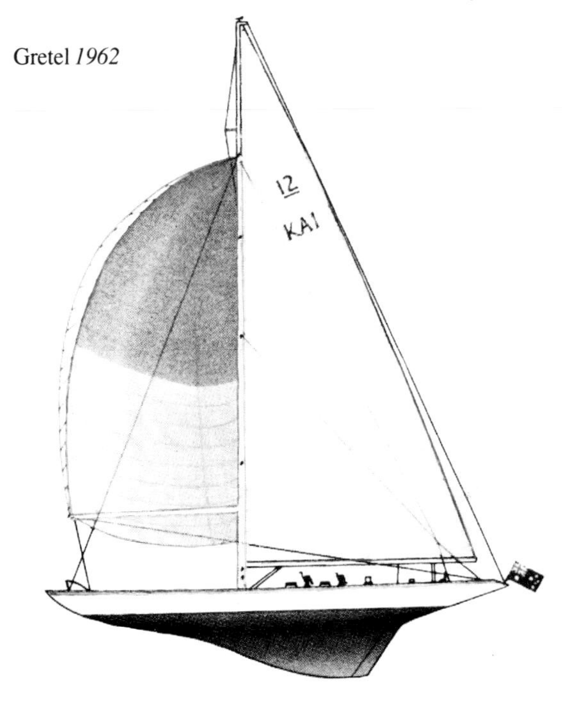

Gretel *1962*

Close reaching aboard Gretel*. ''Pod'' O'Donnell on the unique winch grinding system. Courtesy Australian Consolidated Press.*

and he had a good understanding of the aerodynamic and hydrodynamic factors involved. He was also an innovative engineer. Quick to accept the American offer of assistance, he spent considerable time testing 30 small models in the towing tank at the Stevens Institute of Technology at Hoboken, New Jersey. The tank, crude by today's standards, was also used by Olin Stephens for his 12-Metre designs, but because of the small size of the models at 10 and 20 ft (3.04-6.09 m) and the inability to simulate waves, it could only indicate what might be good shapes.

The 1962 challenger which resulted from these efforts, bearing the sail number KA1 and named *Gretel* after Sir Frank Packer's late wife, was a superb first effort by Payne. As he readily admitted later, he had been working in the dark as the tank results were too vague to give complete answers on the hull shapes necessary for speed through the water, pointing ability and minimum leeway. Payne's design resulted in a yacht that had an easy entry with Vee-shaped sections for'ard, full shoulders around the maximum beam and a long, flat run aft for speed off the wind. At 69 ft 6 in (21.2 m), *Gretel* was the longest 12-Metre until that date to sail for the America's Cup. But Payne had given her long overhangs to add waterline length and speed when she was heeled in moderate and heavy airs. Consequently her measured waterline remained short at just 45 ft (13.71 m), allowing her sail area to be large for light airs and running in all conditions.

Payne did not just pay close attention to the shape of the timber hull. He recognised that match racing not only demanded speed in a straight line, it also called for a yacht that could tack quickly and regain its optimum speed as soon as possible on the new tack. Since the 12-Metres began racing for the Cup the windward legs always promised to be no-holds-barred tacking duels, with the leading yacht always tacking to stay to windward of the trailing yacht, thus dictating the tactics and giving her opponent disturbed wind. Conversely, the trailing yacht would always be tacking away from the leading yacht to try and clear her wind and break free of the leading yacht's cover.

Payne worked very hard to give the yacht's crew every advantage. Some of his systems for sheeting the sails, trimming the rig and tacking the yacht were revolutionary. Among them were the massive headsail winches which had the toughest job on the yacht of sheeting in the big genoas and spinnakers. Instead of having just two men putting their weight onto the winch handles to operate each of the two primary winches, Payne designed a linkage that enabled all four ''grinders'' to operate each winch which made sheeting the genoa in after each tack considerably faster. As well, he developed extremely complicated and sophisticated mechanisms for the mainsheet and

Weatherly. *Photo Rosenfeld Collection. Courtesy Mystic Seaport Museum.*

Weatherly *1962*

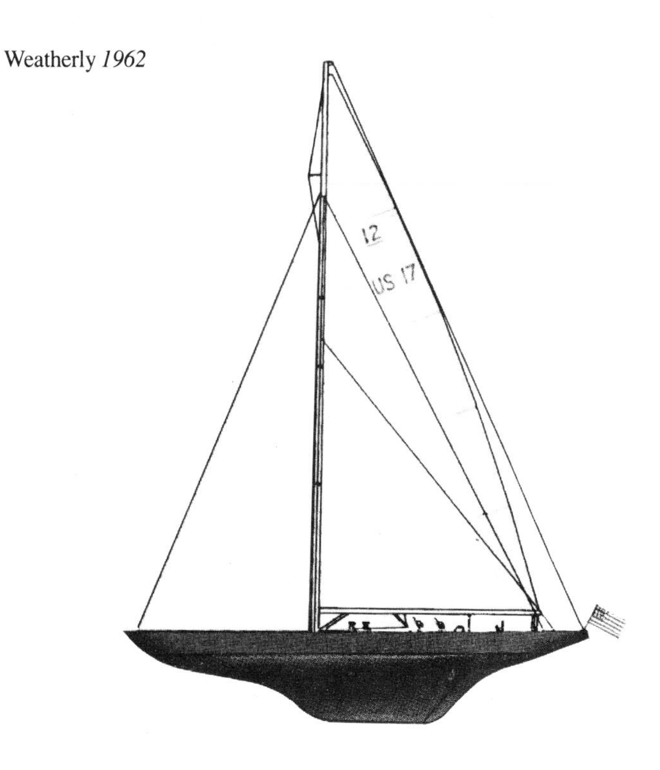

running backstays. Some of the systems were later discarded in the interests of simplicity and saving weight, but Payne's original approach and intelligence produced a yacht with a highly efficient layout.

When the yacht began racing against *Vim* on Sydney Harbour the Australians realised they had been wise to back Payne because his yacht was faster than *Vim*, America's second fastest yacht in the previous America's Cup. As the Australians worked up for the 1962 clash, the defenders largely ignored their progress. In the US only one new potential defender was built: *Nefertiti*, designed and skippered by multi-talented sailmaker Ted Hood. She went up against three Twelves including the Phil Rhodes-designed *Weatherly* which had been considerably modified by A.E. Luders Jnr. Now with the aggressive Bus Mosbacher at the helm, she enjoyed a new lease of life and wore down *Nefertiti* to become the New York Yacht Club's defender. Mosbacher was firmly in control of the defence effort with a loyal and first class crew, good sails and the best possible tactics after a summer of match racing.

After their arrival in Newport, the Australians continually changed their yacht to get everything right in what became a desperate race against time. Payne was a tireless worker and was not afraid to change things, even to the stage of moving the mast 19 inches (48 cm) at almost the last minute to improve *Gretel's* balance for the battle against the slick *Weatherly*.

Not helping the Australians, however, was the attitude of the autocratic Sir Frank Packer who insisted on complete control. Not only did he wait until the day before the first race to name the final crew, but it wasn't until the morning of that race that he named Jock Sturrock as skipper. Sturrock had been the obvious choice all along. Winner of 16 Australian championships in Olympic classes and a bronze medal at the 1956 Olympic Games, he was a renowned helmsman and leader of men. However, Packer's approach hardly inspired onboard confidence.

The first race showed that the Australian effort was not to be a washout like the previous British attempt. *Gretel* lost, but she had been severely hampered by the wash of the spectator fleet, prompting an apology to the Australians by President John Kennedy.

Packer reacted by sacking two key people in *Gretel's* afterguard and the Australians made more changes to their boat. They went into the second race with new heart and it helped them not only to record the first win by a challenger in 28 years, but also to spark real interest in the Cup for all Australians, an interest which would lead to fruition 21 years later.

As in the first race *Weatherly* had the advantage upwind, pointing closer to the wind. In addition, Mosbacher's match racing tactics were superior to those of Sturrock. But downwind, with her flat and long running transom, *Gretel* appeared the faster of the two. On the second run in a stiff breeze the Australian crew picked up a series of big waves after rounding the buoy to surf past the disbelieving Americans. In their haste to get back to windward of *Gretel*, they broke a spinnaker brace which slammed their spinnaker pole into the forestay and bent it in two. By the time the Americans had rigged a spare pole the Australians held an unbeatable lead.

The Americans were regretting not having taken the "kangaroo challenge" more seriously, and Mosbacher had to abandon some of the accepted match racing principles to keep in front. The special winch mechanisms aboard *Gretel* allowed her to tack faster than *Weatherly*, so when the yachts were close when going to windward Mosbacher avoided being drawn into a tacking duel by Sturrock.

In the last race, when *Gretel* was gaining downwind, Mosbacher had to resort to deception to hold them off and keep the Cup. Mosbacher ordered his crew to drop the spinnaker and reach up, away from the distant mark, to fool Sturrock into believing the mark had shifted. Reaching under mainsail and genoa, the Americans could keep *Gretel* behind, and unfortunately the Australians fell for the trick, discovering they had been fooled only when Mosbacher pulled away for the mark at the last minute to stay in front and take the gun and hold the Cup.

For a country which had never been part of the America's Cup it was a magnificent debut. One of America's most experienced America's Cup yachtsmen, Harold S. Vanderbilt, was one of many who praised Payne, commenting "There is little to choose between *Gretel* and the best 12-Metres I have seen in the last 50 years"

The New York Yacht Club quickly reacted by increasing the restrictions on challengers. In the future they could have no assistance from American design facilities, and all equipment, sails and materials would have to be designed and manufactured in the challenger's country. The America's Cup, its keepers announced, was to be not only a test of sailing skills, but also a test of each country's technology.

The Club's critics accused it of continuing its conspiracy to keep the Cup by any means, but this did not dampen enthusiasm outside the United States. Thanks to Payne's design genius, post-war generations taking part in the rapidly growing sport of yachting suddenly saw that perhaps, after all, the America's Cup could be won.

The next challenge came from the British who were determined to expunge the embarrassment of 1958. For the 1964 challenge they again turned to designer David Boyd, but when his new *Sovereign* went up against the chosen defender *Constellation* it was quickly obvious that he had failed to learn the lessons of 1958. *Sovereign* was thrashed 4-0, in the process making dubious America's Cup history by losing the second race by a record 20 minutes. So boring was the racing that an American reporter penned the oft-repeated saying: "watching two yachts race is as interesting as watching the grass grow".

Constellation was the latest design from the drawing board of Olin Stephens. He departed from his traditional lines by having more Vee-shape in the hull forward, and observers of the racing who could stay awake long enough noted that while *Constellation* forged through the chop, the British yacht pitched violently and lost considerable speed as her bow slammed into the waves.

The American effort also re-emphasised the fact that it would take more than a good yacht to win the America's Cup. *Constellation* had superior sails built by Ted Hood and a well drilled

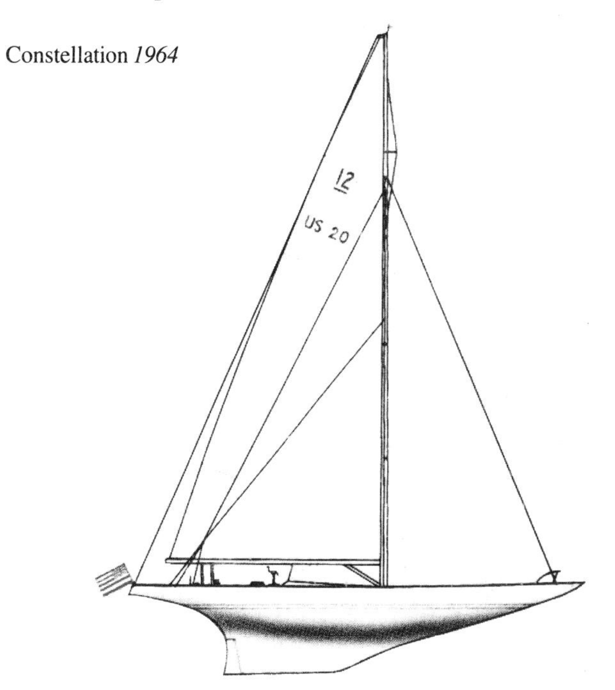

Constellation *1964*

Constellation. *Photo Rosenfeld Collection. Courtesy Mystic Seaport Museum.*

Intrepid. *Photo Rosenfeld Collection. Courtesy Mystic Seaport Museum.*

crew. A new trend also began that year in that her original skipper was replaced before the defence. The determined Americans were being very professional in their approach to an alleged sporting event.

Another development of 1964 was to affect designers of new yachts. In that year the Club began sailing the races on a six leg Olympic course consisting of a triangle, windward and return and windward leg to the finish. The length of 24 nautical miles stayed the same, but there was more windward work and the legs were shorter with more buoys to round. Now, more than ever before, the yachts had to be manoeuvrable as well as fast to succeed, thanks to the greater distance to be raced to windward.

After the anticlimax of 1964, 1967 promised to be an exciting affair with a second challenge from Australia, and Olin Stephens commissioned to design a new Twelve to be skippered by Bus Mosbacher. As it turned out, the year was to be very significant because Stephens developed a yacht that revolutionised 12-Metre design.

Stephens had a year to dream up and tank test the lines for the new *Intrepid* and he put that time to good use thinking about 12-Metre yachts of the past, and particularly what was required

Intrepid *1967, 1970*

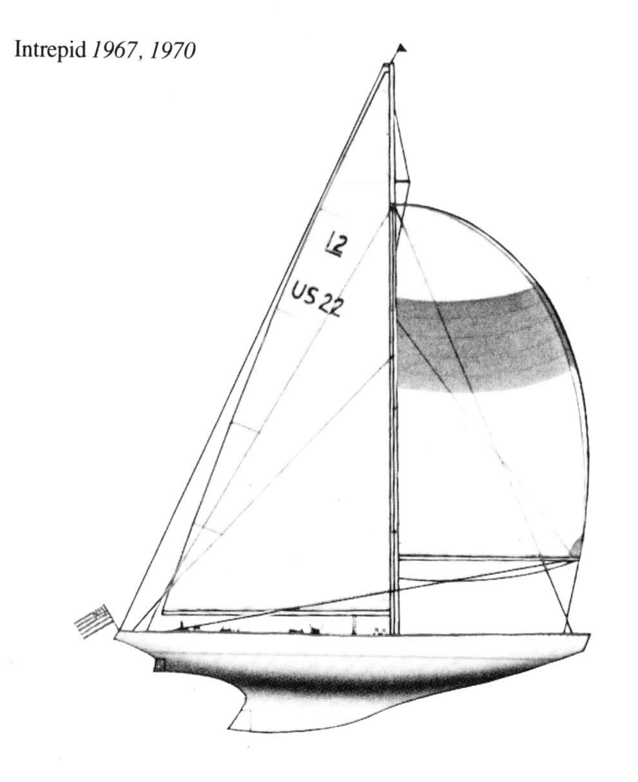

for the conditions of Newport. Stephens knew the Newport summer included a wide variety of weather. Usually June, July and August experienced lighter weather while in September the yacht that had survived the elimination process would generally face stronger winds for the America's Cup itself. For light weather he wanted as little hull drag and as much sail area as possible; for stronger winds he wanted stability so that the hull could carry its sail area without excessive heel and increased drag. When Stephens began work on *Intrepid* he spent countless hours at the test tanks in his search for minimum wetted surface area and drag and maximum sail area and stability. Towing tanks were not new to yacht design. In the 1870s Englishman William Froude devoted his time to evaluating the water resistance to the hulls of ships. Comparing the results of tests in towing tanks with full sized models, he drew up universal guidelines to measuring resistance in tanks that still apply today. Prior to Froude's time the design of vessels was entirely a matter of eye and feel. But he proved that designers could use tanks to test their theories at considerably less expense than "full sized" models.

Froude's tests showed that while hull resistance at low speeds is almost entirely due to skin friction of the water passing across the hull's surface, above certain speeds another factor is introduced. This is wave-making resistance which grows steeper with increased speed. At the bow the water parts and slows, then it speeds up as the hull thickens out to its maximum beam, while there is a sudden decrease in pressure and slowing down as the hull narrows again towards the stern. The water separates from the hull and a quarter wave forms, virtually a wall of water being dragged along by the boat. The earlier this wave is generated the greater it's mass, further slowing the vessel.

Tank tests were treated very warily by most yacht designers, undoubtedly because many did not fully understand exactly how they should assess the results. In addition to their early use by Froude in Britain, in the United States they had also been in use since the early 20th century. Olin Stephens had extensively used the tank at the Stevens Institute of Technology when he collaborated with designer Starling Burgess in the design of *Ranger*, the mightiest J Boat ever to contest the America's Cup.

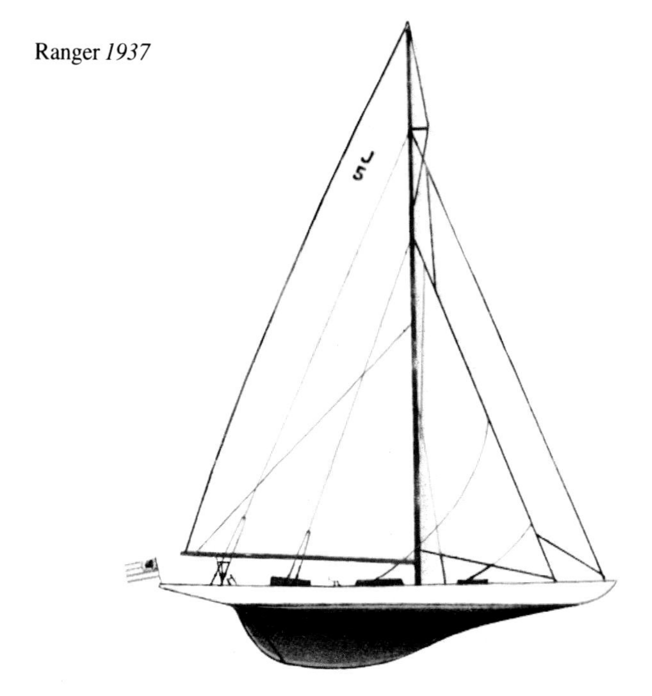

Ranger *1937*

With his calm, analytical approach, Stephens stood out from most designers. He used the tanks for his own means, to answer his own questions. He was not interested in wild experimentation in the hope of stumbling on a breakthrough. Stephens used the tank to evaluate two primary factors in the shapes of his hulls. He divided hull resistance into two parts: the frictional resistance of the water passing over the hull surface and the residual or wave-making resistance.

"The accuracy of the tests is really amazing," Stephens wrote. "Their value has been indicated not only by the success of *Ranger* but also by the outstanding success of boats designed after model tests in classes which, through the building of a great number of boats, have been built up close to their peak. It should be emphasised, however, that a great deal of care and thought must be used to get the greatest advantage from these tests and to avoid being led astray by the results. The tank will not design a boat, it will answer a question."

Stephens also looked long and hard at other types of yachts, particularly ocean racers. All the time he was trying to reduce wetted surface to improve the yacht's performance in the light airs of the elimination series. Traditionally 12-Metre yachts had long shallow keels to stay within the minimum draft requirement. Their trailing edge carried the rudder. The resulting area was larger than required, but designers persisted because they needed this area to keep leeway, i.e. slipping sideways through the water to leeward, to a minimum. Minimum leeway was essential for any 12-Metre yacht, but particularly so following the 1964 decision of the New York Yacht Club to use the Olympic Course for the Cup, with its emphasis on windward work.

In the early 1960s the ocean racing world had been transformed by yachts which did away with the traditional underbody arrangement of hanging the rudder from the trailing edge of the long keel by substituting a short, deep keel with a separate rudder hung behind a supporting skeg well aft. Stephens decided to apply this approach to the 12-Metre and took the short keel version of *Intrepid* to the test tanks along with six other models. He found that his wetted surface had reduced by about 40 sq ft (3.7 sq m) over other Twelves. But, as he feared, he also found that the smaller lateral area of the keel made more leeway.

Again Stephens found the answer in the American offshore racing fleets where some yachts had been experimenting with a small second rudder or trim tab hung on the trailing edge of the keel. The trim tabs, first devised by designers Ted Hood and Dick Carter, operated in much the same manner as the elevators in the tail section of aeroplanes. Sailing upwind, the tab would be set a few degrees to leeward, resulting in hydrodynamic lift that helped the yacht "lift up" to windward. Stephens tested the models and found the extra lift far outweighed the added drag of the tab.

As well as giving lift upwind, the trim tab had its uses off the wind. The helmsman could lock the two rudders together which made steering easy and the yacht more responsive.

Stephens also found he was able to reduce their area even more, further reducing drag.

As well as reducing wetted area and resistance, Stephens wanted to keep the quarter wave as small as possible. In the tank he discovered that by keeping the afterbody as full as possible, with a bustle or skeg leading to the rudder set well aft, he kept the wave making as low as possible. *Intrepid's* quarter wave was the smallest of any 12-Metre built to that date.

Stephens went further in the bow, giving *Intrepid* a pronounced "knuckle", i.e. an almost plumb bow, to lengthen her heeled waterline and keep measured waterline down.

While Stephens worked at the tank, Mosbacher was busy designing a new deck layout which was also radical. Previously all crew and winches had been located on the deck. Mosbacher designed a new layout that would put all winches and seven of the crew, all but the helmsman, tactician and two headsail trimmers, below deck level. The result was not only decreased windage but also increased stability as the not inconsiderable weight of the crew and most of their heavy equipment, including the winches, was lower in the boat. Another innovation saw the mainsail boom lowered to just above deck height to stop wind spillage from the foot of the sail.

The result was a yacht with what appeared to be a ridiculously small keel, ugly lines and a completely uncluttered deck. With the smaller keel the yacht was highly manoeuvrable and Mosbacher could tack and turn it much faster, with less speed loss, than any other Twelve. *Intrepid* was so fast that she lost only one race in the elimination trials, and that was when she broke a titanium mast, another innovation.

Her opponent in the Cup races was the yacht *Dame Pattie*, designed by Warwick Hood, a former assistant to Alan Payne. After *Gretel's* good showing in 1962, everyone looked forward to a tough Australian challenge. However, with *Intrepid*, the Americans had leapt ahead in the design category of the overall formula that equals America's Cup success. Another advantage held by the defenders was their superior sailcloth which easily outperformed the Australian imitation forced on the challengers by the Rule change of the New York Yacht Club.

Hood had designed *Dame Pattie* for lighter airs but his gamble backfired when unusual weather patterns caused by two hurricanes offshore gave stronger winds. *Intrepid* romped away to windward, sailing closer to the wind and faster while heeling less. *Dame Pattie* had no show against the new superboat *Intrepid*. Clearly outclassed, she was quickly dubbed "*Damn Pity*" by those who watched her follow the Americans around every one of the 20 buoys in their four races.

Three years later Australia challenged again and eventually all agreed that this time the challengers had a boat that was superior to *Intrepid* which had again been selected to defend the Cup. The Australian yacht was *Gretel II*, the second 12-Metre designed by Alan Payne, after a number of years of careful thinking and tank testing, following the defeat of his first *Gretel* in 1962.

Gretel II found herself up against *Intrepid*, but this was a different yacht to the superboat that had thrashed *Dame Pattie*. The yacht had been modified by another designer, and many believed the modifications had actually made her slower. Olin Stephens had had nothing to do with the modifications – he had been signed up by a rival syndicate to design another new yacht. Instead, *Intrepid* fell into the hands of Britton Chance Jnr, a rising star in the American yachting scene with a string of successful 5.5 Metre yachts to his credit. While Stephens was one of the establishment designers, constantly refining and developing, Chance was one of the new breed of designers who relied on mathematics and figures to back up their ideas. Chance had worked at the Stevens Institute of Technology as a technician and had far greater faith in its results than other designers.

Dame Pattie *(KA2) leads* Gretel. *Courtesy Australian Consolidated Press.*

With *Intrepid* he tried to improve her all round performance, with particular attention to her heavy air speed. To increase her waterline length Chance moved her rudder aft so that it was behind the measured waterline. By adding fairing strips between the keel and rudder, beyond the waterline, he was able to increase the waterline from 47 ft to 48 ft 6 in (14.3-14.7 m). Because both were behind the waterline the increase was not included by the measurer's tape and his exploitation of a loophole led to anger in the Australian camp.

Stephens, the master of 12-Metre design, had been encouraged to look beyond the successful *Intrepid*. With his new yacht *Valiant* he went for a bigger and heavier boat at the cost of sail area. But she was caught out in the light airs of the early summer, when she was too slow during the elimination series.

Gretel II went the other way. Payne was convinced that increased sail area was the best way to overcome the big chop on Block Island Sound caused by the huge spectator fleets. In his three years of research in the towing tank at Sydney University, Payne had developed a lightweight flyer and *Gretel II* measured in at 62 ft (18.9 m) in length overall, two and a half feet shorter than *Intrepid* and one foot shorter on the waterline with less displacement.

As well as a trim tab, *Gretel II* had a small main rudder to keep drag down, and was demanding to steer. The man chosen for the job was to go on to play an important role in Australia's America's Cup history. He was Jim Hardy, successful Olympic and offshore yachtsman who became Australia's best sporting ambassador overseas. Nicknamed "Gentleman Jim" by the Americans, he was to need all his diplomatic skills during his first America's Cup which became as bitter a battle as the earliest Cups, when English challengers often returned home, vowing never to return unless the New York Yacht Club stopped making, and interpreting, its own rules.

Gretel II was a light weather flyer, more than a match for *Intrepid*. But it was to be a classic example of the better team outsailing the better boat, as *Intrepid* downed her 4-1. The Australians were really beaten before they started. While *Intrepid's* crew won the right to defend after a tough series against three other boats, finally defeating *Valiant* 22-5, *Gretel II* won the right to challenge 4-0 against a French effort headed by ballpoint pen magnate Baron Bich. The Australians accounted for the French so easily that they were still "green" when they went up against the well-drilled Americans led by Bill Ficker.

Once again it was demonstrated that the America's Cup was no "glorious" sporting event, but rather a war on and off the water. After the initial controversy over *Intrepid's* rule-dodging rudder fairing strips, which the defenders agreed to modify, Sir Frank Packer, heading his second challenge, pointed out that the toilet on *Intrepid* was in breach of the Rule as it was not fully enclosed. The toilet was altered and the racing began.

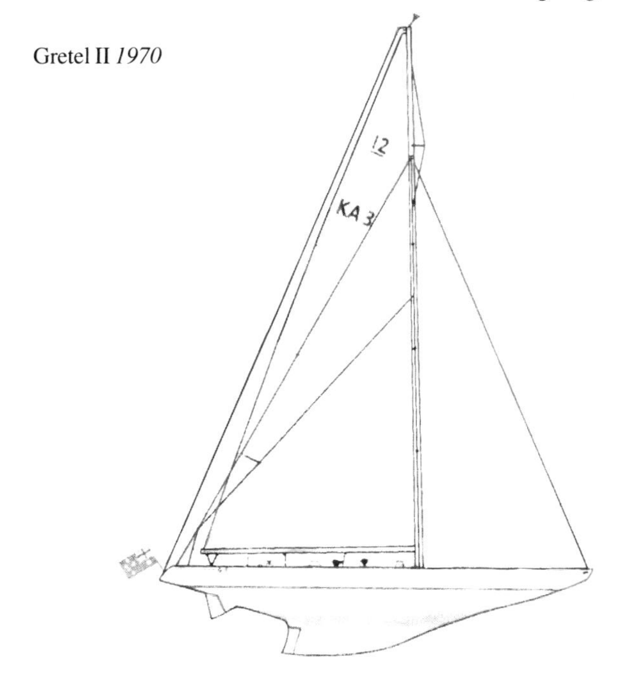

Gretel II *1970*

On the water the protests continued, with both crews lodging formal protests in the first two races. In the first race Hardy protested *Intrepid* for a starting incident, but the committee disallowed it as no contact had been made. *Intrepid* went on to win the race, but not because she was faster. The Australian crew had an appalling day, fouling their first spinnaker set and then losing three minutes while they returned to pick up a crewman who had fallen overboard.

In the next race the Australians had the light 6-8 knot breeeze they had been hoping for, but again the protest flags were broken out after the two yachts collided as they battled for the best position at the start. *Gretel II* went on to win the race, but Australian euphoria turned to outrage when the yacht was disqualified over the start line incident. The New York Yacht Club was roundly criticised by yachtsmen the world over for sitting in judgement of its own yacht. According to Packer: "Appealing to the New York Yacht Club is like complaining to your mother-in-law about your wife."

The next race was a tense affair with Ficker finally taking the honours to put the Americans 3-0 ahead. But *Gretel II's* crew were determined and in the next race they made up more than two minutes on the final leg to come from behind and win the race. The final race saw Ficker back in command, staying ahead of the Australians through superior tactics.

Again an Australian challenge had failed because the complete effort was not there. But Payne's design showed that the American trend towards bigger boats was wrong because the loss in sail area resulted in Twelves that were hopelessly outclassed in all but the heaviest airs.

The approval of aluminium for use in 12-Metre hull construction and international economic troubles delayed the next Cup until 1974. Potential defence syndicates were having trouble raising money until they developed a scheme under which the boats would be owned by tax-exempt foundations, allowing donors to claim their donations in their tax returns.

In Australia, Sir Frank Packer decided he had had enough of the America's Cup. Admitting his challenges had been due to "an excess of alcohol and delusions of grandeur", he sold *Gretels I* and *II* to West Australian real estate developer Alan Bond, who was preparing for his first challenge.

Shaken by the near success of *Gretel II* which could have won the Cup from *Intrepid* if she had had a completely prepared and finely tuned campaign, the Americans refused to let money worries sap their effort. Finally they raised enough to build two new aluminium yachts, rebuild the timber *Intrepid* and alter the discarded Stephens design *Valiant*.

Aluminium became the new wonder material of the 12-Metre class. It had greater strength for its weight than wood so it was believed that building an aluminium hull would result in saving almost two tons in the hull which would then go into the keel and so increase stability. In addition, aluminium was stiffer and, with sophisticated welding techniques, quicker to repair than timber.

Stephens was commissioned to design one of the two new yachts, as well as overseeing the redesign of *Intrepid*. The other new yacht was to be designed by Britton Chance Jnr, who went back to his beloved test tanks to design the yacht *Mariner*. At the same time he referred to his computer, on which he had drawn up a velocity prediction program, one of the initial attempts to evaluate design by computer.

The result was the most revolutionary yacht seen in the America's Cup. Chance concentrated on eliminating the quarter wave, and gave the yacht an unusually wide underbody behind the keel and a deep bustle, abruptly cut off where the Rule insisted it should stop. It was like having a false transom below the waterline. The tank results were most promising, and Chance believed he had fooled the water into believing that the waterline length of the yacht was 10 ft (3.04 m) longer that it really was.

Chance could not have got it more wrong. When *Mariner* was launched her crew, led by media magnate and ocean racing champion Ted Turner, watched the big quarter wave they dragged along with them, complete with rubbish it picked up along the way. The yacht was spectacularly slow.

Chance had believed the submerged step would allow the flow of water to separate, virtually eliminating the quarter wave as on a lightweight planing boat. But at the slower speeds of the heavy displacement Twelve, it just did not happen. The tank got it wrong, and Chance got it wrong by believing the data.Never short of a quip, Turner offered the best line of the Cup campaign: "Britt, even a turd is pointed at both ends." Soon Turner found himself fired and replaced by Dennis Conner while the yacht was quickly rebuilt.

Suggestions by Chance that they should have contingency plans in case he was being fooled by the tank results had been ignored by the syndicate, which quickly found itself out of the running.

"I was misled by the results," Chance agreed. "The tank said the boat was very good and after years of tank testing without any serious reversal I believed the results."

Mariner's failure completely discredited tank testing and resulted in the complete demise of scientific yacht testing for the next ten years. Not surprisingly, it almost ended the career of Chance.

The other designer of a new aluminium Twelve, Olin Stephens, continued his conservative development path and went the other way, following Alan Payne's lead towards a smaller and lighter Twelve. The result was *Courageous* which quickly accounted for the rebuilt *Mariner*. Surprisingly, though, she had trouble disposing of the seven-year-old timber *Intrepid*, only narrowly pipping her for the right to defend.

Seven countries had promised to challenge for the Cup, but only two raised the necessary money to make it to Newport: Alan Bond from Australia and Baron Bich from France. Bond's designer was Bob Miller, later to be known as Ben Lexcen, successful designer of dinghies, 18-Foot Skiffs and ocean racers. His yacht was *Southern Cross*, longer than *Courageous* overall and on the waterline by 10 in (25 cm), heavier and with smaller sail area. Not surprisingly she did not find the predominantly light winds of the 1974 Cup to her liking.

Although the reliable Jim Hardy was in charge of the boat, Bond could not resist interfering by changing crewmen around between races, and the yellow Australian boat went down 4-0 to *Courageous*.

Southern Cross began to perform when the wind increased to 16 knots, but below that she was outpaced in straight line speed and when tacking. Many believed if the series had been sailed in strong winds the result may have been different, but with better light weather speed and good tactics by starting helmsman Dennis Conner and skipper Ted Hood, Stephens' latest Twelve won through.

Technically *Courageous* should have been disqualified. It was learned later that she weighed some 1,800 pounds less than her certificate claimed, but all the New York Yacht Club did was to insist that in future the yachts would be mechanically weighed. At the time they based their argument on the fact that existing mechanical scales were not accurate enough to prove or disprove designers' claims.

The 1974 Cup was memorable for more than the appearance of Alan Bond and Ben Lexcen. With the increasing costs of the Twelves and the associated prestige, commercialism was rearing its head, which to traditionalists was a blight on what they saw as the ultimate sporting contest. In America there had long been intense rivalry between the two major sailmaking companies, the Hood loft led by Ted Hood, and the North loft headed by Lowell North. Both were intensely involved in the America's Cup, and in the lead up to the 1974 defence their rivalry finally spilled out into the public arena. Early in the defender selection series, *Intrepid* with North sails was consistently defeating *Courageous* with Hood sails. Bob Bavier, then skipper of *Courageous*, ordered new North sails for his yacht and believed them to be superior. But then Ted Hood and Dennis Conner joined *Courageous* and Bavier was fired. The syndicate

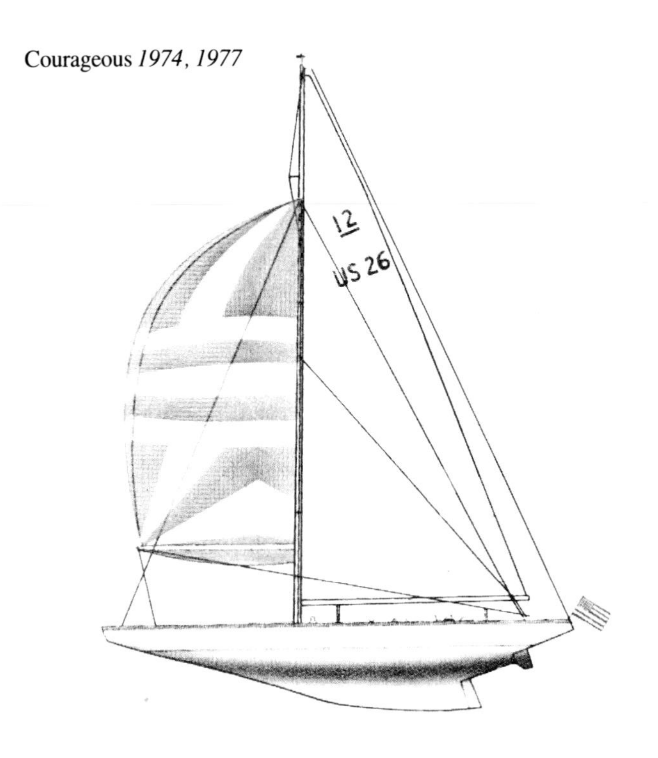

Courageous *1974, 1977*

which had built *Courageous* had put up a lot of money and was running a professional campaign. No-one was sacred, winning was everything.

Before the first race the rivalry blew up. Skipper Ted Hood was told by his syndicate chiefs not to use the mainsail made by his own loft but to hoist the North mainsail they considered better. Hood replied that he was skipper and running the boat and they won the race with the Hood mainsail. Hood was later criticised for making a business decision. It was to be the start of a long festering argument.

As the yachting world prepared for the 23rd America's Cup in 1977, would-be defenders and challengers were busy trying to raise money through sponsorships. The America's Cup had become big business with campaigns budgeted at well over $1 million each. In Australia, Alan Bond and a Sydney syndicate were trying to raise sponsorship for two campaigns from the same country. In Sweden, Metre boat champion Pelle Pettersen was raising big funds from Swedish companies, including car manufacturer Volvo, to mount his country's first challenge. In France Baron Bich continued to bankroll his own campaign.

In the United States, four syndicates continued to attract money through their tax free foundations. All recognised that the increased competition would make it very much harder to win the right to defend and challenge, and all began preparing longer challenges. Previously the American defenders had left the building of the yachts until the spring of the Cup year to give their designers as much time as possible to test their ideas in the tanks of the Stevens Institute. But with the *Mariner* debacle and the discrediting of scientific research, the syndicates planned earlier launchings and longer campaigns to give crews time to optimise their yachts.

In addition, attention was switching from hull design to sails and rigs. In the wake of *Courageous* and *Gretel II*, hull design had largely become conservative, with designers looking for small margins, measuring everything in single figure percentages. But with major developments in sailcloths, the syndicates began putting more money into that area and giving their crews and sailmakers more time on the yachts to test their creations.

Southern Cross *1974*

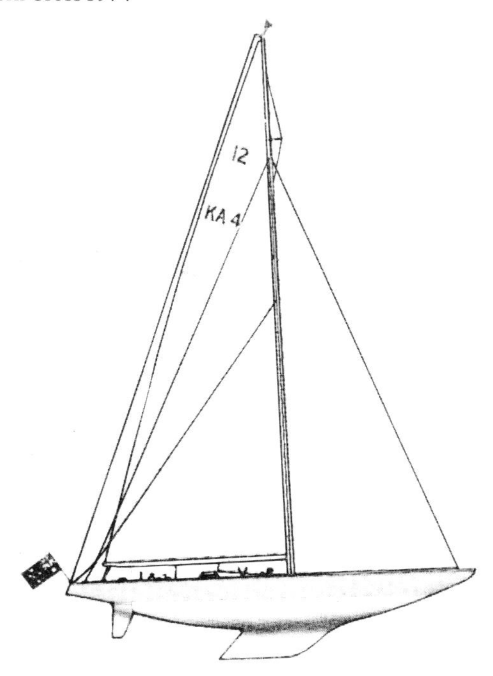

The woven synthetic Dacron and Terylene cloths had dominated sailmaking since taking over from cotton in the 1950s. These synthetic cloths were far superior to natural cloths in that they stretched less and held shape better. As well they did not absorb water. But in the huge sails carried by the 12-Metres stretch was still a problem, and syndicates encouraged cloth manufacturers and their sailmakers to experiment with Dacron and new cloths to eliminate the stretch and so produce consistently faster sails.

Manufacturers concentrated their efforts on two areas. The first was to improve the Dacrons/Terylenes with better fibres and, more particularly, by applying resins to the woven cloth to keep the threads from spreading and the sails from stretching and losing their aerodynamic shape. They also began experimenting with new materials developed for the United States space program. One was Mylar, a particularly lightweight material similar in substance to photographic film, with considerably less stretch than Dacron but with no resistance to tearing. Mylar made its first appearance on the Twelves in the 1977 Cup, but its lack of resistance to tearing from the tiniest of holes meant that it had to be backed with a light Dacron. Its high early failure rate delayed its use until further improvements allowed it to achieve its full impact. Another material was Kevlar, a material stronger per given weight than steel which was able to resist tearing. But it, too, had teething troubles that would take time to sort out.

Nonetheless the sailmakers were beginning to be dominant figures in the 12-Metre scene, with the major lofts assigning key employees to the syndicates to oversee their sail development programs. It became a major battle between the two biggest American and international lofts, Hood and North, with others constantly nibbling away at their superiority.

Both Lowell North and Ted Hood were in Newport in 1977, North in partnership with Olin Stephens in the new yacht *Enterprise*, and Hood with his own design, *Independence*. Hood's syndicate had also purchased *Courageous* and the two yachts worked up against each other with Ted Turner skippering the successful 1974 defender. *Enterprise* made short work of *Intrepid* and in the lead up to the defence most of the bets were on Stephens, the 69-year-old chief designer of Sparkman & Stephens who had seen more of his 12-Metre yachts successfully defend the America's Cup than any other designer. Of six challenges since the 12-Metre class took over the Cup, Stephens had produced *Columbia* in 1958, *Constellation* in 1964, *Intrepid* in 1967/70 and *Courageous* in 1974.

Before the elimination series began *Enterprise* was hailed as a technological masterpiece, but Stephens had restricted himself to an evolutionary design, content to refine his earlier boats instead of pushing for another breakthrough like *Intrepid*.

From overseas there came a variety of Twelves, old and new.

Back for her second tilt was *Gretel II*. By now aluminium had become the standard hull material and Payne gave the timber yacht a new aluminium deck. Payne chose to concentrate on improving the yacht's already proven light air performance. To increase her sail area he reduced her waterline by cutting 3,000 lbs (1,360 kg) from her keel. To make the yacht rate he also increased the size of the rudder and moved it forward, which had the side effect of easier steering. In an effort to conquer the speed-stripping chop of Newport he also narrowed the yacht's bow.

Following trouble experienced by yachts with big deck cutouts in 1974 (one yacht almost sank), the Rule for the 1977 Cup was altered to fill in the decks, with all crew and winches above deck.

Sverige, a Cup newcomer carrying Sweden's colours, was short on the waterline and low in displacement and sail area. Her designer/skipper Pelle Petterson preferred steering with a tiller and had done away with the steering wheel that all others considered necessary for steering such big, heavy boats.

Alan Bond returned to Newport for his second attempt, this time teaming Bob Miller/Ben Lexcen with Dutchman Johan Valentijn who had worked on the design of *Courageous* in his time at Sparkman & Stephens.

The two designers turned to the test tank facilities at Delft University in Holland, testing models of their new *Australia* against their perception of *Courageous* and pronouncing themselves more than satisfied with the results. *Australia* was, they claimed, lighter at 54,700 lbs (24,811 kg) with a correspondingly shorter waterline. The most visible innovation was the lack of freeboard, her designers lowering the deck by six inches (15 cm) to get the 2,000 lbs (907 kg) deck weight lower to increase stability.

Baron Bich also returned to Newport. After abandoning their new heavyweight *France II* in favour of the original *France*, his team virtually sank without trace, losing their elimination series 0-4 against *Australia* with margins as wide as ten minutes.

Gretel II narrowly went down to *Sverige*, and then *Australia* led the Swedes around every mark in the four race final to win the right to challenge.

While the challengers had been fighting it out, so had the defenders with unexpected results. The two new boats were beaten by *Courageous* in the first round of the trials while the sailmakers, Hood on *Independence* and North on *Enterprise*, poured more and more of their backers' money into their sail wardrobes. At times *Enterprise* showed winning speed, particularly when using the new Mylar headsails. But Stephens had given her a smaller headsail area and she was slow out of tacks. Finally North was sacked and the afterguard of *Independence* was switched constantly. But aboard *Courageous*, Ted Turner, buying his own Hood sails and having them recut each night, kept taking the honours.

Those sails were to play an important role in the clash between *Courageous* and *Australia*, which turned into a squelch. *Courageous* won 4-0. She was well sailed with few tactical errors, but the big difference between the two yachts lay in her sails, the defender's setting well and holding their shape while *Australia's* were poorly shaped – particularly the headsails which would not allow *Australia* to point as high as *Courageous*. Lexcen argued with crew and sailmakers to have them changed, but it was not until the series was over that they conceded they were wrong.

After taking a back seat to sail developments in the 1977 campaign, 12-Metre hull design was kept in the background again in 1980, this time by the sheer professionalism of the defence campaigns. It was Dennis Conner, in charge of his own campaign for the first time, who led the way to a new era in the America's Cup. Conner began his full-time campaign two years before the Cup, spurred on by his natural determination to leave nothing to chance.

Conner led a team of complete professionals, his syndicate employing sailmakers, engineers, tender drivers, cooks and physical education instructors. While they trained on *Enterprise*, Olin Stephens designed their new boat *Freedom*, which was launched in time for a summer of racing against the old boat in Newport before both were shipped to San Diego on the west coast, where the crews kept sailing through the winter before returning to Newport for the 1980 Cup summer. Again the yachts were full-sized test beds for the sailcloth manufacturers – this time the new "super sailcloth" Kevlar. Its manufacturers had considerable success laminating it to Mylar and Dacron, and with the considerable weight saving aloft, the sailmakers applied much of their time redesigning their cuts to make the most of the material.

The only other new American Twelve was *Clipper*, a David Pedrick design for Russell Long which was built quickly using the keel, fittings and rig from *Independence*, which had been scrapped. *Courageous*, the design standard for all American designers, was back with Ted Turner again at her helm. But it was *Freedom*, with her professional campaigners, which stood out from the rest. The feeling on the waterfront was that while the boat might not be brilliant she would be unbeatable because of her superior crew and organisation.

Freedom *1980*

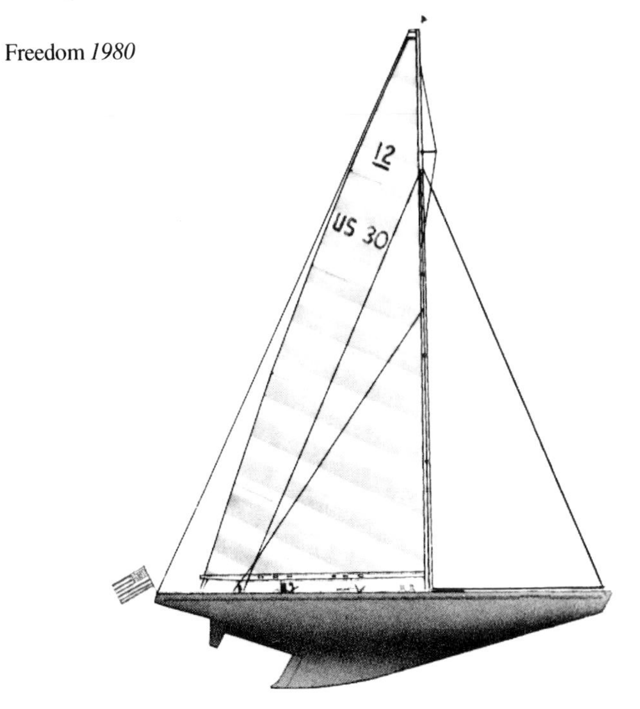

INTRODUCTION

From overseas came two newcomers, Baron Bich's *France III* and *Lionheart* from Great Britain, and two revamped 1977 vintage yachts – Alan Bond's *Australia* and Pelle Petterson's *Sverige*, both extensively modified by their designers. Easily the most interesting of the new yachts was *Lionheart*, built to a design by Ian Howlett which was transformed from an uninspired performer to a very fast yacht when fitted with a special bendy mast. Howlett, with the syndicate's organising committee including Derek Clarke, had found a loophole which allowed him to add an extra 10 per cent of sail area to the mainsail by bending the mast back at its peak. Building the mast from two-thirds aluminium and the top one-third from fibreglass allowed him to produce the "hockey stick" section, and in lighter weather the yacht was transformed by the extra "horsepower".

All other syndicates agonised over copying the British. The Australian syndicate headed by Alan Bond was the only one to do so, in the greatest secrecy as they believed the defenders would copy them if they discovered what they were up to. It was a desperate gamble to gain a design edge over the other challengers and defenders. But it failed, as they ran out of time to make the special sails it needed. The mast was only ready to be stepped a week before *Australia* went up against *Freedom* and her sail-makers were unable to develop the right sails for the rig. *Australia* lost 4-1, winning one light wind race but being outpaced in moderate and heavy airs.

Designer Ben Lexcen and skipper Jim Hardy agreed that if they had had another month to get the right sails for the rig then they could have won the Cup. But they proved yet again that one thing money could not buy in an America's Cup campaign was time.

After the Cup the International Yacht Racing Union responded by eliminating the rule cheating bendy masts through the introduction of girth measurements for mainsails. Low freeboards were also heavily penalised. Both *Freedom* and *Australia* had very low freeboards and there was concern that they were unsafe with their decks so close to the water.

At the same time the New York Yacht Club answered growing international pressure to make the Cup a fair competition by dropping restrictions preventing challengers from using American materials. But this all was to become irrelevant in what was to be the most significant campaign in the Cup's history.

For the first time since *Courageous* was created by Olin Stephens, US effort was channelled into creating a new 12-Metre design that would be a real improvement on the state of the art, which was now *Freedom*. Again it was Dennis Conner who led the way with the support of his syndicate, the Maritime College at Fort Schuyler Foundation. Conner recognised that the effort going into the challenge for the Cup would be unprecedented. He also recognised that because of the large number of potential challengers there was every likelihood that one designer would come up with a breakthrough in design. Consequently, he commissioned new boats from two different designers. One he ordered from Sparkman & Stephens, the successful designers of six Cup defenders. But S&S had changed following the retirement of Olin Stephens and his replacement in "the hot seat" was chief designer Bill Langan. The second designer commissioned by Conner's group was Johan Valentijn, co-designer of *Australia* (1977) and *France III* (1980).

Valentijn's *Magic* was then the smallest and lightest Twelve ever built, measuring 59 ft (17.9 m) overall and weighing just 44,100 lbs (20,003 kg), therefore carrying a heavy displacement penalty. Her designer was looking for the ultimate light displacement boat with maximum acceleration, while retaining stability. It didn't work. The yacht lacked stability and speed.

Langan's boat was bigger, with greater stability to improve her speed in stronger winds, but she missed out badly in acceleration.

Conner remained unimpressed. He did not have a boat that would beat *Freedom*. Such was his determination that he asked both design groups to pool their knowledge and skills to jointly design his third yacht. This was unthinkable for any designers and after tentative discussions broke down Conner opted for Valentijn to draw his third boat.

Other Americans were also trying to come up with successful defenders. Star class champion and tactician aboard *Clipper* in 1980, Tom Blackallar, asked David Pedrick to design a conservative yacht for his team to optimise against *Courageous*, again reworked by Sparkman & Stephens after their falling out with Conner. But the new yacht *Defender* had the worst possible start to life, failing to measure in at 12 metres and having to be cut in half and shortened. The yacht was to go through several modifications in the long lead up to the defence trials, but all the time their sparring partner *Courageous* continued to prove there was life in the oldtimer yet by constantly beating the newcomer.

Overseas there was more happening with three challengers from Australia alone. In addition boats were being built in Great Britain, Canada, Italy, and *France III* would be racing again.

But it was *Australia II* which would lead the way, winning the Cup and revolutionising yacht design by combining the talents of a design genius, who took an entirely new approach to the old problem of designing a faster yacht within the tight confines of the Rule, and the benefits of accurate scientific testing.

Tank and wind tunnel testing in the United States was still in the doldrums following the failure of *Mariner* in 1974. In designing Conner's third yacht, *Liberty*, absolutely no testing of any kind was carried out. "We sat around a table, a committee of six or eight syndicate members – Halsey Herreshoff (navigator and a qualified naval architect), Dennis Conner," Valentijn recalled. "We decided on a mass of numbers. I went home and a week later went to the shipbuilders with a lines plan under my arm and lofted the boat. The amount of design work that went into *Liberty* was zero, just basic knowledge."

Ben Lexcen took exactly the opposite tack. In 1981 he moved to Holland and began work at the Netherlands Ship Model Agency. For the first time money was allocated in Bond's campaign budget for research and at last Lexcen was able to test some of the radical ideas he had long dreamed about.

The Dutch test tanks had a major advantage over other facilities in that they used one-third sized models which gave results that were considerably more accurate and took much of the guesswork out of the interpretation of the data. Lexcen began with a model of *Australia* so that he would have a benchmark for the comparison of his new ideas. Then he designed a conventional Twelve which was to become *Challenge 12*, the Victorian syndicate's yacht which Bond always claimed he could fall back on if the radical boat *Australia II* did not work.

Secure in the knowledge that he had designed a yacht that could challenge, Lexcen then devoted his time to experimenting with ideas that had been in his head for years. It was not haphazard experimentation. He wanted a yacht for all seasons: a light weather performer to win the elimination trials that would also go well in the heavier winds they could expect in the Cup challenge itself.

Under the Rule, small, light boats traditionally went well in light winds but did not have the stability to be fast in stronger winds. To achieve that stability, designers had to go for bigger and heavier boats, with less sail area – boats which did not perform in lighter winds. Lexcen was determined to be the first man to solve the problem.

The problem was the Rule's maximum restriction on draft. On other boats stability was easily achieved by having the weight in a long deep keel. But with the Twelves this was impossible, and designers were forced to go for big, heavy displacement boats which were too slow for the light weather that dominated Newport's early summer and the elimination trials.

Lexcen concentrated his efforts and those of his researchers at the Agency on the keel. As well as using the test tanks, the Netherlands Aerospace Laboratory was recruited to adapt its aircraft design computer programs to yacht design for the 12-Metre project. The finite element program would speed up the evaluation of Lexcen's ideas, giving them a rough idea of the comparative wave resistance of the different configurations. Then the ideas that were most promising could be turned into models for proper testing.

Lexcen tried several types of keel, concentrating on different chords and different lateral shapes. Most successful was what was dubbed "the upside down keel" – a keel that was thicker and longer at the bottom than at the top, where it was attached to the hull. This configuration, with the weight lower down, was more stable, and faster than the benchmark keel of *Australia*, but considerable turbulence was created by the wide tip at the bottom, which caused speed-sapping drag. There was a further problem of tip vortex shedding – the clash of water of different pressures from each side of the keel, as the water on the high pressure side to leeward flowed around the bottom edge of the keel to meet the low pressure windward side and create high resistance. The search began for the solution.

"When we started we didn't know we would end up with winglets," Project Director Dr Peter van Oossanen recalled. "When we arrived at the inverse tapered keel as being good for stability, which was essential for September, we immediately began thinking about how we would then get rid of the huge resistance and tip vortex. We looked at torpedoes, end plates, little bulbs, and stuff before Ben Lexcen asked us to test winglets."

There was nothing new about winglets, except that no-one had thought of applying them to the keel of a yacht. In 1974 the American space agency NASA had published details of its winglet research that solved the similar problem of tip vortex on high aspect ratio aircraft wings.

In the test tanks Lexcen had encouraging results. His keel generated more lift to windward and was considerably more stable with the thicker chord at its base and an extra 7,000 lbs (3,175 kg) of lead in the wings at the lowest possible point. As well as getting the cleanest possible flow of water across both sides of the keel, the wings had the added stability advantage of deepening the yacht's draft when heeled. And further, they reduced leeway by adding to the lateral area.

Of course the wings added drag, which worried Lexcen for light weather performance and downwind speed in all wind strengths. The tank tests confirmed his fears and Lexcen looked closely at the hull to reduce wetted surface. His answer was to dispense with the bustle behind the keel, removing wetted surface and reducing displacement, which had become redundant owing to the increased amount of lead in the keel. The resulting shorter waterline length was translated into increased sail area and Lexcen was satisfied that the increased drag had been more than overcome. Another by-product was that the yacht would be far more manoeuvrable than any other 12-Metre with a traditional long, low aspect keel.

Scientific research showed Lexcen had achieved a breakthrough. The acid test was to see whether that research had been accurate or whether it had deceived those who believed in it. In the end it took 2,000 sailing hours in Australia to get everything right and prove *Australia II* clearly superior to her stablemate, the conventional *Challenge 12*.

When *Australia II* arrived in Newport she immediately proved to be superior to the rest of the world. In the elimination series of three round robins she won 44 races and lost five. No other boat could match her manoeuvrability, her speed out of tacks, her height to windward and her speed in all conditions.

Dennis Conner and the other American syndicates watched the races and Conner admitted later that he knew the Australians would be very dangerous. As *Australia II* marched inexorably towards the Cup, attention was diverted ashore by the New York Yacht Club's challenge to the keel's legality, but its campaign to discredit the keel and its designer foundered.

Conner, in a yacht which had nothing to do with scientific research, had a trouble-free run to win the right to defend. Blackaller's *Defender* underwent major surgery three times but was still the first to be eliminated, leaving the 10-year-old *Courageous* to unsuccessfully face Conner. His yacht *Liberty* also underwent surgery, but of a very unscientific nature. Valentijn carefully watched the boat's motion while racing and decided before the eliminations to lop three feet off the overall length in the stern. He decided it wasn't doing anything for speed, just increasing unwanted weight.

Conner had also looked hard at the problem of having a boat that would perform in all wind strengths, but he had a different answer to Lexcen's – multiple rating certificates. Predicting the weather they would have in the next race, *Liberty*'s crew could add or remove internal ballast and adjust the sail area to suit the new configuration. No-one had ever done this before and opposing Americans and Australians alike were angry that it was going on. But there was nothing in the Rule to prevent it.

History shows that this was not enough. *Australia II* was clearly the superior yacht and won the 25th America's Cup 4-3 after a thrilling series. It could have been a walkover for the Australians if they had not lost the first two races through equipment failure. As it was, they had to stage sport's greatest comeback to win the Cup.

It was a triumph for Lexcen, who proved that original, lateral thinking could lead to a breakthrough. In the United States there was much lamenting that designers had continued to ignore the offerings of scientific research. In some corners, scorn was poured on Conner for defending in a boat that had been designed "by committee" without any attempt to experiment for a breakthrough. Conner answered that they had built boats to try to head off any breakthrough. *Spirit* had been a big boat, *Magic* a small light displacement boat. Neither had worked. *Australia II*, which was even lighter than *Magic*, fooled them with the stability given to her by her winged keel.

Following the bitterness of the debate over the winged keel before the Cup, Lexcen and Bond finally had the argument settled once and for all later that year at the annual meeting of the sport's governing body, the International Yacht Racing Union. The IYRU voted that the 12-Metre class was a development class and that the winglets were perfectly legal. Two restrictions were applied to them: they could not be wider than 11 ft 9 in (3.6 metres) and they could not be retracted. However, in order to keep the existing ocean racing fleet from being made obsolete overnight, the Union decreed that only Metre Rule boats could use winged keels. Lexcen assigned his keel patent to the IYRU. At the same time the use of different certificates during a series was banned.

Following the approval of the winged keel, the overnight rehabilitation of scientific research in yacht design began. As more than 20 syndicates around the world prepared to tackle Australia for the America's Cup, the designers were overwhelmed with offers of assistance from research organisations sensing a whole new market. Research programs totalling millions of dollars got underway as designers pressed computer operators and tank technicians to discover the secret of Lexcen's winged keel and then refine it, looking for another breakthrough.

At the same time other keel configurations tried on radio-controlled model yachts were also tested, including the canard or "window" keel.

The new design research industry spawned another new industry: protection of the results of the research from the prying eyes of other syndicates. When *Australia II's* team first covered her winged keel with a cheap sheet of green plastic they could never have guessed what they were starting. In the lead up to the 1987 America's Cup, the yachts in Fremantle are kept in submarine style pens, with sheets of galvanised iron driven into the seabed and locked outer doors to prevent divers from sneaking an unauthorised look. But not *Australia II*. She remains on show for all to copy, taunting others to do better.

When the yachts put to sea they are photographed from helicopters by members of other syndicates to study what their opposition is up to. Constant surveillance is necessary as most syndicates continually change the configurations of their yachts, trying a range of keels in their search for any extra margin of improved performance.

By early 1986 the number of challengers for the Cup had been reduced to 13. The high cost of sailing – America's Cup style – had begun to take its toll. Budgets for the 1987 America's Cup range up to $20 million.

Two yachts will begin racing on 31 January 1987 to decide the next winner of the America's Cup in a best of seven series of races. Until the last possible minute, both will still be experimenting, still looking for an edge. And even after it is all over, many will still have their yachts covered and refuse to give details of their design. After all, they may want to keep their secrets until the 1991 America's Cup.

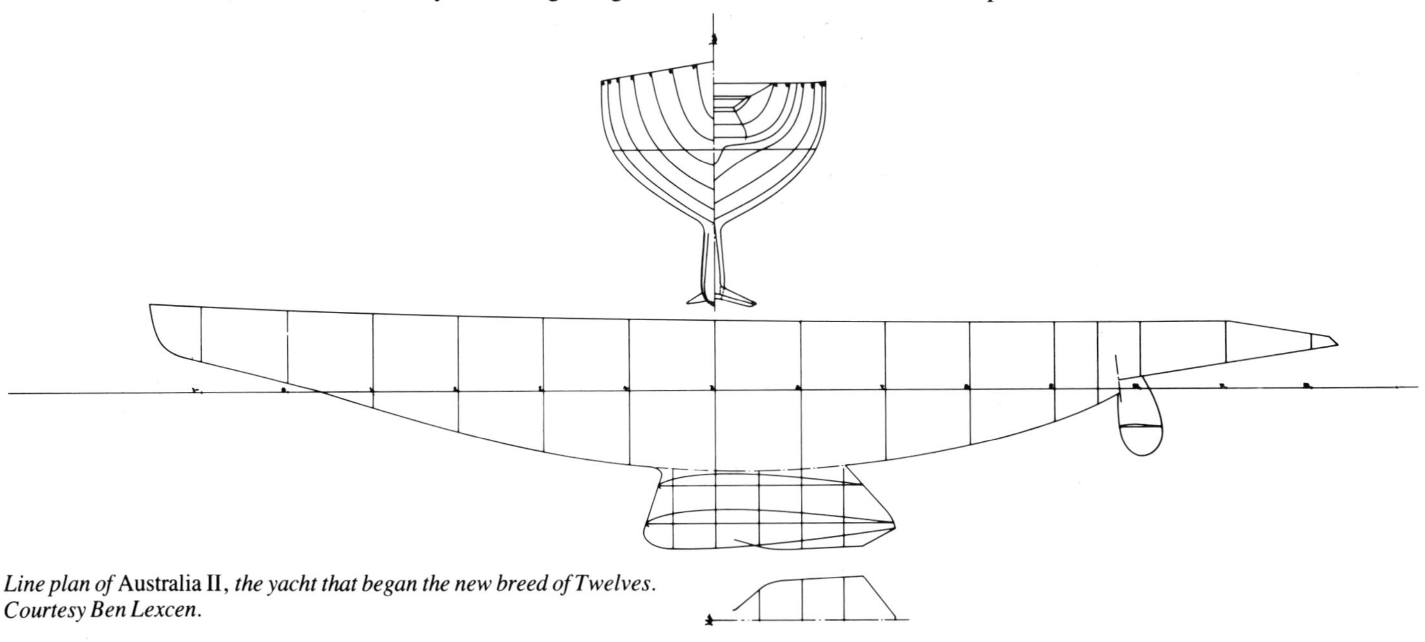

Line plan of Australia II, *the yacht that began the new breed of Twelves. Courtesy Ben Lexcen.*

AUSTRALIA

Hard Act To Follow

When *Australia II* finally removed the America's Cup from the New York Yacht Club after 132 long years, it marked the success of a long and ongoing partnership between two remarkable men, Alan Bond and Ben Lexcen.

It was a partnership often referred to by Lexcen as one in which he was the faithful court painter to the Medici prince. To strangers they appear total opposites: Bond the aggressive and successful businessman with high profile ventures around the world; Ben the shy man, only comfortable when "messing about in boats".

In fact they share many similarities. Of similar age, both are ambitious, albeit for different reasons, and both have gone through their lives determined to avoid being restricted by accepted standards.

Bond was always the upfront businessman – prepared to take on the world to prove himself right and then determined to go on to the next successful venture to prove the past had not been a fluke. Bond long suffered the handicap of being a pioneer, the first of a new breed of Australian millionaire – aged in his thirties, West Australian and completely unconcerned by his lack of acceptance by the "establishment" located on Australia's east coast which traditionally controlled the nation's finances and commerce. Throughout his career it had refused to take the brash young West Australian seriously, constantly predicting his messy downfall. Despite one very close shave in the mid 1970s, Bond continued to prove them wrong and today heads a vast empire with interests around the world in brewing, mining, resources, technology, the media and property development.

Bond became interested in yachting in the early 1960s when he sailed small yachts on Perth's Swan River. In 1968 he commissioned Ben Lexcen to design him a lightweight 58-Footer to beat Royal Perth Yacht Club champion Rolly Tasker. The result was the successful yacht *Apollo* which began a long partnership between the two men.

Lexcen has always been determined to succeed – as a yachtsman, sailmaker and yacht designer. Like Bond, throughout his career he has refused to take accepted standards for granted, preferring to think beyond the current norms and eventually prove his theories correct.

Bond discovered the America's Cup in 1970 when he was preparing *Apollo* for the Newport-Bermuda Race. With Lexcen he looked over the yacht *Valiant* and decided to challenge for the America's Cup. Following the success of Lexcen's first ocean racers, Bond decided Lexcen was the man to design the boat.

It was in 1974 that Alan Bond first challenged for the America's Cup. The little known West Australian property developer had purchased both *Gretel* and *Gretel II* from Sir Frank Packer to use for crew training while Ben Lexcen (then called Bob Miller) designed his first 12-Metre. She was to be named *Southern Cross* after the pattern of stars that points the way southwards in the heavens over Australia and is featured on Australia's national flag.

Alan Bond – refused to accept defeat.

Bond was thinking as much about using the America's Cup to promote a major business venture as he was about winning a yachting regatta. He had bought a large area of sand dunes at the little known town of Yanchep, 45 kilometres north of Perth. He renamed it Sun City, built an artificial harbour, subdivided the dunes, planted some grass and began building houses. It was a risky speculation and Bond moved his entire 12-Metre operation to the unlikely area to prepare for the challenge through the new Sun City Yacht Club, then situated in a boatshed on the edge of the blustery Indian Ocean.

The performance of *Gretel II* in the previous challenge, when she took a race from the Americans and showed the potential to be generally faster than *Intrepid,* was to make it harder for Alan Bond in his first year. The Americans had had a fright and their 1974 defender would be picked only after the most rigorous trials.

Altogether seven clubs challenged for the Cup but owing to the worldwide recession only Bond and Baron Bich from France turned up.

Bond did not wait for the racing before going into battle. Then aged 32, he used the Australian media and their American affiliates to great effect to criticise the New York Yacht Club at every available opportunity. The Club's members and committees were accused of being most unsportsmanlike in their determination to hang on to "their Cup". The New Yorkers were shocked, not knowing how to treat this brash young Australian.

It is now history that *Southern Cross* with Jim Hardy at the wheel ran into the new superboat, *Courageous*. The Australians also ran into a match-fit team of Americans including Dennis Conner, who was starting helmsman and tactician. *Southern Cross* was slower than her opponent in the predominantly light airs. Observers believed she was faster in

Ben Lexcen – revolutionised 12-Metre design.

heavier airs but had few opportunities to show that speed.

Like so many others before him, Bond could not refrain from overruling his yachtsmen when they began losing races. He ordered rig and crew changes between races, even manning the winches himself in one race. But it did no good and much to the relief of the NYYC, *Southern Cross* went down 4-0. They believed the brash young Australian who had been promising to annihilate them at his first go would be too embarrassed to show his face in Newport again. But the tenacious Bond was never one to admit defeat.

As it turned out, Bond's first challenge for the America's Cup did not end in 1974. Three years later, as he was preparing for his second challenge, news leaked out in the USA that *Courageous* had been 1800 pounds underweight when she had raced. Bond was incensed when he learned that the New York Yacht Club knew of this before the racing, but had blamed the measurers and considered the matter insignificant. Bond claimed the yacht had not been a 12-Metre when she had raced and therefore should be disqualified. His request that the Club should forward the Cup to him was refused. The Club did concede that in future all yachts would be weighed. But it did nothing for the relationship between the two parties nor for the New York Yacht Club's image.

Getting Lexcen to design his new Twelve was no easy matter. Shattered by the thrashing of *Southern Cross,* he left Australia to live in England. Bond literally had to drag him back to begin designing their 1977 yacht. As co-designer, Bond recruited Dutch born Johan Valentijn, who had previously worked on 12-Metre design for Sparkman & Stephens in the USA. He and Lexcen used tank testing facilities at Delft University in Valentijn's home country for their design.

Australia was short on the waterline and started a new trend to less freeboard. But it was no help. With Noel Robins at the helm, she went down 4-0 to *Courageous* with the "Mouth from the South", Ted Turner, in charge.

Courageous led around every mark of every race and handed out what appeared to be a drubbing to the Downunder pretenders. But Bond was encouraged by what he considered to be an improvement over their first challenge and, in true America's Cup tradition, announced that he would return in 1980. As he saw it, in 1974 they had been beaten by margins ranging from one minute to more than seven minutes. In 1977, the biggest margin was two minutes 32 seconds.

A downturn in the Australian economy and business difficulties meant money would be tight, but Bond was determined to keep his America's Cup education underway and Lexcen began to modify *Australia* for a second tilt at the Auld Mug. Lexcen was now working full-time for Bond. At the same time Bond kept building up the team, with Jim Hardy returning to the helm, former British schoolteacher John Longley preparing to run the foredeck for his third challenge and others such as sail trimmers Peter Shipway and John Bertrand girding up for further attempts. Running the challenge for the first time would be Warren Jones, an aggressive businessman whose company had been taken over by Alan Bond before the 1977 challenge. He had gone to Newport to watch how that challenge had been handled.

Lexcen, a one-man band again following the decision by Valentijn to change nationality once more to design a new yacht for Baron Bich of France, made a number of important underwater alterations to *Australia.* He altered the keel, enlarged the trim tab and rudder, and moved the rig forward 30 cm. Lexcen also took on the job of tactician, although Bond for a time considered replacing him with Bertrand.

The Alan Bond of 1980 surprised the waiting Americans with his cool demeanour. The whole Australian effort was one of getting on with the job and at all times they remained realistic. As Ben Lexcen put it: "There's not a real good chance, but it's better than the past two attempts that I've been involved in." Jim Hardy, who had initially been reluctant to take the helm for another try, commented: "I think *Australia* is a very fast yacht. To me the lack of really tough match-racing practice has been the biggest single factor in the challengers not being able to beat the defenders, so if the others co-operate as promised we'll be in better shape."

On the water the competition had become much tougher. Traditionally the best America's Cup racing took place in the defender elimination series. But the Cup was beginning to attract worldwide attention. As well as the three-year-old *Australia,* the Swedish yacht *Sverige* returned to Newport, Baron Bich was back with a new *France 3* and Britain returned to the America's Cup with *Lionheart,* sporting a radical mast with a fibreglass top section which bent dramatically, enabling them to add more than 100 sq ft (9.2 sq m) in unmeasured mainsail area. When the British stepped the mast it transformed *Lionheart's* performance. The Australians estimated it gave them 15 minutes improvement around the full length course.

The American groups agonised over whether to build similar masts. Lexcen knew it would give the Australians an edge they had never had over the defenders. He persuaded Bond it was worth the gamble and, to keep the Americans from following suit, they built their own mast in absolute secrecy in Newport, well away from prying eyes.

Now into his third America's Cup campaign, Bond agreed with Lexcen that to win they would need an edge over the Americans. To be equal in boat speed was not enough because they now realised other factors gave the defenders an automatic advantage. The first was their local knowledge of the waters and weather patterns in Newport. Secondly, match-racing had long been popular in the United States, with a well-established circuit of regattas. By contrast there was not one match-racing regatta in Australia. And thirdly, they knew the effects of campaigning away from home with the attendant homesickness and other distracting problems.

The new mast was ready just in time to be stepped after *Australia* won the right to challenge. But that left only a week to cut new sails and tune the rig before going up against Dennis Conner in *Freedom*. It was not long enough. The Australians could not get their sails right and went down 4-1. Americans and Australians alike agreed that the yacht could have won the series if they had had another month to get the rig ready.

Bond was not put off. Although conceding it could well be his final fling, he announced that he would challenge again in 1983, this time with John Bertrand, the Melbourne sailmaker and Olympic bronze medallist, steering the boat in place of Jim Hardy, who said he had "heard enough losers' guns". "Gentleman Jim", as he is commonly known, had done a magnificent job for Australia, steering challengers in 1970, 1974 and finally 1980. But towards the end of that period he watched the America's Cup becoming more and more professional, with big sponsorships making it a highly commercial event. That in turn was leading inevitably to what he perceived to be less sportsmanship on the water, and he was just not interested in competing at that level.

Estimating the challenge would cost $5 million in 1983, Bond remained undaunted. To help pay the bills he sold *Australia* to England but kept the computer readouts of her performance in the misguided belief that they would provide a yardstick for their new 12-Metre, to be designed again by Ben Lexcen.

Bond made a big change to his approach for the 1983 challenge by allocating $1.5 million to research. In 1978 he had met Dr Peter van Oossanen, head of research at the Netherlands Ship Model Agency which was then the world's largest and most sophisticated marine research facility. A qualified naval architect, van Oossanen had spent many of his working years in Australia and knew Ben Lexcen well. Bond had planned to give Lexcen use of the Dutch facilities in his redesign of *Australia* for 1980, but tight funds had stopped that.

This time Bond wanted a design edge over the defenders and knew he would have to pay for that to happen. In 1981

Lexcen moved to Holland for four months. The end result of his research was to scandalise the New York Yacht Club, develop a war of words and legal jargon unprecedented in sporting history, and finally play a vital role in ending sport's longest winning streak.

Lexcen had long played around with "weird and whacky" ideas in yacht design, but for the first time he had the budget and the resources to put some of those ideas to the test in the one-third scale models and long towing tanks of the Netherlands Ship Model Basin. The result was two 12-Metre designs, one conventional and the other so radical that it was to revolutionise 12-Metre design and lead to a complete re-evaluation of underwater shapes and appendages of all racing yachts.

Lexcen did not have it all his own way when he developed the upside down keel with wings. Taking time out from the 1981 Admiral's Cup to fly to Holland to discuss the development, Bond, Jones and Bertrand grilled van Oossanen. Bertrand in particular was sceptical. He had maintained all along that given a good conventional boat the Australians could win through better crew work, self-confidence, and the use of sails that would be at least the equal of the defenders for the first time.

Bond believed he needed a superior yacht but understandably wanted to hedge his bets. Consequently he decided to build not only the potential breakthrough yacht and name it *Australia II*, but also the second boat, which was slightly longer and heavier, with a conventional keel. That boat, *Challenge 12*, was bought by a Melbourne syndicate for $400,000. When they ran short of money, Bond chartered it back and equipped it to race against *Australia II*.

It took six months of close racing between the two yachts before *Australia II* showed herself to be superior. Basically the crew learned to sail her on a higher angle to windward than they were used to. With good sails and the crew in tune with the yacht, they were formidable to windward. Off the wind they were only average, and so began a major program of spinnaker development and improvement of offwind techniques. Bertrand said their downwind performance would be their Achilles heel in Newport if they did not improve. As it turned out, it became their second secret weapon.

Secrecy was paramount to the syndicate. They knew that other syndicates would be able to copy their keel concept up until just six weeks before the actual Cup. Throughout the building and campaigning *Australia II's* keel was kept shrouded, and all who worked and sailed on her were contracted to maintain absolute secrecy. This policy would drive the New York Yacht Club to despair, and cause the American crew aboard *Liberty* to adopt a siege mentality and commit costly mistakes on the water.

At the same time the syndicate kept quiet about their yacht, foregoing all the usual razzmatazz aimed at extracting much-needed sponsorship from Australian and multi-national companies. In contrast to their earlier campaigns, this was a completely professional operation.

Australia II

Bond deliberately kept the size of the team down to a manageable minimum. In all, 32 men and women made up the official team that went to Newport in 1983. Warren Jones and John Longley were in charge of administration, with Longley handing over his administrative tasks to Jones in Newport to concentrate on sailing in his fourth Cup. Bertrand, a highly motivated and intelligent yachtsman, picked his crew carefully. Back from 1980 were 18-Foot Skiff champion Rob Brown, Skip Lissiman, Scott McAllister, Phil Skidmore and Peter Costello. The vital role of tactician went to Hugh Treharne, a successful Sydney sailmaker ranked with Bertrand as one of the best yachtsmen in Australia. The job of navigator went to Grant Simmer, twice Australian Lightweight Sharpie champion with an understanding of computer analysis that was demanded by the sophisticated computer performance analysis programs developed for the yacht by van Oossanen and the syndicate's full-time computer expert, Glen Read. Another newcomer to play a key role was Colin Beashel, twice Australian champion in the highly competitive Laser dinghy class and world champion crewman in the 5.5 Metre class. Beashel's father Ken, a leading Sydney shipwright. went to Newport in charge of the yacht's maintenance.

Despite opposition from Bond and Jones, Bertrand got his way to have sport psychologist Laurie Hayden join the team to help them prepare for the Cup. Bertrand was very well aware of the overaweing effects of the aura that surrounds the America's Cup, with its long years of tradition, and the inferiority complex of Australian yachtsmen in previous challenges against the unbeaten Americans. Also providing valuable support was Sir James Hardy, who saw much from the tender that others missed. He was also to fill in for Bertrand for a time when he could not sail during the elimination series.

For the back-breaking task of "grinding", the operation of the massive winches that trim the headsails, Bertrand began a new America's Cup trend by going outside yachting circles to recruit two rowers, Will Baillieu and Brian Richardson, who had stroked the Australian eight in the 1980 Olympic Games.

Inferior sails had always hindered challenges for the America's Cup and the Australians were determined not to be caught short in 1983. New Zealand sailmaker Tom Schnackenberg became an honorary "Aussie" and oversaw the Australian sail loft, pioneering the design of tri-radial and vertical-cut mainsails, and headsails that were in many instances superior to those on the American defender.

The Australians were confident that for the first time they would go up against the Americans fully race-fit after a demanding elimination series. Lining up against them in Newport were the Victorians with *Challenge 12* and a Sydney effort with the yacht *Advance*, Italy, England, Canada and France. As it turned out, none was a match for *Australia II*, which swept through the eliminations with more than 40 wins and only six losses, finally defeating the British yacht *Victory 83* for the right to challenge. From the outset *Australia II* had no trouble with the opposition. She had superior boat speed in all conditions and was unbelievably manoeuvrable, spinning like a top, keeping her speed through tacks and pointing closer to the wind than any other yachts when beating to windward. In stark contrast to previous challengers, the team went into the racing "hot to trot", with no last minute changes to the boat or people.

When the ability of the Australians and the speed of their yacht became obvious early in the eliminations, three months before the Cup, attention quickly switched from the action on the water to the happenings ashore, which quickly became dubbed the "Keelgate Affair". The problem was the winged keel. The New York Yacht Club believed it was a peculiarity under Rule 27 and could not be measured fairly. If it could, they maintained, it would measure in well over the limit. This was long after the yacht had been measured and approved by an international team of measurers, in accordance with the rules of the New York Yacht Club. Appeals by the Club to the International Yacht Racing Union were rebuffed on the grounds that the Club should abide by the rules it had laid down.

The Club then attacked the syndicate with the claim that the keel had been designed by the Dutch at the Netherlands Ship Model Basin and not by Ben Lexcen. Publicly Lexcen shrugged off their accusations, but privately the strain told. Already under a lot of pressure designing and building masts and acting as general adviser to the group, the sensitive Lexcen was admitted to hospital shortly before the Cup began, to be treated for high blood pressure.

The NYYC's hierarchy was deeply split over whether they should even race against *Australia II* and the Cup was very nearly called off at the last minute. In its dealings with the news media and the public, the Club paid dearly for its high-handed attitude of previous years. Many Americans joined in the Australian outcry against its efforts to have *Australia II* disqualified and the other potential challengers also supported the Australians.

1983 veterans Colin Beashel (left) and Hugh Treharne, leading the way in 1987.

Business end of Australia II *with* Australia III *to windward.*

Some in the Bond camp felt the whole campaign was aimed at distracting the Australian yachtsmen. But they made sure they did not fall for that. Bertrand insisted that the yachtsmen concentrate on their sailing, leaving Warren Jones and his lawyers to handle the controversy which was front page news all over the world for months. Jones handled the affair superbly, at all times staying one step ahead of his antagonists. Finally, shortly before Australia was declared the challenger, he produced his trump card when he made public a telex from the *Liberty* syndicate to the Netherlands Ship Model Basin asking to buy the winged keel design to put under one of their yachts. This was in direct contravention of the rule stating that yachts had to be designed by a national of the same country. It was the end of the affair and the New York Yacht Club lost badly. Dennis Conner later claimed it was Warren Jones who had made the difference between Australia winning and losing the Cup.

The Americans were badly demoralised by the affair and by watching the yacht they considered illegal continue to make all other foreign yachts look second rate. Naval architect and navigator of *Liberty,* Halsey Herreshoff, summed up their feeling of despair when he wrote: "If the closely guarded, peculiar keel design of *Australia II* is allowed to remain in the competition, or is allowed to continue to be rated without penalty, the yacht ... will likely win the America's Cup in September 1983."

So the stage was set for the yachting battle of the century, with the public around the world backing the Australian underdogs against what most perceived as the unsporting New York Yacht Club. Dramatic as the shoreside battle had been, the best was still to come, and the 1983 America's Cup turned out to be a highly emotional, heart-stopping event that was better in fact than the best fiction from Hollywood's scriptwriters.

Bond was convinced they would win. "In my opinion, this is the breakthrough we have been waiting for. We will win 4-0 and with our manoeuvrability and height to windward will lead around every windward mark." Lexcen knew he had produced a yacht that was superior to the American defender *Liberty*. Bertrand was confident and knew he had moulded a crew that was not only good but also sure of their own abilities as individuals and as a team.

As it turned out, the Australians got off to the worst possible start, losing the first two races through equipment failure. But the boat was obviously as fast and manoeuvrable as they had hoped, and the defenders knew they faced a faster boat. The story of Australia's great comeback from 3-1 down is now sporting legend. The last race could so easily have been the result of the vivid imagination of a leading Hollywood scriptwriter.

Honours at the start were even, Bertrand going left, Conner right. Conner realised he had made a mistake and tacked four lengths behind to follow the Australians. Towards the mark, Bertrand failed to cover Conner who got the break he wanted, rounding the mark 29 seconds ahead of *Australia II*. Conner stayed in front, rounding the second last leg to begin the square run 57 seconds ahead. It appeared the Cup would stay in American hands.

But the Australians were not finished, and as they ran downwind they closed the gap on Conner with better boat speed. Then Conner failed to cover the Australians, who picked up a stronger breeze to sail in front of the Americans. It was unbelievable for all except the crews of the two yachts. The Australians kept their minds on the job, while arguments broke out aboard *Liberty* as they prepared to tackle *Australia II* on the last windward leg.

That last beat to windward will forever stay in the minds of yachtsmen all over the world. Conner rounded 29 seconds behind and began to throw everything at the Australians in a ferocious tacking duel, trying to force them to make a mistake. He not only threw dummy tacks at the Australians; at one stage he tried to lure them into the spectator fleet. In all, the yachts tacked 47 times. But the Australians kept their cool and crossed the finish line 41 seconds in front to wrap up the greatest sporting comeback of all time.

The Australians were ecstatic, Conner and his crew shattered. Back at the dock, thousands of people treated the Australians like heroes. The grin on Alan Bond's face as he ordered the yacht to be lifted out of the water without her shroud for the first time was wider than the mysterious wings that rose from the murky depths.

Ben Lexcen summed up the feelings of many when he said he had been worried all along by Dennis Conner, not *Liberty*. Lexcen said no-one but Conner could have forced the series to seven races.

For Bond it was a lifetime dream come true. Just before the 1983 Cup races he had said that it would be his last attempt. Personally he felt he could do no more to win the Cup. With *Australia II*, an excellent crew, good sails and sound administration, he finally proved what he had been saying all along – that the America's Cup was winnable.

A hero's welcome greeted the *Australia II* team when they returned to Australia with the Cup, which promptly went on a tour of capital cities. When the yacht returned, it too went on tour to be admired by tens of thousands of people, who regarded the America's Cup win as proof that Australia was still a nation of winning sportsmen, despite constant disappointments on the world's cricket pitches, golf links and tennis courts.

Bond went to work planning his defence of the Cup, while local and national governments began to struggle with the problems of turning a sleepy harbour town into an international sporting venue capable of coping with an estimated 500,000 visitors over a six-month period. Bond arranged to house his defence at new headquarters in the Fremantle fishing harbour, which would host the world's post-*Australia II* 12-Metres. No fewer than 26 yacht clubs around the world began planning serious challenges to win the America's Cup.

Bond kept most of his team together, the most notable loss being John Bertrand, who was not interested in devoting another three years of his life to another America's Cup campaign. "For 14 years I've been involved with trying to win the Cup", said Bertrand. "Finally we did it. We climbed the mountain, conquered our Everest and that takes lots and lots of effort. Technically it takes a year and a half to two years full-time and at least half of that is away from your family. I just can't give up that time again."

Bertand did remain with the syndicate as an adviser. As helmsmen, Bond nominated 1983 veterans Treharne, Beashel, Lissiman, and recruited local champion Gordon Lucas.

Bond planned a two yacht campaign for the defence. While other potential defenders would emerge, he felt that to be competitive he had to have two yachts pushing each other to new limits. In *Australia II* he knew he had the benchmark of 12-Metre design which everyone else would have to copy and then improve on. But he could not rely on that yacht for a defence, because it was designed for the light airs and flat seas of Newport, not the blustery winds and choppy waves of Fremantle.

That meant it was back to the drawing board for Ben Lexcen, while John Longley, Skip Lissiman and Warren Jones began developing the infrastructure for the defence effort.

Bond was not content to rest on his laurels. First he expressed the hope that the other defence syndicates planned in Western Australia, South Australia, New South Wales, Victoria and Queensland would be competitive to ensure the strongest possible defence. Then he had the first of many rows with the Royal Perth Yacht Club, accusing it of taking funds from Australian companies that should have gone to the syndicates.

A similar wrangle, also long-running, developed between Bond and the West Australian and Australian Governments, with Bond accusing them of failing to support them by

Early development for the defence – Australia II *and* South Australia *return from a day's racing.*

dropping taxes and duties, as was happening to benefit challengers overseas.

Bond planned a $10 million campaign which included a new *Australia III* and possibly an *Australia IV.* Already Lexcen had been working on an improvement of *Australia II,* and had booked time at the Netherlands Ship Model Basin (now called the Maritime Research Institute Netherlands) to test his ideas.

But first he designed a new yacht for the South Australian syndicate. Under an arrangement between the two groups, Lexcen would design the new yacht, she would be built by Steve Ward who built Bond's Twelves, and Bond's yachtsmen would show the newcomers how to sail it. They would then race *Australia II* against it while their own *Australia III* was being built by Ward. In return, *South Australia* would be a test bed for Lexcen's ideas for *Australia III.*

When *South Australia* was launched she was longer and slightly heavier than *Australia II.* Her keel was kept shrouded, but in her first races she was able to spin as fast as *Australia II.*

Lexcen was enthusiastic. "It's faster than *Australia II* in a straight line, both upwind and downwind. We still have to get some weight out of the boat which will make it faster downwind, and when they learn how to sail it they will start to beat *Australia II* around the track."

Lexcen was right. When *Australia II's* veterans joined the inexperienced South Australians aboard their yacht for intensive racing over half and full length America's Cup courses, there was nothing between the two yachts, with both sharing the honours in some tough racing.

At the same time, Steve Ward was completing *Australia III,* Lexcen's latest, which some said would be another radical from the wizard of 12-Metre yacht design while others claimed it would be a natural progression from *Australia II.* Syndicate spokesmen were saying little, except to insist that they did not know whether the winged keel would even work off Fremantle in 1986/87 because it had not been a success before 1983 when *Australia II* raced *Challenge 12.* The team that had rewritten the rules about secrecy in the America's Cup was staying firmly in the lead, out to keep everyone guessing what their next move would be.

And as if to rub in the superiority of their lead over other America's Cup aspirants, each night *Australia II* was lifted from the water with her keel uncovered, symbolically daring others to be brave and do better.

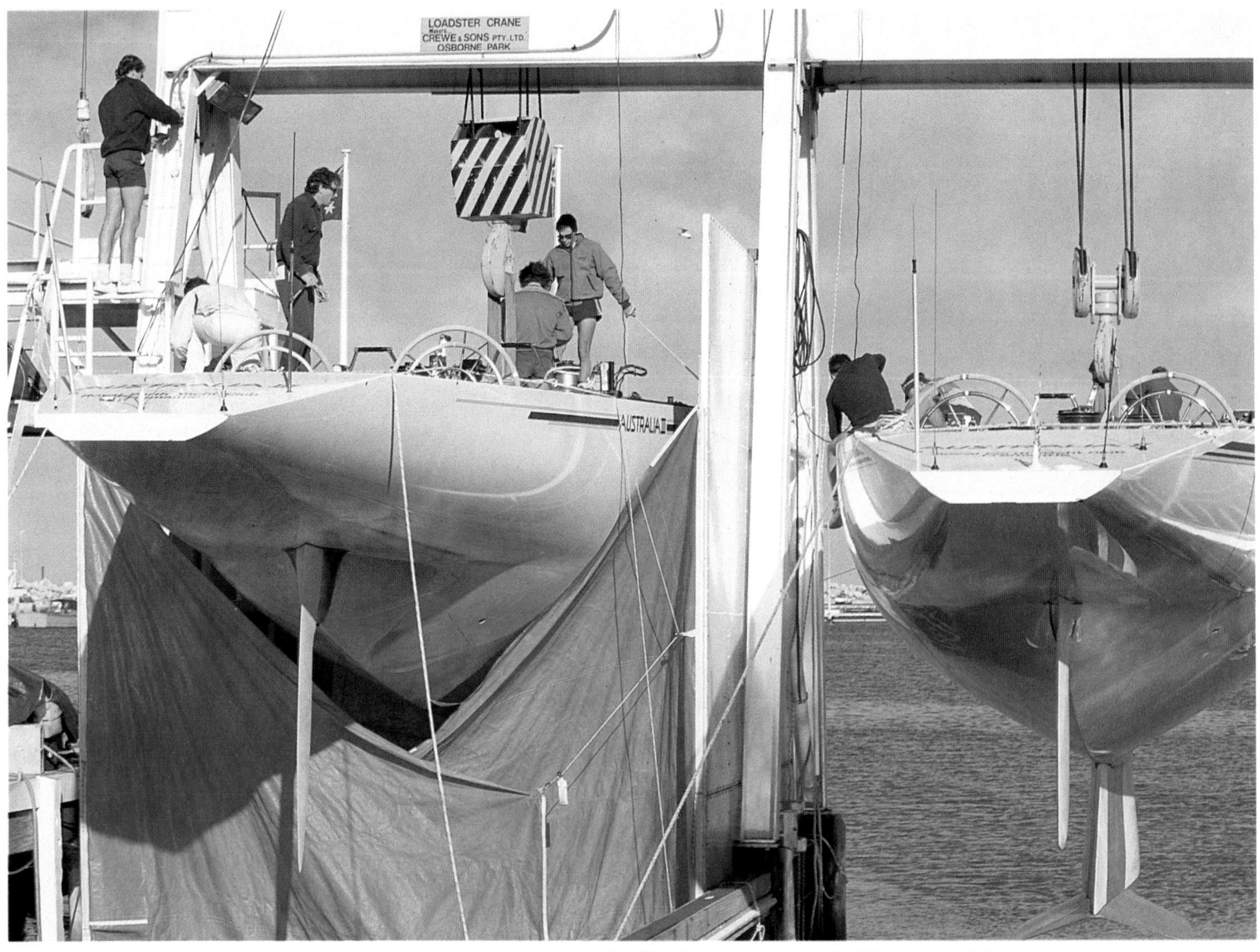

Australia III's *secrets kept covered to keep the world guessing while 1983 Cup winner* Australia II *hangs free, defying others to do better.*

Finally on 27 September 1985, two years to the day on Australian time that *Australia II* won the America's Cup, *Australia III* emerged from Steve Ward's yard, with her keel covered, and was trucked to Fremantle for launching and rigging as she lay alongside *Australia II*. After a day of feverish activity the organisation and professionalism of the team was graphically demonstrated when, just before sunset, Ben Lexcen took the helm of the new yacht as it was towed out to sail on Gage Roads. All aboard were ecstatic when they returned to the dock in the dark.

Lexcen enthused: "She sails beautifully, she's perfectly balanced. I took my hand off the wheel for a mile downwind and she sailed perfectly straight. As the sun was hitting the water it felt as though we were going at 5,000 miles an hour. I know they always feel fast then, but it was fantastic. We'll need a couple of months to optimise her, but if it's not faster than *Australia II* and *South Australia* then I've just wasted 18 months of my time."

Two days later, on the anniversary of the day the Australians were congratulated by US President Reagan on the lawns of the White House, the official christening of *Australia III* took place at the Royal Perth Yacht Club in a glittering ceremony that was televised live around Australia.

The inevitable question was quickly answered by Lexcen: "Yes, it does have a winged keel, although it is different to the one we used in Newport. A better solution will come along. Maybe it won't be at this America's Cup but I'm sure that my one stab at a different thing is not the final solution."

After the mandatory toasting in champagne (and beer from Bond's Swan Brewery), the two yachts were sailed on the Swan River, just kilometres from the city of Perth, in an exciting display that took thousands of enthusiastic spectators back to 1983. It also showed the two to be very similar in appearance, physically and cosmetically. Both had the same colour schemes: gleaming white hulls with gold and green stripes along the topsides. Where *Australia II* had a green kangaroo painted on her bows, *Australia III* bore the boxing kangaroo which had symbolised their successful challenge in 1983.

In size and shape, too, the yachts were similar. *Australia III* was obviously longer by approximately 18 inches and heavier, to be stronger for the rough Fremantle conditions. She also showed more volume in the ends. In rig size the two appeared very similar and the changes to her deck layout were minor.

Australia III *and* Australia II.

Australia III

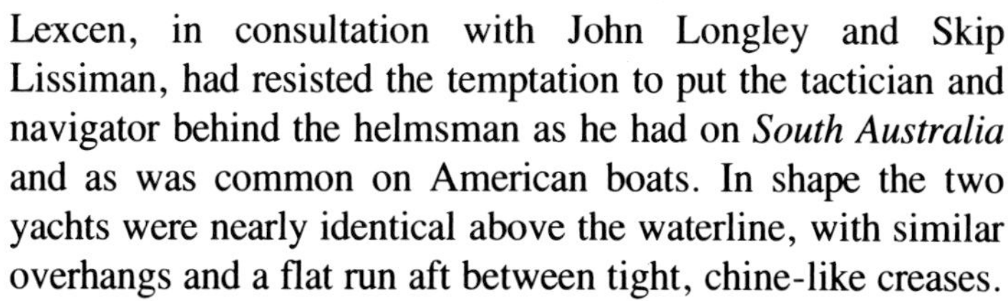

Lexcen, in consultation with John Longley and Skip Lissiman, had resisted the temptation to put the tactician and navigator behind the helmsman as he had on *South Australia* and as was common on American boats. In shape the two yachts were nearly identical above the waterline, with similar overhangs and a flat run aft between tight, chine-like creases.

If anything *Australia III* showed more bustle between keel and rudder, which was considerably larger than that hung below her predecessor. "Everyone is getting bigger rudders," Lexcen explained. "They were too small in the past and the boats would wander a lot. The spoon shape like *Australia II's* was very good in theory but it was too small, so now I've gone for a deeper and more pointed blade."

Allowing for the rougher waters off Fremantle, *Australia III* had approximately 10 cm (four inches) more freeboard than her little sister. She also had a little more sheer in the bow.

When *Australia III* was launched she carried her rig on a spare mast from *Australia II*. The reason was simply that her new mast, designed by Ben Lexcen and built by Steve Ward, simply had not been completed in time, and the project was put on hold to ensure the new yacht was launched on schedule. Lexcen had long been dissatisfied with the masts available commercially. In 1983 he had spent months building masts after discarding the commercial spars that were too soft and unsafe for his liking. Finally he bought the bare sections and built the masts himself. In addition he designed all the fittings and complicated rigging systems including the hydraulic jumper struts controlling the mast above the hounds.

For *Australia III,* Lexcen again threw himself into a complete mast design program, this time beginning with bare sections manufactured in Melbourne. Lexcen and another local spar manufacturer believed they had a big advantage over foreign rigs, as the aluminium manufacturer had the only ovens in the world long enough to heat treat the 27 metre sections in one piece. Other masts available to the syndicates were built in two pieces scarfed together. But Lexcen believed this to be a disadvantage in the windy conditions off Perth, and when four masts were broken on other yachts while sailing in the summer of 1985-86, he was proved right. The advantages of the single length mast were that it removed a weak point at the join, kept the curve smooth and eliminated unnecessary weight aloft in the form of the sleeve.

Lexcen and other designers were tightly restricted by the Rule which limits mast dimensions, taper, weight and centre

AUSTRALIA III
Royal Perth Yacht Club
Fremantle

of gravity. Rather they had to concentrate on strength and keeping as much of the weight as low as possible to reduce the heeling moment of the weight aloft.

Lexcen's masts were built by taking four longitudinal strips, glueing them together and then supporting the glue joins with a mind-boggling 5,000 rivets. Commercial spars were traditionally welded together for reasons of speed and economy. But Ward and Lexcen believe rivetting to be stronger because there is no weak point left by the heat of the welding process.

In addition to the skills of Ward and Lexcen, aircraft engineers and riggers were co-opted from national airline TAA to help rig the spar. Lexcen was determined that everything would be just right, which meant having fittings and systems that were totally efficient, minimised wind resistance and were as light as possible.

''It's a real challenge making these masts,'' said Ward. ''The boats are stiffer and there are unbelievable loads on the rig in the big winds and choppy seas. There is just no give in the rig at all, so the compression loads are enormous.''

After *Australia III* was launched, she began an intensive campaign of racing against *Australia II* and *South Australia,* which had been modified during winter with the relocation of the internal ballast in her keel to make her more stable. Each day two of the three yachts would be out racing together, on straight line course and around buoys. The first bout between *Australia II* and *Australia III* saw a protest decide the series in favour of the new yacht, particularly satisfying for her crew as they were carrying a small sail plan on a discarded *Australia II* mast.

Lexcen was happy with *Australia III.* ''She is a very slight, safe development of *Australia II*. She's similar to *Australia II* with characteristics to make her suitable for sailing in Fremantle and improvements to her rig and gear. It's just a logical next step, by no means adventurous.

''For the defence elimination series we have designed a boat for strong, 30 knot winds, but we still have to be able to perform in light weather so that has been taken into account in the design. We're finding that *Australia III* is better than *Australia II* above 12 knots of true wind, that's the cross over point.

''It's hard to spread the spectrum of performance. You can go for an absolute heavy weather boat and have no performance in the light. In addition, if you go for the heavy stuff then your downwind performance is ruined because you are throwing away sail area. And you have to be able to perform on all points of sailing.''

As Lexcen helped the crews tune *Australia III,* he was also hard at work on another yacht. Alan Bond never ruled out the building of *Australia IV,* but would wait to see how *Australia III* went against the opposition in the World Championships scheduled for February 1986, exactly 12 months before the Cup defence. Lexcen was very keen about the possibility of a new boat and was putting in many hours of work on his own

Australia III

Warren Jones

Gordon Lucas

Colin Beashel

Hugh Treharne

computer in his Sydney office. At the same time, like most other syndicates, he had a booking at the Dutch tank testing facility. That would give time for a crash building program of 100 days before sailing and optimising the yacht for the selection series beginning 18 October 1986. While *Australia III* represented the safe approach, he was more enthusiastic about *Australia IV.* ''It will be very different. I think it could be as big a breakthrough as *Australia II.*''

While the Bond camp raced against each other, their rivals in the Kookaburra syndicate gave up their attempts to race them and went off to race the foreign syndicates, in particular the Italian Azzurra group and the *America II* yachts of the New York Yacht Club. The Bond group was highly critical and said they would never race the Kookaburras if they continued to help the challengers.

''Part of our psychology against the enemy is the element of surprise and by racing the Americans they are eliminating that edge,'' said Warren Jones. ''By racing the *Kookaburras,* the challengers would be able to determine how fast we are, just by comparing the results against their own,'' said Alan Bond.

Early in the summer the Bond group received two setbacks to their campaign. The first came with an electrical fire in a container containing headsails and spinnakers. Several sails were destroyed, and with the attrition rate in Fremantle's strong winds, their sail development program, under the leadership of Tom Schnackenberg, was put back by more than a month. A little later the new mast for *Australia III* snapped in a shoreside accident after being measured. As it turned out, the mast was stepped only days before the World Championships.

Midway through the summer the sailing team of 28 was divided into two crews to get the competition going for the

It's not hard to understand why the crews call it "Adventureland."

World Championships. Steering *Australia III* was Colin Beashel, the 26-year-old natural yachtsman who had been mainsheet trimmer in 1983. Beashel had become favourite for the steering job after an impressive year in Fremantle and on the international match racing circuit. Backing him aboard *Australia III* were 12-Metre newcomer, former Olympian Carl Ryves, and 1983 veteran Grant Simmer, again filling the role of navigator/technician. The crew of *Australia II* was also a blend of the new and the old, newcomer Gordon Lucas steering with 1983 veterans Hugh Treharne and Skip Lissiman making up the afterguard.

Leading up to the championships the syndicate was happy with the progress of *Australia III* which they found consistently faster than *Australia II* and *South Australia* in moderate and heavy winds. Day after day they would be out racing, with some of it torrid as the crews threw their yachts around the courses and at each other, sometimes with collisions and protest hearings the result.

The World Championships were a crucial test for them: after all the politics and verbal battles died down they would sail against the New York Yacht Club's *America II* (US42), the Italian yachts *Italia, Azzurra II* and *Victory 83, Courageous,* New Zealand's *KZ3* and *KZ5*, Canada's *True North, French Kiss,* and *Challenge 12* sailing under English colours.

The regatta was a complete success with *Australia III* winning the series without even having to take part in the last race. With her positions showing 4,2,1,6,1,1,DNS, she won easily from New Zealand's *KZ5* and *America II* with stablemate *Australia II* in fourth position.

The seven-race series was sailed in a complete variety of

Spinnaker hoist on Australia III.

conditions and *Australia III* showed she could handle them all except possibly the light breezes of heat four in which she stayed in sixth position all the way around the track.

She won the regatta, not through significantly better boat speed, but through expert sailing and no gear breakages. It was a completely professional effort while others made mistakes in tactics, lost men overboard in the roughest races, and broke equipment and sails. To other syndicates it was a chilling reminder that the Bond group still led the world in professionalism. Those syndicates which had difficulties in campaigning one yacht could only admire from outside the Bond syndicate's wire fences and locked gates as they put two 12-Metres to sea each day with the best possible equipment. Certainly *Australia III* was one of the fastest yachts, but others occasionally showed similar or better speed. *Australia III* was not sufficiently superior to make her people happy.

Bond announced that they were still considering building another boat to look for that "design edge" which had served him so well in 1983. Jones was more specific: "We are very comfortable with *Australia III*. Twelves cost a lot of money and money makes 12-Metre yachts go. Deciding to spend a million dollars to make *Australia III* go faster or spend a million dollars building *Australia IV* is pretty difficult."

After watching the first two races, Lexcen had disappeared from the scene, flying out to the test tanks in Holland to finalise his design for *Australia IV* about which Bond remained coy. Returning to Australia, Lexcen was typically blunt. "None of those boats went well in the heavy weather. *New Zealand* and *French Kiss* looked better than they really were because of their tactics. There were no breakthroughs. None of those boats would be good enough to challenge or win the Cup. There will be better ones in the final summer. I know we will have a better yacht and others will do the same. Any syndicate at the Worlds which does not have a better boat than they had this summer will be wasting their time coming."

Lexcen also had some harsh words for the syndicates that did not get to Perth for the 1985-86 summer. "Dennis Conner says he knows how he went against *Australia II* in 1983 and that he is happy because his new boats have significantly been beating *Liberty*. That's nonsense. On only one day in 1983 did he race *Australia II* when she was sailed properly, so Conner is living in dreamland thinking he knows how fast we are. As for his boats, I think they're all crook. They are heavy, they have no sail area, they're all like *Southern Cross*. He's wasted a lot of money, but maybe his new boat will be up to it.

"As for the others, Blackaller in *USA* has the biggest dog since Goofy. *Eagle* (Rod Davis) looks OK and while I don't like their keel he can change that easily. England's first *Crusader* is just a nice looking *Australia II* but I don't think it's good enough to challenge, and as for their second boat, it's so weird, who would know? The French boat is not quite good enough, the New Zealanders have too much money, too many people with too many egos. If their boats were built from aluminium and not fibreglass then maybe I'd be worried. As for the Italians, they haven't a chance. They look nice, but they should stick to their clothing.

"I might be wrong but I think it will be *Australia IV* against Kolius and *America II*. They have a class act and their boats are alright."

Immediately after the championships the Bond boats finally met the *Kookaburras* in a series of races organised by the Royal Perth Yacht Club. Although the Bond syndicate said they were experimenting with sails and crews, the Taskforce syndicate claimed victory for *Kookaburra II* over *Australia III*. Lexcen remained unconcerned over statements by Taskforce principals, claiming that they were way ahead of the Bond group in their keel development campaign.

"We've been making small changes while they have been experimenting a lot because they started behind. We didn't want big changes because we were developing our sails and crews. Every time they experimented we would know what they were up to and would be able to measure the result, just as if we had carried out the experiment ourselves. Look at the widely differing performances they are having; sometimes their boats go really well and sometimes equally badly, because they are changing keels. We've got a good handle on what they are doing, our spy network is good so we have saved a lot of time. They could trick us, but that's hard to do when they are sailing their boats properly."

Finally in April, Alan Bond formally announced what everyone already knew: *Australia IV* was being built by Steve Ward. This, Lexcen promised, would be "a different boat from a different family, quite radical".

As construction of *Australia IV* continued towards its August launch date, *Australia II* was finally retired, returned to Ward's shed for refurbishing before eventually going to a new museum in Canberra. When she arrived at Ward's she found herself with plenty of company. The American yacht *Courageous* was in the yard bearing a sheriff's note attached to her mast for non-payment of debts. Both *Australia III* and *South Australia* were also locked in the shed undergoing modifications, undoubtedly including changes to their keels.

Aboard Australia II *in 1986, still the world's fastest 12-Metre in light airs.*

Cockpit of Australia IV *shows big computer read-out and four genoa tracks for fine sheeting angles.*

Australia IV was finally launched at the end of August, leaving just enough time to tune her for the trials. The yacht was bigger than *Australia III,* although showing the same lines above the waterline as her predecessor. Lexcen said he had gone right back to the basics of 12-Metre design, putting his earlier concepts out of mind as he dreamed up the new boat.

The biggest surprise was in the rig: the yacht was fitted with a triple spreader mast as well as the customary adjustable spreaders supporting the mast above the shrouds. ''Now that the rule incorporates the weight of the spreaders you would be mad not to have them. They make the mast much more controllable.''

It was an interesting move by the Australian guru of 12-Metre design. Triple spreaders were first seen on the New Zealand Twelves the previous summer. But the New Zealanders said they were necessary to support their first inadequate spars. When they fitted new masts they returned to the normal configuration of twin spreaders with jumpers.

After the first week's sailing, skipper Colin Beashel said it would take time to get the boat to her potential but that it was ''definitely not slow.''

From the outset Bond had entered two yachts in the Defence selection trials. That left his syndicate looking in good shape to defend the Cup, depending on the performance of *Australia IV.* In *Australia III* the syndicate knew it had a yacht as good, if not better, than the others they had raced the previous summer. Should *Australia IV* prove to be a failure, they always knew they had her predecessor to fall back on.

At the end of the summer Bond was asked whether, in the light of the number of designers and research organisations helping the foreign syndicates, he had considered calling in other designers or technical experts to work with Lexcen on *Australia IV.* His reply was angry. ''Looking at the results of the World Championships, I don't see any designers who come near our own 'in-house' genius, Ben Lexcen.''

But what about facing an onslaught estimated at more than $200 million dollars and featuring such leading organisations as NASA and the various aerospace companies? ''We just have to make sure that we have the best possible boats, equipment, sails, people and administration and then we have to be tough enough to withstand that onslaught.''

And what about his chances of success? ''I think they stand at 60-40, which is good because in the past we could only ever manage 50-50.''

KOOKABURRA

No Stone Unturned

Before 1983, only two Australians had ever shown real interest in the America's Cup: Sir Frank Packer and Alan Bond. The latter's tenacity saw him lift the Cup from the New York Yacht Club's grip on his fourth attempt. On returning to Australia in triumph, Bond remarked that he hoped other potential defenders would emerge as strong contenders for the right to defend the Cup. His point was that for any successful defence the team would have to have been through the toughest possible competition before meeting the top challenger.

Bond need not have worried. Another Australian syndicate, with remarkable parallels to his own, quickly got off to a flying start and after three years of development have become worthy contenders for the right to defend the "Auld Mug".

It was never easy for the newcomers. Bond himself went to considerable lengths to make them earn their spurs and the competition between the two groups made previous rivalry between Bond and the New York Yacht Club pall to insignificance.

The new syndicate was officially called Taskforce '87 Limited. Informally it was named the Kookaburra syndicate, as its yachts would be named after Australia's best known native bird, a king in its bushland.

Like Alan Bond, Kookaburra boss Kevin Parry is one of the growing breed of Western Australian businessmen who are self-made multi-millionaires. Older than Bond, he lives nearby in "millionaires' row", part of Dalkeith on the Swan River. A keen sportsman, he represented his State in baseball and has sponsored local sporting events including golf, baseball, bowls and yachting through his support of the record circumnavigator Jon Sanders.

Parry is a tough customer. As a young man he took his father's ailing carpentry business and turned it into a success before broadening his horizons. Best known for the chain of discount department stores that dominates retailing in his home state, the Parry Corporation's interests today include media ownership, land and property development, satellite and other high technology. Some of his business is through joint ventures with others, including Alan Bond.

Unlike Bond, Parry shuns personal publicity. Uncomfortable in the spotlight, he tries to push all media attention onto his lieutenants.

When Australia won the America's Cup, Parry did not own a boat. Today he owns a motor cruiser and three 12-Metre yachts, all called *Kookaburra*. Parry has sailed on the yachts only once. His interest is not in sailing, but in the technology and the way the Cup fits the philosophies of his businesses. He also wants the first Downunder Defence of the Cup to be successful because of the attention and the business it brings Western Australia.

Parry did not rush into his America's Cup bid. Renowned as a shrewd decision-maker, he prepared carefully before committing himself. The first thing he knew was that he would have to find the right people for the job.

Western Australia is a strong yachting State, but Parry knew

that Australia as a whole had few yachtsmen skilled in 12-Metres. High on his appointment list was Iain Murray, one of the most talented natural sailors in Australia with a list of first class victories as long as the remarkable 18-Foot Skiffs in which he had made his name. Murray also had 12-Metre experience. He had been skipper of the ill-fated yacht *Advance* from Sydney, the first potential challenger to be eliminated in 1983. The yacht was so outclassed that its crew, cheerful to the end, nicknamed it *Retard*.

The failure of *Advance* could not be held against Murray. The campaign had been hopelessly underfunded and designer Alan Payne was forced to go for a radical design in the hope that it would work. It didn't, and Murray found himself in the unprecedented position of being a loser.

However, with two years of 12-Metre campaigning behind him he was Parry's obvious man for the job. When Murray signed up early in 1984, the Taskforce Syndicate became a reality with a budget of $4 million. Today, with a budget of $20 million for three 12-Metre yachts, the Parry/Murray team exudes confidence. Their whole campaign, in the words of 27-year-old project director Iain Murray, has ''left no stone unturned''.

Hurt by the *Advance* campaign, Murray insisted that the Taskforce effort should be completely professional. He was only interested in getting involved on his terms. His credentials were impeccable. He started sailing at the age of ten in small dinghies on Sydney Harbour and in just his third year he designed and built his own Cherub and won the National championship. It was no fluke, as he went on to 12-Foot Skiff victories before taking the 18-Foot Skiff world by storm in 1976. In this completely open class which encourages continuous development, Murray designed and sailed his own skiffs to six world championships, five Australian titles and five State championships, a record in the class. With crewmen Andrew Buckland and Don Buckley, he built a successful business around his own exploits, leading the Eighteens into the age of exotic materials, stabilising wings, and sheer speed that would see them firmly established as the fastest monohull yachts in the world.

When the challenge of the Eighteens grew jaded, Murray moved into offshore racing keelboats, capping a short career by winning every heat and division in the prestigious Clipper Cup, Hawaii, 1983, in the Sydney yacht *Bondi Tram*. That was when he began racing with Peter Gilmour, one of the best young yachtsmen in Western Australia. In 1984 they finished fifth in the world championship of the highly competitive Soling class in Italy, and Gilmour was also involved in the first talks about the 12-Metre campaign with Kevin Parry. Gilmour was to be Murray's tactician and while their first Twelve was being built they proved they were not just dinghy sailors when they won the 1984 World Etchells 22 championship against some of the world's best yachtsmen.

Pinched and narrow stern above the waterline of Kookaburra I. *Tactician and navigator situated behind helmsman unlike earlier Australian yachts and Bond syndicate preference to have helmsman aft.*

Kevin Parry

John Swarbrick

Iain Murray bringing back a drenched and exhausted crew after a day's duelling with Kookaburra I.

Spinnakers provide the best advertising on the 12-Metres when they are not racing. Kookaburra I's *Channel Seven spinnaker obscured by that of Taskforce.*

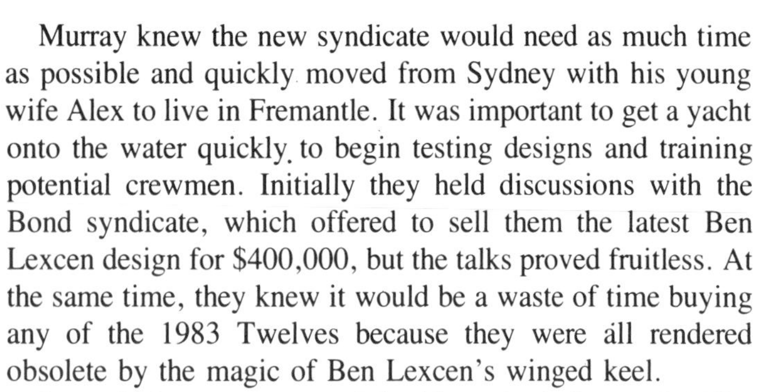

Murray knew the new syndicate would need as much time as possible and quickly moved from Sydney with his young wife Alex to live in Fremantle. It was important to get a yacht onto the water quickly to begin testing designs and training potential crewmen. Initially they held discussions with the Bond syndicate, which offered to sell them the latest Ben Lexcen design for $400,000, but the talks proved fruitless. At the same time, they knew it would be a waste of time buying any of the 1983 Twelves because they were all rendered obsolete by the magic of Ben Lexcen's winged keel.

Instead Murray, a successful self-taught designer of skiffs, had definite ideas about 12-Metre design, as did John Swarbrick, an equally young naval architect and member of a successful WA yacht designing family. Neither had previously designed a 12-Metre but they promised to make a formidable team. In addition, they knew that by using the Maritime Research Institute Netherlands (named the Netherlands Ship Model Basin when used by Ben Lexcen in the design of *Australia II*) they would have access to the world's most sophisticated yacht design research and testing facilities. With its computer analysis program and its highly successful 3:1 model testing tanks, they could comprehensively test their ideas before committing themselves to the $1 million expense of building a full-sized yacht in aluminium.

Because of the cost of using the facility and the inevitable long distance communications difficulties, the Taskforce syndicate also helped develop existing research facilities in Australia such as the limited tank testing facility at the Australian Maritime College in Launceston, Tasmania, and the Defence Department's Aeronautical Laboratory in Melbourne.

Their first step, like more than 30 other yacht designers around the world, was to study the reasons for the success of *Australia II*. They realised her breakthrough keel had thrown the accepted norms of 12-Metre design out the window, so they set out to recreate the Cup winner on their drawing boards. Murray says they were able to accurately copy her from photographs and magazine drawings, and by studying the yacht itself; soon after its return from the United States, *Australia II* went on a nationwide travelling roadshow to be admired by hundreds of thousands of Australians. Mingling among them were spies from all potential syndicates, measuring her with their eyes and, according to rumours, theodolites after the crowds had gone home.

According to Murray, they copied the yacht and then

Hot action aboard Kookaburra II *as her crew tacks to cover the syndicate's first yacht in match racing practice.*

applied their own ideas to her before Swarbrick flew out to test the ideas first on the computer and then with one-third sized models in the 220 metre long tanks. Most of their own ideas, according to Murray, were not successful.

"We were able to be very original in our approach to the whole question of 12-Metre yacht design," he says. "I've never really accepted other people's ideas of what was best. Sparkman and Stephens are probably the greatest design company in the world in the past 20 years but I've never really wanted to work for someone like them."

From the outset, Murray and Swarbrick knew that for the rougher conditions of Fremantle they would need a boat that was bigger than *Australia II*. They also knew that they would need some form of winged keel because of its increased stability, but they did not know how it would work in the rough chop of Gage Roads off Fremantle.

"No-one knows," Murray said at the time. "It will be a year before we know for sure, and even then, if it does work, people will be playing around with the concept. We are going to see some pretty weird and wonderful keels between now and the Cup."

As Swarbrick spent four months in Holland testing their design and many variables, he also looked ahead to the second yacht they planned to build. With *Kookaburra* I they wanted to catch up with *Australia II*. Their second boat would give them the opportunity to be more original and to make significant improvements.

Taking time out to fly to Holland on a regular basis to check on Swarbrick's progress, Murray concentrated on putting together the team they would need. Recognising that Alan Bond's superior organisation had played an important role in winning the Cup in 1983, Murray insisted on an efficient organisation. He divided the effort into seven key areas – yacht design, rigging, sails, boat construction, computers and electronics, sailing and operations. From the outset, his recruiting was not restricted to Australia.

In England he beat the British to Derek Clarke, a top yachtsman and highly innovative engineer. The nuclear physicist and engineering graduate had represented his country in the Olympic Games before becoming involved in the America's Cup in 1979, when he joined Britain's Lionheart challenge. Clarke designed and built *Lionheart's* rule-beating bendy mast, which gave the yacht an unpenalised extra 90 sq ft (8.36 sq m) of mainsail in the unmeasured mainsail roach.

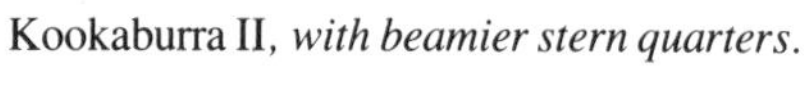

Kookaburra II, *with beamier stern quarters.*

Bowman sorting out halyards under spinnaker on Kookaburra I.

Nobody had thought of it before, and when Ben Lexcen saw it he quickly copied it for *Australia I*. But it was too late for the rig to be tuned and the Australians won only one race in the 1980 Cup against Dennis Conner's *Freedom*.

In 1983 Clarke sailed aboard the British contender *Victory 83* as navigator, and after Murray's approach he became a naturalised Australian to join Taskforce in the same role. In the modern day Twelves, particularly on the smaller courses off Fremantle, this job involves analysing the computer readouts from the yacht's sensitive instruments and relaying necessary information to the other ten men on the yacht.

Clarke was also put in charge of rigging, a responsible position calling for new standards of engineering excellence to build rigs that would withstand the constant strain of Fremantle's 25 knot winds and rough seas. Not content with the standard of commercially available items, Clarke's riggers and engineers began to design and build all their own fittings, from the smallest pulleys to the $150,000 masts.

From America, Murray recruited Howie Marion to look after their sail development program. Marion had been in charge of research for the Horizon international sailmaking group. Sail development is critical to successful 12-Metre campaigning and, as with the masts, there was additional challenge in the strong winds of Australia. Marion quickly moved to Fremantle to join Taskforce while Australian Rob Hook left the North Sails loft in Sydney to take charge of design.

Another American to sign on with Murray was former US Marine Chris Todter. Todter had lived in Australia for some years, successfully designing and manufacturing a range of small, computerised marine instruments. In Fremantle, Murray put him in charge of computers and electronics, a vital part of any 12-Metre campaign as proved in 1983 when *Australia II's* systems were so clearly superior to those of defender Dennis Conner that he ordered his instrumentation and onboard computer to be replaced just two weeks before he raced against the Australians.

Yacht performance instrumentation has become incredibly sophisticated since Australian yachtsmen first heard of it in 1962 when *Gretel* raced against *Weatherly* which had a mysterious "black box" in her cockpit to help her crew. Today, micro computers are linked to all the instruments to analyse the yacht's performance at all times, with additional data being relayed to a bigger computer aboard the constantly shepherding tender for

Iain Murray

Derek Clarke

Black lines painted on sails are filmed by two mini video cameras at masthead and top spreaders.

delivery to a more powerful computer ashore. As well as helping crews to analyse their performances, the computers help designers to find and measure their strengths and weaknesses and assess modifications to their yachts.

To build the yachts, Murray went to two of Australia's most respected boatbuilders, Toby Richardson and Graeme "Frizzle" Freeman. In typically thorough fashion, Parry had established Parry Boatbuilders under the same roof as the syndicate's administration, design and computer development centre in South Fremantle. Both Richardson and Freeman have built some of Australia's finest racing yachts and both are good yachtsmen. Freeman was tactician aboard the Victorian Twelve *Challenge 12* in 1983 before assuming the role of adviser for the elimination series. In 1986 he was sailing master aboard the maxi *Apollo* when it took line honours in the AWA Sydney-Hobart bluewater classic. Richardson is a trimmer on the *Kookaburras* when he can leave the work to his staff of 14; Freeman often fills in as an alternate tactician.

The sailing program was initially the responsibility of Peter Gilmour with the assistance of National Yachting Coach Mike Fletcher. (Fletcher had taken over as tactician of *Challenge 12* in 1983, but he and Freeman remain staunch friends.) As well as overseeing a program aimed at getting the yachts to their full potential as quickly as possible, they were also responsible for finding and training the right men to drive the yachts, not easy in a country where 12-Metre sailing has always been very limited.

Operations, or in other words getting it all together, went to businessman and keen yachtsman Terry Newby.

According to Murray, their management structure differs widely from the other Australian syndicates. "We operate on a self-management levelling system where everyone has their responsibility and their job and they get on and do it. It's probably one of the hardest sports in the world in that the race actually starts three years before the event. There is no other race like that in the world, so to keep motivated you need a very well thought out program. All our people are intelligent, so to treat them like store dummies would be to insult them. And they are all excellent sportsmen in their own right."

Design was the bailiwick of Iain Murray and John Swarbrick, but their policy was always to gain additional input from others who could help. Principal among these was the Sydney-based naval architect Alan Payne, who gave Australia two potential winners in *Gretels I* and *II*, and the unfortunate *Advance*. Swarbrick later paid tribute to Payne for "lending us a vast amount of experience. He helped us think in directions other than the accepted and also how to best analyse what we were finding out in the research stages."

On the water, Murray, Gilmour and Fletcher went for the best people they could find. From the outset Murray was to be helmsman and skipper, with Gilmour his tactician. However, when it was established that they would have the budget for a two or possibly three boat program, they kept looking for alternatives. It was not easy. Few Australian yachtsmen had ever set foot on a 12-Metre and to make things more difficult, they were competing against the Bond and South Australian groups.

As second helmsman, Murray imported Englishman Lawrie Smith, who had helmed *Victory 83* in 1983. One of the world's leading helmsmen, Smith is a renowned match racing expert and joined the syndicate full time after being helmsman on one of the British yachts that teamed up to win the 1985 Southern Cross Cup.

Starting with the best people he had sailed with on *Advance*

Pulling Kookaburra I *into her security berth resembling German U-Boat pens of World War II.*

and others from *Challenge 12*, Murray kept recruiting and attracted some of Australia's best big and small boat sailors. At this time the Bond and South Australian groups were also trying out everyone they could aboard *Australia II* and the new *South Australia*. Murray, quickly learning to use the power of the press, kept his recruiting going by accusing the Bond group of using its crewmen like cannon fodder, "burning them up and spitting them out".

By the time *Kookaburra I* was launched in February 1985, more than a hundred yachtsmen had elected to try out for the crew. Meanwhile, Parry had one advantage over the other syndicates – he had his helmsman. In the Bond camp they tried out more than ten helmsmen to replace John Bertrand, who had retired from sailing after 1983, before reducing it to a shortlist of four.

When the public got its first look at *Kookaburra* (sail number KA11) on launch day they saw an elegant gold-hulled yacht that was obviously larger than *Australia II*. Following the Bond syndicate's psychological success in 1983 by keeping their keel shrouded, the Parry syndicate went two steps further, completely shrouding the yacht's underbody before putting her into a dockside pen made of galvanised iron sheets sunk into the seabed.

In deck layout she differed from *Australia II* principally in positioning the navigator and tactician behind instead of in front of the helmsman. Computer performance analysis was based around a microcomputer below the aft hatch, behind the cockpit. On deck, giving the people in her afterguard control, were four monitors and a keyboard mounted on a circular disc that turned for operation from either side of the boat. Power for all of this was provided by batteries and a small generator. Readouts from the instruments were clear to all in her crew from four "Jumbo" repeaters on the mast below the boom. They could be set individually for any readout from the hull and masthead instruments such as hull speed, wind speed true and apparent, and wind angle true and apparent.

Her stern was tapered and rounded, with a long overhang, a complete departure from the squared off *Australia II* which had chines in her transom overhang and flat run between. *Kookaburra's* waterline measured in the same as *Australia II* so with her long overhangs she had obviously been designed to pick up waterline length and speed when heeled in the stronger conditions of Fremantle.

The syndicate released statistics showing her to be, as expected, a larger yacht than the Cup holder:

KOOKABURRA

Length overall..... 67 ft (20.42 m)
Length waterline.. 44 ft (13.41 m)
Beam................ 12 ft 3 in (3.73 m)
Displacement...... 54,000 lbs (24,494 kg)
Sail area........... 1,800 sq ft (167.22 sq m)

AUSTRALIA II

Length overall..... 64 ft (19.50 m)
Length waterline.. 44 ft (13.41 m)
Beam................ 12 ft 2 in (3.71 m)
Displacement...... 52,300 lbs (23,723 kg)
Sail area........... 1,772 sq ft (164.6 sq m)

The christening day was a proud one for the Parry syndicate and its young "prime movers". At last they could begin sailing and find out whether they had been on the right design track – if they could find someone to race. Alan Bond said it would be some time before his team could consider racing *Australia II* against the newcomer because they had a contract to race and train with *South Australia*. So Murray went sailing against the Italian yacht *Azzurra* and a war of words developed between the Bond and Parry camps. Kevin Parry complained that Bond was putting his own interests before those of Australia. Alan Bond retorted that his yachts would never race Parry's if they persisted with sailing against foreign contenders, as it would be giving them the opportunity to assess Australian progress.

Parry was incensed. "He's scared and what he is doing is not in the interests of defending the Cup."

"We have to race to get our people going," Murray said. "If Bond won't sail against us then we will have to find someone else. I don't care who it is, we have to race."

At the time of *Kookaburra's* launch, *Australia II* and *South Australia* were sparring daily off Fremantle. Often they would be tailed by an inflatable runabout with Murray's sailmakers and key men watching the two yachts, their crews, trim and sails. Soon after *Kookaburra* began sailing, Murray began to shadow them in his own Twelve, sailing 250 metres away from them in an effort to compare his boat speed. Trouble developed one day when Murray climbed into the tender to tail the other boats. The Bond tender shepherded him away from the yachts, telling him he was much too close. Murray complained of being put in a very dangerous situation. Finally the Royal Perth Yacht Club had to step in to end the public wrangling and draw up guidelines to control "spying".

While work was continuing on the design of the second *Kookaburra*, the syndicate decided to send the first on a fund-raising promotion on the east coast where most of the corporate decision-makers are based. Parry had been finding it difficult to raise sponsorship so he decided it was time to fly the *Kookaburra* flag in Melbourne, Sydney and Newcastle. In Sydney, *Kookaburra* sailed a series of short races against *Australia I*, the 1977/80 challenger that had been purchased by Syd Fischer as a trialhorse for his Sydney-based syndicate. It was almost a public relations disaster for *Kookaburra* as it ran into possibly the world's fastest light weather 12-Metre in just that type of weather. The racing was inconclusive but *Kookaburra* appeared slower and yachting writers were quickly calling the boat "a dog". Murray and Swarbrick drew their own conclusions, ignoring outsiders, and followed their original plan to have the yacht modified. They described the changes as minor but numerous. Whatever they were, they must have done the trick because when she returned to the water in the spring of 1985 to race *South Australia* the crew found themselves very competitive.

Meanwhile, work continued on the second yacht which Murray promised would be slightly bigger than their first and quite a departure from it, with a variety of keels to test.

All the time the budget continued to grow, particularly in the light of the decision to build three yachts. What began as a $4 million campaign escalated four fold until, with a year to go to the 26th America's Cup, Murray put the figure at a cool $20 million. Of this, between $16 and $17 million would go out in cash, the balance would be supplied in goods. Murray put down the dramatic rise in costs to their philosophy of "leaving no stone unturned in our determination to be successful".

Like most 12-Metre syndicates around the world, Taskforce found it hard to raise corporate sponsorship. Being seen as the underdog to Alan Bond's syndicate made raising the necessary cash a frustrating task. But in mid-1985 Taskforce had its first major win when Ted Thomas, the general manager of the Sydney television station ATN 7, convinced his network that they should put their resources behind Taskforce in the form of cash and free air time. More correctly, Thomas was putting their support behind Iain Murray, and it was not for the first time. It was Thomas who had given the young Murray his break into the spectacular 18-Foot Skiffs. Murray's skiffs were called Color Seven, the TV station's logo, and all his exploits were televised on the Seven Network.

Typically, Thomas threw himself into Taskforce with great gusto. One of his first projects was to get his engineers to refine their revolutionary remote camera system for racing cars to suit use on the transom of the yachts, beaming their pictures and sound live to viewers of the Seven Network around Australia. More importantly for the syndicate, they were suddenly getting mass exposure on television sets around the country, and that included the sets of other potential sponsors.

With the launching of the second *Kookaburra* late in 1985 and the plans for a third yacht well underway, Taskforce was looking good. Having the second yacht meant they could modify one yacht and immediately measure it against the other to see whether the modification was successful.

The second yacht, numbered KA12, was of similar size to the first but the syndicate never released her actual specifications. When the two *Kookaburras* first went sailing, the new boat seemed to have a larger sail area because her boom appeared approximately three feet (one metre) longer than that on the first boat. Swarbrick explained the apparently bigger sail area on *Kookaburra II* by two things: the first, cosmetic, as the yacht's meeting point of transom and sheer was further forward than on the original yacht; the second, and more significant factor, was that the mast on the second yacht was stepped approximately eight inches further aft.

"Half the problem in 12-Metre design is in getting the balance right," Swarbrick says. "You find it balances OK in the tank, but put it into rough water and it will be hopeless. The tanks are helpful only to a point: it's not until you get into full size models that you can really measure balance. It's made more difficult by changing the configurations of the keel, too. You have to be able to slide the keel fore and aft to get it in balance, and at the same time this is affecting the configuration of the rig, so it's all one big juggle, balancing all these variables to get it right."

A two boat campaign calls for a lot of people. Murray had 80 fulltime staff keeping the two yachts racing each other while the third was being built and his talent scouts' antennae were still twitching. Ashore, the group was self-sufficient with 15 in the boat building team, six patternmakers, 12 sailmakers, six sparmakers and riggers, and six maintenance men to keep the yachts ready to take to the water.

The 1985/86 season was critical for Taskforce. Most of the foreign syndicates would be sailing their first yachts in Fremantle, concluding with the World 12-Metre fleet racing championships. For Murray's men it was also the time for a tough racing program against the others, particularly the South Australians and the New York Yacht Club; in fact, anyone but the Bond syndicate, who refused to play ball.

As they continued to work their yachts up they were encouraged by their success. Their designs, particularly the first yacht, were competitive, and their sail program began to improve. In the early days they had considerable setbacks with sails that could not stand up to the strong winds. The composite Kevlar/Mylar materials would quickly self-destruct as they flogged in the strong winds and sail designers had to concentrate on their engineering to get the sails to last more than a week. At $15,000 a mainsail, it was an expensive learning curve.

"The first sails we had were hopeless – great in shape but built for somewhere else," new executive director Malcolm Bailey summed up. "They could not handle the strong winds and were just throwaway items for a long time. It's only this year that they started getting it right."

Most interest in the World championships in Australia focused on how the *Kookaburras* would go against the Bond syndicate's *Australia II* and *III*. It was the clash everyone, including the people aboard the yachts, was waiting for. However, under a new rule of the International Yacht Racing Union, and against the wishes of the syndicates, the rating certificates of yachts taking part in the championships were to be made public before racing began. Murray was determined that no-one should see the certificates and measurement details for his boats, so while he entered the championships, he refused to give his certificates to the Australian Yachting Federation. It caused a furore but Murray was adamant: he would not give away any secrets in his design.

Finally, a fortnight before racing began, the IYRU relented and agreed that the certificates would remain confidential. But it was too late for Taskforce; they announced that they were committed to their ongoing campaign of development. So while 16 yachts from Australia, France, Italy, America, Canada, Great Britain and New Zealand took part in the most spectacular 12-Metre racing ever seen, the *Kookaburras* cut a comparatively sorry sight as they match raced each other just a few miles away.

Murray and his men kept a close watch on the yachts during the racing but Murray remained unimpressed by the first wave of post-*Australia II* 12-Metres, commenting "The boats out there were almost sub-standard, not one of them was good enough to defend or challenge for the Cup. There were no good boats out there. And even if good ones turn up later this year, the Worlds have demonstrated that they will only be as good as the people who know how to harness them correctly and get out of them what they want. There are obviously only a handful of groups who can do that. Bond would be best, followed by the New York Yacht Club. They are going to be tough to beat."

Murray insisted that they gained more in their own match racing than they would have achieved in the fleet racing. But it was still bad for the morale of the syndicate, and it did nothing to help the fundraisers who had been hoping for a respectable result to show potential sponsors that they would be supporting a syndicate that could win the America's Cup.

Alan Bond's *Australia III* won the championships. The *Kookaburras* bounced back with a vengeance in their first head-on clash with *Australia II* and *III* in a series of short races organised by the Royal Perth Yacht Club. After the World Championships Bond had changed his tune and said that they would race Parry's boats. "I have always maintained that we would race them when the time came, when we would all have things to learn," Bond said. "That time has arrived."

Although there was an agreement not to announce the results, Taskforce publicly claimed to have won 14 races to *Australia III's* 12. The racing was inconclusive to be sure, with all syndicates experimenting with sails and crews. But at last the Kookaburra syndicate was getting the credibility in the eyes of the public that it so badly needed.

At the time, Murray was in Holland finalising the design for the third yacht with Swarbrick. On his return, work began in Parry Boatbuilders on *Kookaburra III*, with the launch date set for the beginning of August. Not content to put all their hopes in any one yacht, the first *Kookaburra* was also pulled out of the water for nine weeks for extensive modifications, to get it ready to be the syndicate's second entrant in the defence elimination series.

Throughout, the designers had concentrated on developing

Tactical computer console with monitor and keyboard at hand for navigator.

each boat, using the other as a benchmark by which to measure their success or lack thereof. Each boat was constantly changed during the work-up and after the summer of 1985/86 both Murray and Swarbrick described the two boats as being very even, with *Kookaburra II* slightly faster in the heavier airs.

Swarbrick says they concentrated on changing keels: either the whole appendage, half a keel or just the wings. He says that during the summer the performance of the first yacht improved dramatically when they changed the bottom half of her first keel. "There were inherent problems in her original keel, but when we changed it the improvement was very dramatic and overnight the two yachts changed roles. Nothing we have done to the new boat has made such a difference."

Over the summer as they worked on the design for their third yacht, Swarbrick concentrated almost solely on keels, building ten different models to test with a "lot of modifications to test further". As well as tank testing them, Swarbrick put them through the wind tunnel at the Aeronautical Laboratory in Melbourne. "This was an improvement because I was able to test bigger models, half sized models, which are certainly more accurate."

Swarbrick built fibreglass models of the keels and instead of towing them through water, used the tunnel to blow wind over them at speeds of up to 200 mph. Using special microphones and earphones, Swarbrick would listen for any hiss which would indicate speed reducing drag. First he would check the smoothness of the surface, which is critical, and then study the angles and chords of the area in question to examine why it should be creating drag. Sometimes it would be a poor surface finish, at other times it would be bad angles of the wings or incorrect attachment to the main keel. Swarbrick says laminar flow is all important – that is having the layer of water dragged along the hull run as far aft as possible before breaking up and creating drag.

Swarbrick is very wary of tank testing. "The tanks are not wrong but you have to be very careful about what they tell you. Their problem is the small size of the models and because the tests are in flat water. From what we have found, what tests best in the towing tank and the wind tunnel can be right up the creek, completely wrong, so designers must make sure they're not fooled by the figures they are getting. There is still nothing to beat full size testing, that's for sure."

One of the men most involved in the Kookaburra development, Peter van Oossanen – the director of the

Kookaburra III *about to be launched in August 1986.*

Maritime Research Institute Netherlands – says they have done an enormous amount of research. "I think it's an effort that has gone really well. If one man like Ben Lexcen had been in charge of the research activities that Taskforce had to do there would be no way he could cope because there is this ongoing work in the tanks at Launceston, at the aeronautical lab in Melbourne, there's our program including both numerical and tank testing and there are all these naval architects in Australia doing all sorts of calculations for them. They have put more models through the water than anyone else, close on 30 in all.

"I think Iain Murray is the supreme design co-ordinator, taking more decisions in the design area than most people realise. Their boats are not extreme, they're sensible boats that will 'hang in' in all wave conditions and having one or two features which a lot of other boats don't have."

Murray says they have concentrated throughout their campaign on "creating yachts based around low drag hulls with high lift being optimised for match racing in all weathers". He believes their design approach has given them one significant advantage over all other yachts they have raced, Australian and foreign: the ability of their yachts to recover speed after tacking. "It's mind blowing. In 16 knots of breeze on flat water we are now losing less than half a knot in a tack. It's come about gradually. A tack used to cost us at least one knot, but not now, and it's all been part of our ongoing program of modification and measuring."

The manoeuvrability of *Australia II* played a very important role in winning the America's Cup. On the shorter courses in Fremantle where the yachts reach their laylines in half the time it took in Newport, quick tacking is absolutely essential for success. It's not the whole story by any means, but it's part of the overall picture.

The third *Kookaburra* bearing the sail number KA15 appeared similar in size to the first two yachts when it was launched in August. According to Iain Murray it was very similar in specifications and not radical, rather it was different in shapes and appendages. "It is not as radical as we have tested but it is not conventional by any means."

Although much of the yacht's underbody was shrouded while the yacht was out of the water, it was obvious that it had longer overhangs fore and aft than the earlier two boats. In its for'ard sections, particularly, it had a shallower forefoot and a comparatively long flat section aft of the stem. In the stern it showed similar easily rounded chines, although again with longer overhang.

At the yacht's launching, syndicate chairman Kevin Parry said the new boat combined all the good points from the first two boats. But he added that he would not be surprised to see *Kookaburra I* or *II* still carrying the laughing Kookaburra flag into battle.

The yacht's configuration could still be changed beween the series of races over the long summer.

Murray says some of the things they tested in the tank proved to be startlingly fast but only in certain conditions and had to be discarded. He says it is essential to have a boat that will perform in all conditions, not just the heavy winds of the famed Fremantle Doctor.

Swarbrick says most of their time has been spent working on the appendages. "With rudders we have gone the full circle and finished up with what we started with, a high aspect fin. Everyone has their own ideas and it can be pretty frustrating sometimes proving them wrong when you have had a gut feeling all along that they have been going up the garden path. But after last summer I've been very satisfied with our progress."

Swarbrick says their aft underbody shapes depend on the type of keel and rig configurations they use. He gives no details, content to say that in their yachts they have the most manoeuvrable 12-Metres on the water in Australia.

The search for the best boat will continue until the last race to decide the defender of the America's Cup. As well as entering two yachts, Murray and Swarbrick have been changing their boats continuously in search of the best potential defender. Changes to the first *Kookaburra* included moving the mast aft approximately eight inches. As Swarbrick says, it's still up to full sized models to get the balance right.

Iain Murray is determined that the whole Kookaburra approach will result in success. So too is the shy man of the 12-Metre scene, Kevin Parry, who has put his trust in the man 27 years his junior.

Ask Iain Murray what he will do after 1987 and he shrugs his broad shoulders. He hasn't had time to think about it. He's been too busy at what he has been doing all his life – preparing to win on the water.

"I have no idea of what I'll be doing, there's no great plan. These three boats are the boats I love. They're the great development class of the world where you can think freely in any direction and try something you can't do with other boats."

The story of the Taskforce syndicate inevitably concentrates on Iain Murray. He does not encourage that; he prefers to get on with the job. He has a big task, and only two other men carry as much responsibility in their 1987 America's Cup campaigns: Dennis Conner and Marc Pajot. Of course Murray also has a great opportunity to record his name in history.

Murray is responsible for spending a lot of money, most of it provided by a man who does not even like sailing. Murray is not troubled by that, and he knows he has full support from the man he has grown to admire. "Kevin doesn't know anything about sailing, he's just a great sportsman. He loves this, he knows all the guys and his attitude is that we must leave no stone unturned to succeed. He has an amazing attitude. With the amount of money we're spending it is a big commitment and, you know, he's not ever phased by that."

Spinnaker peel aboard Kookaburra III.

If one of the *Kookaburras* does not defend the America's Cup the Taskforce team will be shattered by the defeat. It will be small consolation that they will have succeeded in pushing their conquerors to their absolute best in time to face the challenger. In three years they have achieved what most others would not even attempt and what some have given up on along the way. They have started from scratch and put together a fully professional 12-Metre campaign with credibility – lots of credibility.

KA-8

SOUTH AUSTRALIA

New Kids In Town

The fact that the syndicate established in 1984 to organise South Australia's first ever America's Cup effort knew nothing about 12-Metre design was no deterrent – its principals knew they had the contacts to buy a boat from the best 12-Metre yacht designer in the world.

For $600,000 the syndicate entered into an agreement with Alan Bond's syndicate to purchase a Ben Lexcen designed Twelve, built by Steve Ward who had constructed *Australia I*, *Challenge 12* and *Australia II*. The contract also gave the Cup newcomers a complete set of sails designed by Tom Schnackenberg, who had developed *Australia II's* sails in 1983. In addition, it provided them with the use of the Cup winner *Australia II* for crew training while their own yacht was being built, followed by a period of time during which both boats would race together in Adelaide and Perth.

It was a very sensible arrangement for the South Australians. Not a big yachting State owing to the location of the capital city on the tempestuous St Vincent Gulf, most of its sailing was done in dinghies and none of its sailors, with one notable exception, had even set foot on a 12-Metre yacht. The exception was Sir James Hardy.

Born on 20 November 1932, Hardy grew up as a natural yachtsman. After winning several State and National championships and being reserve yachtsman in the 1964 Tokyo Olympic Games, he catapulted to the forefront of Australian yachting in 1966 by beating a star-studded international field to become World champion in the 505 dinghy class.

The following year Hardy stopped at Newport, Rhode Island, to watch the second Australian America's Cup challenge. *Dame Pattie* was no match for the superboat *Intrepid*, but Hardy was fascinated by the racing and American skipper Bus Mosbacher, the last of the great amateur America's Cup skippers. "Watching Bus Mosbacher on the dock and then on the water really fired me up," Hardy recalls.

In 1970 Hardy realised his new ambition to sail in the America's Cup, steering the Alan Payne designed *Gretel II* against *Intrepid*, this time helmed by Bill Ficker. It was a series of highs and lows. The real high came when *Gretel II* won the fourth race. But the low had come earlier, in the second race when *Gretel II* won the race but lost it the next day in the protest room. The yachts had collided during starting procedures, *Gretel II* at the time in the hands of starting helmsman Martin Visser.

"Until the day I die I will back Martin Visser," Hardy said later. "I still believe the Americans reached the correct decision on the facts that were put forward. But we put up no case at all. We should have been represented by an American attorney. The Americans sat up all night going through all the photographs and the next day they presented shots that made us look awful. We'd gone to bed confident. If we'd presented a good case there would have been a different outcome."

In 1973 Hardy met Alan Bond, who invited him aboard his Ben Lexcen designed *Apollo II* as sailing master. It was the start of a long relationship between the two men, who would

undergo both elation and crushing depression in pursuit of their common goal of winning the America's Cup.

In 1974 Hardy steered Bond's America's Cup challenger *Southern Cross* but lost 4-0 to *Courageous*. In 1977 he was not in the Bond camp for the West Australian's second challenge; he was not even in Newport. With long time friend and advertising whizz kid Roger Lloyd he had been trying to raise money for a people's boat to be called *Matilda*. The bid was unsuccessful and particularly galling for Hardy after his 1974 defeat. Understandably he began feeling bitter about the elusive "Auld Mug".

However, in 1979 he was winning again, this time as helmsman aboard the yacht *Impetuous* which was a member of the Australian team which won the Admiral's Cup in England. Self-confidence and enthusiasm restored, he accepted Alan Bond's invitation to steer the heavily modified *Australia* against *Freedom* in the 1980 America's Cup. On this occasion he would have alongside him as tactician long time friend Ben Lexcen, formerly an innovative sailmaker who had cut Hardy's sails when he made his mark by becoming World 505 champion in 1966. Once more he went close to victory, but again "Gentleman Jim", as he had been dubbed by the Americans, was to go into the history books as a loser with the scorecard 4-1.

It was enough for the 48-year-old winemaker/yachtsman, who declared: "When that loser's gun goes in the last race it might as well have been aimed at you. You're dead."

But the America's Cup is tantalising and Sir James Hardy played an important role in Alan Bond's 1983 victory. Hardy stayed on as a director of the syndicate, and became a valuable adviser to the team including skipper John Bertrand. Watching *Australia II* from the tender and from *Challenge 12*, he picked up many points for her crew, and when Bertrand was ruled out of part of the selection series on medical grounds, Hardy stepped in to steer and kept *Australia II* on her victorious course. Then, before each Cup race, he would steer *Challenge 12* as she sailed alongside *Australia II*, tuning up for the battle with *Liberty*.

On his return to Australia, Sir James Hardy was approached by Roger Lloyd with the suggestion that they should put together a defence campaign for South Australia. Hardy was horrified. Had his friend forgotten 1977, when they had been humiliated by their unsuccessful efforts to put together a "People's Boat"?

But Lloyd, the head of Adelaide's biggest advertising agency, was persuasive. He also counted on successfully appealing to his friend's love of his own State. Although living in Sydney where he headed the family winemaking company, Hardy had always been extremely enthusiastic about his home State. After his knighthood for services to the sport of yachting in 1981, he was freely tipped as a future Governor of South Australia.

Hardy remained unconvinced, but agreed to consider being involved – on the proviso that they be tied as closely as possible

All weight to weather for stability when going to windward.

South Australia's *battleflag*.

Sir James Hardy

Phil Thompson

John Savage

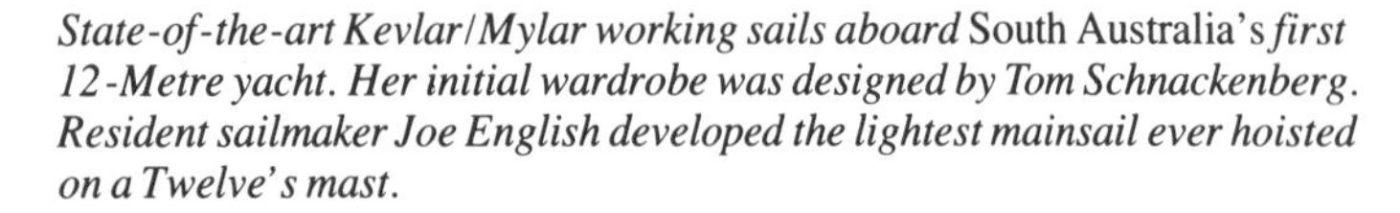

State-of-the-art Kevlar/Mylar working sails aboard South Australia's *first 12-Metre yacht. Her initial wardrobe was designed by Tom Schnackenberg. Resident sailmaker Joe English developed the lightest mainsail ever hoisted on a Twelve's mast.*

Facing page: Backstay outrigger on transom to protect mainsail roach was found to be unnecessary and was later discarded.

to the Bond syndicate to capitalise on their America's Cup expertise built up over 11 years through four Cup campaigns.

While talks with the Bond group began, Lloyd put together a very impressive proposition to local companies to get backing for a defence contender. The emphasis was to be parochial, with a South Australian yacht crewed by South Australians and backed by South Australian dollars, goods and services. That gained the support of the State Government and a grant of $1 million, and Lloyd quickly found himself being promised the $3 million target he had set for May 1984 if the campaign was to go ahead.

"Five years ago this challenge could never have been mounted," Lloyd said later. "It wouldn't have got to first base because for decades Adelaide was controlled by a handful of men who sat on the same boards and did it all their way. Since the late 1970s this has changed dramatically. Those old warhorses have gone and a new breed of aggressive young businessmen and women are taking over Adelaide."

Another development was to illustrate the truth in Lloyd's words. In 1985 Adelaide was host to Australia's first Formula One Grand Prix motor race and it was a spectacular success.

As well as receiving $600,000 from the South Australians for providing them with a new 12-Metre yacht, the Bond syndicate knew it would gain out of the deal as well. Ben Lexcen could test his ideas for his successor to *Australia II* before completing work on his new *Australia III* for Bond. And when the yachts began racing, the South Australians would also provide a sparring partner for the West Australians while they tried out new people for their two boat program.

Back in Adelaide, the now enthusiastic Hardy was recruiting yachtsmen, writing to every yacht club in the State inviting applications for the crew of the yacht to be named *South Australia*. More than 80 people replied and more than half were given their chance to join the crew. The syndicate wanted to keep theirs a truly South Australian effort. "I want the crew to evolve," Hardy maintained. "I don't want to go to the so-called heavies around the countryside offering lumps of sugar to get them on our boat."

Still, Hardy knew it would be difficult to put together a good crew from a State in which there was virtually no big boat racing. From Western Australia he recruited Scott McAllister, bowman on *Australia II* before breaking his arm in an accident on the yacht in the 1983 selection trials. With three America's Cup campaigns behind him, McAllister had valuable

experience and would double as operations manager for the syndicate. Queenslander Mal Kampe joined to trim headsails and look after the yacht's running rigging when ashore. From Sydney Joe English, an Irish sailmaker with vast yachting experience, was recruited for the afterguard and to control the sail development program.

Helmsman was to be 41-year-old Fred Neill, one of South Australia's most successful yachtsmen who, like Hardy, had been a helmsman in Australia's 1979 Admiral's Cup win, although on another yacht. Hardy would look after tactics, although he maintained that he would rather be replaced and resume his 1983 role of adviser.

On 28 April 1985, the new royal blue *South Australia*, bearing her State's red and gold colours on her topsides and the sail number KA8, was christened at Port Adelaide. Thousands turned up for the occasion, while many more watched the event on national television. Everyone turned out again the following weekend when *South Australia* was joined by *Australia II* for an exhibition sail off Adelaide's beaches. The new yacht led for most of the race until a crew error let the 1983 Cup winner through to take the gun. It was an omen of things to come.

No-one was saying much about the yacht, although it was obviously bigger and heavier than the lightweight *Australia II*. Like the Bond boat, *South Australia* had her winged keel shrouded by a canvas "skirt" when lifted out of the water. What the skirt could not conceal was that in addition to having more freeboard, below the waterline Lexcen's new yacht had more bustle and fuller ends than *Australia II*, adding to her displacement. In addition her transom was more rounded than that of *Australia II*. An unusual feature was the mounting of a large outrigger on the transom, well above the waterline, to carry the backstay. Lexcen had given the yacht a longer boom and believed the backstay might rub against the bigger roach of the mainsail, causing friction which would be disastrous for the Kevlar sailcloth needed to keep the high-stress leech in shape. Later it would turn out to be unnecessary and removed.

In deck layout the new yacht was a departure from Lexcen's designs for Bond in that the navigator and tactician were behind the helmsman. *Australia II* kept the two men in front of the twin steering wheels, but the South Australians opted to keep them at the rear of the cockpit where they had plenty of room to move and easy access to their performance evaluation computer in the aft hatch leading into the transom. Moving the

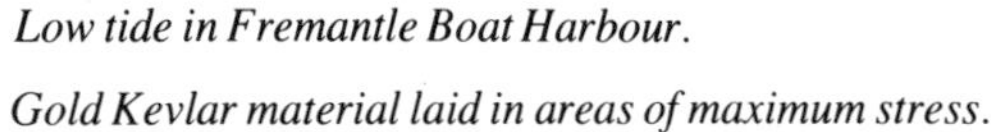
Low tide in Fremantle Boat Harbour.

Gold Kevlar material laid in areas of maximum stress.

steering position forward made things more cramped for the rest of the crew working the middle of the boat, and a later modification was made to give them more room. The hydraulic systems for controlling the rig appeared to be the ultimate in 12-Metre sophistication, with all sail trimmers having duplicates of the controls and measuring dials.

The yacht also had the latest in winch power to drive its big rig. Winch systems had been ordered from the Australian company Barlow, which chose to fit the yacht with Barient winches made by its American subsidiary company. Components such as pedestals and angle boxes were manufactured locally. The two primary winches for trimming the big headsails and spinnakers were each Barient 19, three-speed winches which were coupled to a gearbox to give six speeds with extremely high and low ranges. In traditional style a gearbox enabled the four grinders to operate each winch which, when tacking headsails, would come under loads of up to 4,000 lbs (1,814 kg).

Coming under considerably more load would be the winches controlling the running backstays, leading from the stern of the boat to a mid-point up the mast to control forward mastbend and forestay tension. Loads on these winches operated by the tactician and navigator behind the skipper, can be as high as 10,000 lbs (4,530 kg), and it is critical for the new windward runner to be pulled on as soon as the yacht tacks to keep the mast from pumping and possibly breaking. As well as the self-tailing winch, the runners were operated through a block and tackle. After quickly winding on as much runner tension as possible with the winch, the tactician would then use the hydraulics to fine tune the load on the runner, measured through forestay tension. The South Australians decided against linking their runners with the three-speed mainsheet winch for fast operation like some American syndicates.

To make the mastman's job as easy as possible, his cluster of Barient winches around the base of the mast were fitted with spring loaded, self-tailing jaws, allowing automatic adjustment of the jaws to take ropes of different diameters, including the halyards, spinnaker pole topping lift and downhaul.

As well as having more freeboard and slightly more sheer than *Australia II* to help keep out the rough waters of Fremantle, big coamings were positioned in front of the sail hatches for'ard of the mast.

Immediately after *South Australia's* launching the two yachts began an intensive round of racing. Her designer was

Headsail change in moderate breeze.

Deck-sweeping main boom typical of modern Twelves.

typically enthusiastic. "It's faster in a straight line than *Australia II*, both upwind and downwind," Lexcen commented after the first races. "It's a nice boat and it has everything on it. When you compare it to *Australia II* it's like comparing a Boeing 747 to a dugout canoe. We still have to get some weight out of the boat which will make it faster downwind, and when the guys learn how to sail it they'll start to beat *Australia II* around the track."

In this statement Lexcen summed up the biggest problem facing the South Australians – putting together a crew that was America's Cup standard. During the following months in Fremantle they had mixed success as they raced against *Australia II* and, after her launch in September, *Australia III*. In some races over short and full courses, experienced Bond yachtsmen like Hugh Treharne, Colin Beashel, Gordon Lucas and Carl Ryves would join the crew of *South Australia*, often turning her into a boat that would beat *Australia II*.

One problem which quickly showed up in the strong winds off Fremantle was that the boat was too tender and lacked stability in the winds she had been designed for. "I didn't believe the results in the (test) tank but I went with them and they were wrong," Lexcen summed up. The answer was to fit the yacht with a new keel over the Christmas break, taking trimming lead out of the hull and putting it into the keel to lower the centre of gravity.

At the same time a new Sparcraft mast was fitted to the boat, replacing a "stand-in" spar that had been discarded by *Australia II* in 1983.

The syndicate had begun with North sails designed by the Bond group's Tom Schnackenberg, the sailmaker who had played such an important role in the 1983 win. When they moved to Fremantle in mid-1985 they purchased a former supermarket and converted it to a loft run full time by Joe English. With two assistants, English began refining existing sails and building new ones in consultation with Col Anderson, owner of the Hood loft in Melbourne. Anderson had made most of the sails for *Challenge 12* in 1983, some of which were later used on *Australia II*.

Recognising the importance of a good sail performance program, the South Australians sailed off Fremantle every day with the sail trimmers photographing various sail shapes during races, the draft and its position within all working sails measured by the horizontal "speed lines" on the sails. A special camera recorded pertinent data including boat speed, trim and running backstay tensions directly onto the negative. At the end of each day, English would study the photographs processed in a darkroom at the loft and decide whether to recut the sails overnight. It was a long process, refining existing sails and using the growing bank of knowledge to build new sails as well. All the time English was looking to design sails that would be lighter, saving weight aloft to reduce heeling momentum.

In addition, like the Bond and Parry syndicates sailing off Fremantle, the South Australians found they had a big problem keeping the sails not just in shape, but in one piece. Fremantle's blustery conditions ravaged the high-tech sails, ranging in price up to $15,000 for a mainsail made of Mylar/Kevlar and Dacron laminates. Both Mylar and Kevlar are superior to woven cloths in terms of resistance to stretch. But they are not durable materials, and in the constant pre-start luffing and tacking around the course, with the sails flogging in the strong "Fremantle Doctor", the crews found that their sails needed almost daily recutting to put them back into their designed shape. Initially the average life of headsails in windy conditions was just two weeks. No-one believed the America's Cup was a cheap sport, but the decline of the Australian dollar was bad news for all Australian groups. The exotic sailcloths were all manufactured in Europe and the USA, so syndicates had to increase their budgets to pay for the largely unexpected wear and tear of sails.

Encouraged by better performances with their new keel, early 1986 offered the moment of reckoning for the South Australians. They knew their yacht was capable of winning races, but their record in match racing bouts against *Kookaburra* and *Australia III* was dismal. Morale was low, there was a generation gap causing tension amongst the crew aboard the boat and, coming under presssure from sponsors looking to justify their investments, the syndicate bosses let it be known the the World 12-Metre Championships in February 1986 would be the acid test.

In the Championships they would be competing with the Bond syndicate and against potential challengers from America, Italy, New Zealand, Canada and Great Britain.

The series turned out to be a disaster for *South Australia*, which finished eighth overall, while her near sister ship *Australia III* won the regatta in impressive style, not even having to start in the final heat of the seven race series. *South Australia's* best result was a fourth in the fourth race, but even then she managed to slip back from second place through some poor sailing.

Despite her new keel the yacht still appeared to lack stability and also seemed unable to point as high as the leading boats. But the damning point which no-one could ignore was that while *South Australia* languished in the middle of the fleet, the near identical *Australia III* was out in front. It was time for tough talking after bad results in the first three races, and sailing director and tactician Sir James Hardy led the self-criticism by standing down as tactician in favour of former two-time Lightweight Sharpie National champion Robby Duessen. It was a typically honest gesture by yachting's "Mr Nice Guy", but it didn't solve the syndicate's problems, and apart from their fourth in the next race they stayed near the back of the fleet.

The man who stood to lose the most credibility from the failure, Roger Lloyd, said later they had gone into the regatta knowing they would not win because they were light in the skills department. It was, he admitted, "a time of anguish" Undaunted, he said they had deliberately honoured a commitment to the South Australian Government by going into the Championships with their local crew. They knew they would be found wanting, and the time had now come to look elsewhere.

"It's not a dud boat," Sir James Hardy insisted. "*Australia III* and *South Australia* are virtually identical but their crew has vital America's Cup experience. We have to lift our performance in the skills department." Promptly signed up were some top calibre yachtsmen. They included Western Australian Jack Baxter, three times navigator on earlier America's Cup challengers; Bill Edgerton, an Australian who had long earned a good living on the tough European offshore racing circuit; and Phil Thompson, a leading Sydney skipper in the Etchells 22 one design keelboat class who had been mainsheet hand aboard *Challenge 12* in 1983 and who had previously spent some time trying out for the Bond group.

Inevitably there were casualties – the most prominent being helmsman Fred Neill who left the group to join the Eastern State's syndicate as manager. It was a tough time for the man who had put his neck on the block and had it lopped off.

Shortly after the Championships the Royal Perth Yacht Club organised an informal series of races for the Australian defenders. Most attention was on the long-awaited battle between the Bond and Parry syndicates. But for the South Australians there was at least satisfaction in winning seven races, beating *Australia II*, *Australia III* and *Kookaburra II*, though finishing fourth overall on the unofficial race tally. It went some of the way to restoring crew morale and they were also pleased by the result of adding more lead to *South Australia's* keel which made her more stable than she had been in the World Championships.

The yacht then underwent drastic cosmetic changes, being painted a burgundy red to play the role of *Liberty* for the filming of a television series on the 1983 America's Cup. One crewman delivered the classic line: "At least we know we will win three races."

Still in her "*Liberty*" livery, the South Australians completed the summer racing against *Crusader*, the first of two British Twelves to arrive in Fremantle. The South Australians claimed to have decisively won a series of races. For all concerned it was important therapy in their recovery.

During the winter break, the yacht was sent back to Steve Ward for refurbishing and minor modifications. Syndicate boss Roger Lloyd said the keel was slightly modified to make it "virtually identical to *Australia III's* – there would barely be a millimetre of difference". He said the syndicate would later have the option of adding a new keel identical to that of

Powering to windward in early training. Sir James Hardy checks mainsail leech and trim.

Lexcen's new *Australia IV* should that keel prove to be better.

At the request of Roger Lloyd, *Australia II's* 1983 skipper, John Bertrand, spent four days analysing the syndicate and concluded that the problem was lack of skills: "That boat is good enough to defend the Cup." In line with Bertrand's recommendations the syndicate added to the afterguard, recruiting 1983 *Challenge 12* helmsman John Savage and his navigator from that campaign, Gary Simmonds. Thompson and Savage were to decide between themselves who would steer at what times while the other called the tactics. Both were pleased with the arrangement.

The South Australians' regrouping was profound. Gone was the old afterguard to make way for the new boys. But Roger Lloyd, Fred Neill and Sir James Hardy had performed a huge task, taking a group of yachtsmen which had never even set foot on a 12-Metre to give their State a credible 12-Metre campaign. Hardy had always known that they would have to bring in outside experience, but he was determined to have as many South Australians as possible involved.

Unfortunately, Hardy was to find himself spending little time with the syndicate while they regrouped. A pinched nerve in his neck forced him out of action soon after the series against the British. When it failed to respond to physiotherapy his doctors operated, but three months later he was still in pain. A side effect left him almost powerless in one arm.

In the summer of 1986/87 the yachting knight will be adviser to the team – the role which he handled so well in 1983. Steering the yacht and calling the tactics will be John Savage and Phil Thompson, both in their second America's Cup campaigns.

Anyone who has been involved in an America's Cup campaign will tell you that it is far more demanding than any other form of yachting and requires years to develop the necessary skills and experience. In just three years the South Australians have struggled to overcome their lack of experience. At times it has been a traumatic experience. After all, no-one likes to lose. The mere fact that the South Australians continue to survive has surprised some outsiders. But they have came back from defeats on the water, poor crew morale and budget blowouts from $5.5 million to $7.5 million.

Lloyd believes they have done everything possible to succeed in 1987. And he looks beyond. "We've been building a base in South Australia for future challenges. We've been giving our people America's Cup experience and we've involved everyone in our State. Our challenge has 150 sponsors, more than the rest of the Australian syndicates put together. I hope the increasing costs don't stop us challenging again; we have always wanted to build on everything we've learnt so far."

There is no reason why the South Australians cannot ensure their ongoing Cup commitment. They have a crew well trained by Hardy and Neill, boosted by a strong afterguard. They also have a boat that is the equal of the 1986 World Champion and which could be improved even further, depending on the success or otherwise of Lexcen's latest thinking.

Most Australian yachtsmen scoffed when they heard of the South Australian America's Cup campaign. The fact that they will make it to the starting line for the selection trials should be enough to end any criticism. They have succeeded where so many others, not just in Australia, have failed.

STEAK 'N KIDNEY

Syd's Bid For Sydney

Designer Peter Cole with Steak 'N Kidney's *framework.*

When the America's Cup changed hands in 1983, the resulting euphoria in the new home of the "Auld Mug" led to a rash of syndicates in almost all Australian States. Everyone, it seemed, wanted to get in on the act.

However, within months, reality set in. The America's Cup had become big business overnight and the response from the corporate world was, to say the least, cautious. Most companies were not interested in taking the risk of backing newcomers with no track record in this unique sport, while successful and seasoned campaigners like Alan Bond would be having another go.

South Australia surprised other States by gaining the backing of the State Government and major local businesses. But on Australia's east coast, syndicates in New South Wales, Victoria and Queensland found it hard going. All quickly ran into the problem that even if they did beat the favourites in the West and successfully defend the Cup, their yachts would still be representing the Royal Perth Yacht Club and the America's Cup would stay in Western Australia.

Eventually the Victorian and Queensland syndicates admitted defeat, throwing what little they had gained into the Sydney-based effort, which became the Eastern Australia America's Cup Defence syndicate. However, the money moguls of the financial capital of Australia remained unimpressed and the man behind the syndicate was left almost alone to keep his ambition alive.

The role was not unfamiliar to Syd Fischer, who had almost singlehandedly run his first America's Cup campaign the previous year. One of Australia's most successful ocean racing yachtsmen with his string of beautiful *Ragamuffins*, Fischer first became interested in the America's Cup in the 1970s. His interest heightened towards the end of the decade due to a long-running personal battle with Alan Bond. In 1977 the two clashed publicly after a collision between their yachts during the trials to select the Admiral's Cup team. Then in 1980 in Newport, Rhode Island, Fischer was studying the America's Cup scene closely but ran foul of Bond who, after another public altercation, banned him from his dock.

Fischer returned to Australia incensed and openly critical of Bond's handling of the unsuccessful campaign with *Australia*. Anyone watching the growing feud could not help but notice the similarities between the two highly successful men, with their high profiles and big egos. Both had made much of their money through property development. While Bond had diversified, Fischer had specialised in property from the time he was a 21-year-old, self-employed carpenter until he headed one of Australia's largest and most successful property investment, design and management groups based in Sydney.

No-one was surprised when Fischer announced a campaign through the Royal Sydney Yacht Squadron for the 1983 America's Cup. Originally the syndicate planned a two-boat

Fundraising Eastern State style with the yacht the centre of attention in the heart of Sydney.

STEAKIDNEY
SUPERSTATION
SUPERSTATION

Stern view of Steak 'N Kidney *shows clean run aft, typically clean Cole lines.*

bid, with Alan Payne as the designer and world 18-Foot Skiff champion Iain Murray as the skipper. But, as in the past, the Sydney public treated the whole campaign as something of a bore, and it was gradually scaled back to a one yacht effort. The shortage of funds denied Payne the opportunity to scientifically test his theories and he was forced to pull 18 ft (5.4 m) models through salt water at Brisbane Water, north of Sydney. The lack of money convinced Payne that he had to gamble and the resulting yacht, *Advance*, was tailored for light airs.

The gamble failed. The financial problems continued and it was only the generosity of individual syndicate members that kept the crew housed and the yacht racing, albeit without the sails and equipment that other challengers, except the similarly impoverished Canadians, enjoyed. On the water *Advance* was slow, unable to pace the other challengers, and was dubbed *Retard*. As the crew struggled against the odds, Fischer fell out with the syndicate, suggesting that they cut costs and withdraw before being eliminated. His suggestion was turned down and the boat went on to be the first to be bundled out of the elimination series, managing to win only two races.

Fischer said he was determined to try again. First he purchased the 1977/80 challenger *Australia* from the British syndicate and had it shipped back to Sydney. Then he had *Advance* stripped of her fittings and rig, which he shipped home, while consigning the hull to a 12-Metre graveyard in Newport. Back in Sydney, Fischer found himself alone in his determination to overcome the odds and challenge again. Embarrassed by their 1983 mauling, the Royal Sydney Yacht Squadron declined to actively support him again. But Fischer began to live up to his reputation of overcoming the toughest odds, and used his own money to start his campaign. At the same time, the first of several fundraisers for the syndicate began trying to cajole Sydney's corporate world into helping pay the bills.

To design his yacht, Fischer turned to Peter Cole, a man who, in his own words, "had played around with the Rule in recent years and drawn the designs for a couple of boats". Cole said one design had almost become a reality. As it turned out, he was "awfully glad it hadn't".

A very quiet, shy man, Cole is almost the opposite of the aggressive Fischer. He had long been associated with 12-Metre campaigns, but in the role of sailmaker for a number of Australian challengers from *Gretel* to *Advance*. Born in Sydney in 1929, Cole left school to begin an apprenticeship in sailmaking and in 1950 started his own sail loft. It was successful, and in

STEAK 'N KIDNEY

Gary Sheard

Syd Fischer and Cole.

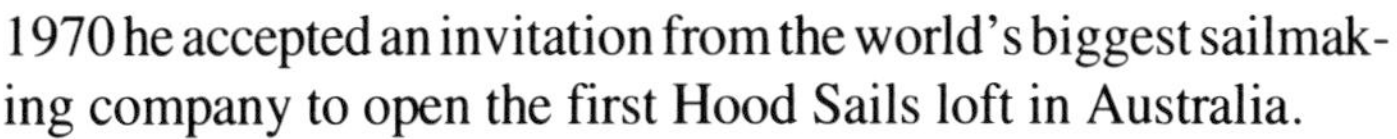

Tack of headsail well aft of "business-like" bow.

Narrow waterline beam and easy lines through the water by Sydney's representative.

1970 he accepted an invitation from the world's biggest sailmaking company to open the first Hood Sails loft in Australia.

Cole began designing yachts in the 1950s and went on to achieve success, including wins in the Half Ton division with his designs in 1974 and 1976. In 1977 he turned to design full time, drawing a number of successful production yachts including the Cole 43 and the East Coast 31.

In May 1984 he began working for Syd Fischer full time. Like all designers, he found his 12-Metre thinking outdated by the winged keel of Ben Lexcen. "It was certainly a good way to go; it re-wrote the numbers. It had a lot of good things like lower centre of gravity and more stability without added displacement, it added hydrodynamic lift and cut down induced drag. On the bad side it had increased wetted surface, but reducing that elsewhere meant the good outweighed the bad.

"It's interesting that all breakthroughs in yachting seem to grow from earlier developments. Take Henry Sheil. Twenty years earlier he was on the right track with a new keel which veed out at the bottom to blunt foils which stopped vortex loss."

To test his new theories, Cole went to the same testing facilities used by the other Australian designers – the Maritime Research Institute in the Netherlands.

Cole had an advantage over some new 12-Metre designers in that he had a proven design to compare against his own efforts. When Fischer bought Lexcen's *Australia* from the British, part of the package was a set of line plans for the yacht which was, according to Cole, "better than most people realised, particularly in light weather." At the Maritime Institute, Cole also had a one-third size model of the yacht, which had been built as Lexcen's benchmark for his design of *Challenge 12* and *Australia II*.

Not only did Cole know the numbers he should get from the model on the computer and in the test tank, but he could also compare those numbers against full-scale performance as he knew how the yacht had gone against two other Twelves, the British syndicate's *Victory 82* and *83*, when *Australia* had been their trial horse.

Cole started by comparing four hull and six keel designs against *Australia* on the computer panel program of the Netherlands Aerospace Laboratory, which worked closely with the Maritime Institute. Studying the results of these tests in Australia, Cole says he settled on two hulls and keels to tank test against the refurbished model of *Australia*, to confirm the results of the computer. Cole visited the Institute for five weeks in 1985 to study the testing and results.

In Sydney, work began on the new yacht which would carry the sail number KA14. In Western Australia the Bond, Taskforce and South Australian syndicates were already well into their sailing and construction programs and were openly critical of the Sydney syndicate for its late start.

As well as developing their new designs, these syndicates had an important advantage over the latecomers in the east – crewmen. The shortage of experienced 12-Metre yachtsmen in Australia meant the first syndicates had the pick of the crop as well as the time to recruit and train newcomers in this exceptionally demanding form of yachting.

While construction of KA14 continued, Fischer used *Australia* to try out hopefuls on Sydney Harbour, most of them from within local ocean racing ranks. But he found particular difficulty in signing people aboard for the important afterguard – the helmsman, tactician and navigator. Fischer had talks with several top yachtsmen, but was beaten to the punch by rival syndicates for people like former Olympian Carl Ryves (to Bond) and leading Etchells skipper Phil Thompson (to South Australia).

In typical fashion, Fischer was never openly put off. "I'm not concerned, I don't want a crew of egomaniacs like others." Nor was he worried about the lateness of the campaign, which he valued at $7 million. "This is just a boat race, it's nothing else but another regatta. All other ballyhoo is superfluous," he declared.

Finally, in April 1986, KA14 was launched and the low key approach re-emphasised at the christening in the shadows of Sydney's famous Opera House. It was, all agreed, a "no frills" affair. Unlike most other launchings the bands did not play, the champagne did not flow, and the syndicate chairman did not make a rousing speech. The yacht was simply painted in white undercoat, still lacked some deck fittings and rode high out of the water, waiting to receive her internal trimming ballast.

Unlike most other potential defenders and challengers for the 26th America's Cup campaign, the syndicate announced the yacht's specifications:

Length overall	68 ft (20.7 m)
Length waterline	44 ft 11 in (13.7 m)
Beam	12 ft 4 in (3.76 m)
Displacement	55,114 lb (25,000 kg)
Sail area	1,750 sq ft (162.5 sq m)

These specifications placed the yacht at one foot longer than *Kookaburra I*, both overall and on the waterline, with similar beam and slightly smaller sail area. Like all new boats she was bigger than *Australia II*, in this case by four feet overall but by just one foot on the waterline, carrying long overhangs. According to the published figures she was a little more than 1,000 lbs (453 kg) heavier in displacement than *Kookaburra I* and 3,000 lbs (1,300 kg) heavier than *Australia II*.

The keel and afterbody were kept shrouded while the boat was on dry land. However, she was rarely lifted from the water, as her mooring was a disused naval base on the south side of Sydney Harbour which did not have lifting facilities. As part of this "no frills" campaign, a chlorinated bag wrapped around the hull had to suffice to prevent weed growing on the yacht.

Asked why he was funding the campaign himself while others relied heavily on sponsors, Fischer replied simply: "Someone from the east has to do it, so it might as well be me. A lot of people doubted we could mount this challenge. They tend to rubbish the opposition. I think the Cup brings out the worst in people. There is a bit of personal rivalry in this, but I've beaten Bond a lot more times than he's beaten me."

The yacht's lack of preparedness at the christening was explained by the fact that Fischer's fundraisers needed credibility – and that meant having the new boat on the water. As Fischer said, people had to see the yacht before they would believe what they were being told.

In the wake of *French Kiss'* success in opening the way to greater recognition of commercialism in the America's Cup, the Sydney yacht was not to be named until a new sponsor was found. Soon after it began racing against *Australia* on Sydney Harbour and off Sydney Heads, the yacht displayed the name *Sunshine* on her hull and a spinnaker carried the logo of the Sydney afternoon newspaper, the *Sun*, while the syndicate remained coy about making any formal announcement. Suddenly the logos disappeared. Her official name, her disappointed fundraisers agreed, would not be *Sunshine*.

Less than a fortnight after the yacht began working up, disaster struck when a crew error resulted in a broken mast. An old spar from Fischer's *Advance*, strengthened with triple spreaders, had been used while the syndicate completed its own spars. In terms of lost sailing time, the mast breakage was a disaster. However, the new syndicate manager Fred Neill, one of Australia's leading offshore helmsmen who had just left the South Australian syndicate after being relieved of their Twelve's helm, put on a brave face. According to Neill, they needed the time to fair (smooth) the hull before the yacht was to go on a ship to Perth.

In reality, this was just another indication of the lateness of their preparation. Sydney's yachting fraternity groaned aloud, murmuring about being witnesses to another poorly funded *Advance* campaign.

But the campaign soon received a shot in the arm from an unexpected source. Cashing in on a major drive of sponsorships for all types of sport was the new sports marketing group Powerplay. Less than a year earlier it had leapt to public prominence by buying an ailing Australian Rules football club, the Sydney Swans, spending the maximum possible amount of money on them and seeing the team turn from also-rans to top contenders for the 1986 season finals.

Powerplay decided it was worth becoming involved in the Sydney yacht and took over the marketing rights to the syndicate. Things started happening quickly. Before being shipped to Fremantle the yacht was taken from the water and put on public display in the heart of Sydney for all the people to see "their America's Cup contender", with a shroud covering its keel, "the secret weapon that would win the America's Cup" for Sydney.

In yet another ceremony, Powerplay dropped its bombshell, the yacht's new name. It was called *Steak 'N Kidney*. A puzzled

Designer describes deck layout as "standard 12-Metre" with navigator and tactician behind helmsman.

crowd was assured that this had nothing to do with meat pies; this was an old rhyming slang nickname for Sydney. The spirit of the name, they were told, signified that this was "a boat for the people, the real people of Sydney, not the millionaires like the Western Australians who could afford 12-Metre campaigns in their own right". The message was that now the people of Sydney had their own America's Cup yacht it was up to them to get behind it.

Journalists rushed into print and onto television screens to express their disbelief. Alongside such names on the America's Cup as *America, Columbia, Enterprise, Constellation, Intrepid, Courageous* and *Australia II, Steak 'N Kidney* was downright embarrassing, they declared. Interstate and overseas America's Cup commentators mocked the new name.

Not embarrassed at all were the promoters of Powerplay. They had said they wanted to get the public of Sydney behind the yacht and, initially at least, they had succeeded.

Lost amidst the hype was the announcement of a skipper for the yacht. He was to be Gary Sheard, a top yachtsman in Olympic Soling keelboats from Victoria, who had finally signed up after a long courtship by the syndicate. Navigator was to be Greg Halls, who had sailed as "naviguesser" aboard Fischer's maxi *Ragamuffin* and managed Fischer's marine business. No tactician was nominated, although several yachtsmen had tried out briefly for the role. They included New South Welshman Graham Jones, a 6-Metre match racing helmsman and offshore yachting champion, and Leigh Dorrington, a Melbourne sailmaker who had been a national champion in the Lightweight Sharpie class and who also had extensive experience on ocean racing yachts.

The people of Sydney were allowed little time to appreciate their yacht first-hand. In less than a week she would depart for Fremantle, although not before another christening to give everyone a further opportunity to dig into their pockets.

Embarrassment finally struck *Steak 'N Kidney's* enthusiastic promoters when the yacht was loaded on the ship taking her to Fremantle. They had done as much as possible to attract media attention to the farewell, including the hire of four divers who took to the water to keep away "camera-carrying divers from foreign syndicates desperate for a look at Cole's keel". As it turned out they were not needed.

When the crane lifted *Steak 'N Kidney* from the water, the shroud encasing its keel gave way under the weight of water trapped inside. The shroud tore apart, exposing every inch of the yacht to the television and press cameras. A grim-faced Syd Fischer said nothing. Revealed to one and all across the nations's television screens on that night's news broadcasts were the results of Peter Cole's work and Syd Fischer's investment.

Cole's winged keel differed markedly from the trendsetter slung below the hull of *Australia II*. It had more lateral area, with considerably smaller wings beginning further aft along the base of the keel.

While *Australia II's* wings began halfway along the keel base, those on the new *Steak 'N Kidney* began about three-quarters of the way back along the keel's length and protruded slightly beyond the keel's trailing edge. The well-rounded wings were quite thin in chord and not as wide as those of the 1983 Cup winner. They curved down evenly to an angle of approximately 10 degrees, possibly creating a slight tunnel effect on their lower edge.While the wings were less than half the area of those of *Australia II*, and would carry much less weight, the profile of the keel was also quite different. The leading edge angled forward at approximately 8-10 degrees, considerably less than that of *Australia II*. Similarly, the trailing edge carried far less angle outwards.

In addition, it appeared that the yacht had an articulated trim tab, with a second hinge down the centre of the tab aimed at giving the keel more lift to windward. Articulated trim tabs had been tried before on 12-Metres, including the 1974 Australian challenger *Southern Cross*, but all had been discarded. Cole later refused to confirm or deny this observation.

The yacht had a deep forefoot beneath a slight bump at the waterline measurement point, and beamy midsections. Aft of the keel the yacht also differed markedly, with a deep bustle leading back to the rudder. Lexcen had virtually eliminated the bustle from *Australia II* to counteract the increased wetted surface and drag of the wings. On *Australia III* and sistership *South Australia* he had added bustle for better steering control in the rougher waters of Fremantle and to account for some of the increased displacement.

In Fremantle, the *Steak 'N Kidney* crew quickly began establishing themselves in their new dock and quarters. An early priority for Cole was to begin his own sailmaking program. The Sydney sail loft which had been developing their program had tossed in the towel through frustration with the direction of the campaign after the broken mast had abruptly brought a halt to the new yacht's sailing program.

Within a week the Easterners were to learn the power of Fremantle's strong sea breezes. They began training in light airs one morning, only to find the breeze building to 34 knots by mid-afternoon. That day's sail finished abruptly when their boom broke.

The failure was no fault of the crew or the spar itself: 34 knots of wind is well above the unofficial top limit for America's Cup racing. But it was a timely reminder that they would have to ensure their boat was free of breakages by the time they began racing to earn the right to defend the America's Cup.

For the yacht's designer it was an anxious time, putting his first real 12-Metre up against those of other syndicates which had already had many months of hard training and tuning on what had become their home waters. One of the first competitive programs was to be against *South Australia* with her new afterguard and recharged crew.

Getting Peter Cole to talk about his design is difficult, though he rankles at the inevitable restrictions of secrecy surrounding his 12-Metre work. Where he can he gives details, yet like so many other designers, he apparently looks forward to the end of February 1987 when he will be able to speak about his design without being censored.

Getting him to discuss some of the ideas he tried, and rejected is easier. Yes, he says, he looked briefly at the canard keel as fitted to the second British boat designed by model yacht expert David Hollom. He didn't like it, he says, "because of a poor angle of attack".

No, he didn't go for wide wings as some had tried including *America II*, because "they would be a worry in the slop with their big wetted surfaces, top and bottom. You have to get that wetted surface out of somewhere else in the boat and that quickly becomes difficult."

Above: Early sails from Sydney sailmaker looked promising. Cole took over in Western Australia.

Left: Thumbs up before moving to Fremantle for their moment of truth.

The angle of attack of the wings is one aspect he has obviously concentrated on. "The angle of attack (horizontal plane of the wings) is very critical. In any kind of chop the angle changes constantly and that can be critical. In the test tanks the bigger wings may be alright because they are at a fixed angle. But real life is different. Take, for example, hydrofoil ferries such as those on Sydney Harbour. They have wings, yet their angle lifts the boat right out of the water. On yachts the wrong angle can wreak havoc. I preferred to go for smaller wings and bigger keel area."

Yes, he agrees, his yacht does have long overhangs, particularly the stern counter. "Overhangs are cheap under the 12-Metre Rule – the only payment is a little extra weight for the structure. But they do increase speed when the yacht heels with the extra waterline sailing length, and they do help damp down the hobbyhorsing in a seaway."

Cole says they could change Steak 'N Kidney's keel if necessary because, after all, it's only bolted on. But unlike some, particularly the *America II* and Taskforce syndicates with their "Lego" boats enabling them to change whole keels or wing configurations overnight, Cole doubts that the syndicate would go to these lengths.

"I'd hate the job, what with fitting trim tab controls and the like. But we could change if we had to, it would just take us longer. However, our approach is different. I would have loved to have gone on looking at funny keels, but we had to draw the line somewhere. We had to decide which was the best we had, so that we could come over here and get on with it."

Cole says that in deck layout his yacht is deliberately fairly conventional. He believes most 12-Metre layouts have settled into two modes, depending on whether the navigator and tactician are located aft or for'ard of the helmsman. *Steak 'N Kidney* has the helmsman in front. The Lewmar winches are, he says, pretty standard, although the important runner winches at the rear of the cockpit differ from some by having a third, very low ratio instead of just two speeds, along with an additional hydraulic system for fine tuning. Cole says in designing the layout he was careful to take into account the big loads on equipment. "Reliability will be very important. For some of the period on most boats, breakdowns will be a problem. So we must make sure that when the racing begins our fittings are not too light or too heavy, and that everything holds together."

According to *Steak 'N Kidney's* creator she is designed to be at her best in a wind range of 17-22 knots. Allowing for the fickle wind gods, which all yacht designers have tried to second guess, how does she go outside that range? "At the bottom end of the range (in light airs) she was a pleasant surprise, fast and having excellent acceleration. Above that it's too early to tell; we haven't done enough sailing in heavy airs."

That lack of sailing time, despite Syd Fischer's protestations to the contrary, may be a major problem. Considering that other major syndicates have been preparing – on the water as well as on land – since 1983, this one boat program with a little known crew and such a late start almost palls to insignificance. Other Australian groups say it is not even worth taking into consideration. However, Cole is quietly confident that he has come up with a boat which can do the job, although he would obviously like the budget to keep looking for an edge – a breakthrough.

He receives solid support from his principal researcher, Dr Peter van Oossanen, the head of the Maritime Research Institute of the Netherlands. Van Oossanen says he believes Cole has designed a 12-Metre that could defend the Cup. But he quickly points out that to do so the syndicate must have in place all the other components that make up a successful campaign: sails, people, tactics and support.

That is the herculean task facing syndicate chief Syd Fischer, undoubtedly one of the most determined and successful yachtsmen in Australia today. But the America's Cup is like no other sport or form of yachting because of its financial demands and remarkably long period of preparation. Considering the calibre of the opposition, Fischer and his people will need to be quick learners to catch up.

STARS AND STRIPES

Personal Point To Prove

tars&Stripes

Thousands of hours of match racing on Hawaiian waters.

The mere mention of the name, Dennis Conner, brings to mind the America's Cup. The man has towered over the scene almost continuously for the past decade. More words have been written about Conner than any other person in the Cup's history. In America he is listed among the all-time sporting greats, a shining example of an unknown overcoming all odds to fight his way to the top.

In 1983 the story took a downturn turn when he lost the America's Cup. But the book was not closed: Conner vowed to add another chapter by becoming the first man to win back the Cup.

After a successful career in Olympic classes, ocean racers and match racing championships, Conner became involved in the America's Cup in 1974 when he was starting helmsman aboard *Courageous* which defeated Alan Bond's first challenger *Southern Cross*. After a break in 1977, he was invited to skipper the potential 1980 Cup defender of the Maritime College at Fort Schuyler. Given almost complete control of the campaign, Conner swept away the last vestiges of pretence that the Cup was an amateur event sailed for honour and glory. He introduced the long term campaign to the Cup, sailing for more than 200 days before beating *Australia*. In 1983 the number of sailing days grew to more than 300 as the draper turned professional America's Cup skipper strived to find a yacht that was superior to his 1980 craft *Freedom*.

It's history now that Conner's long and costly three yacht campaign was not enough to overcome the superiority of *Australia II's* winged keel, combined with the most professional challenge ever mounted. It was the end of the New York Yacht Club's grip on the Cup and, in the eyes of his critics, the end for Dennis Conner.

Yet there was no argument over the fact that Conner had almost overcome impossible odds. One mistake in the last race with the score at 3-3 let the Australians get back in front and win the series 4-3. *Australia II's* designer Ben Lexcen said that night that he had not been worried about *Liberty*, but Conner had been another matter: ''He's a tricky little devil''.

Nineteen-eighty-three was not just a traumatic year for Conner; it was also a tough time for the key American 12-Metre designers as the truth sank home that they had been dealt a death blow by the Australians. The designers correctly accused the syndicates of complacency, denying them the funds for research to improve existing designs. Faced with

"Tacking – duck!"

spiralling costs for the long professional campaigns, major sail design programs and, in the case of Conner, an unprecedented number of boats, the syndicate bosses had found their time taken up with raising the money needed to keep their campaigns afloat.

For all Americans involved, it was a period of bitterness, accusation and counter accusation. Conner had already fallen out with both his designers, and later blamed the Cup loss on their lack of vision in not matching the quantum leap of the "superboat" *Australia II*.

When it was time to plan his revenge he knew his former approach of concentrating on sailing skills had been outdated by the need to focus on design. Taunted by the title of his book which had been published before his defeat, *No Excuse To Lose*, he was determined not to make the same mistake again. He wanted design input from every possible source.

"Nineteen-eighty-three showed that 12-Metre design was not a question of being a garage industry any more," the deposed Cup king said. "In-house designers such as Sparkman & Stephens and Valentijn simply do not have enough horsepower. The America's Cup has changed dramatically. The sailing is now a minor proportion of any campaign while the fundraising and design are now the major parts."

To design his new boats, Conner put together a committee of four designers headed by his long-time lieutenant John Marshall, the head of North Sails who had sailed mainsheet for him in all his campaigns before stepping off the boat after 1983.

First to be recruited were two designers with totally contrasting 12-Metre experience. One was David Pedrick, responsible for four Twelves including *Courageous* (1974) and *Enterprise* (1977) when he worked for Sparkman & Stephens, *Clipper* (1980) and *Defender* (1983) in the name of his own company.

The second was Britton Chance Jnr, with one and a half Twelves to his name. In 1970 he had redesigned *Intrepid*, which went on to successfully defend its second Cup. Four years later he realised his ambition to draw his own Twelve. Chance turned to the test tanks and his own unsophisticated velocity prediction computer program to draw the lines of the boat. A firm believer in the results of the tanks, he thought he had a breakthrough. According to the tank, chopping off the yacht's underbody in the stern would fool the water into thinking the yacht was longer on the waterline than it really was. The yacht *Mariner*, skippered by Ted Turner, succeeded in propelling Chance to inter-

John Marshall

Dave Pedrick

Britton Chance

Bruce Nelson

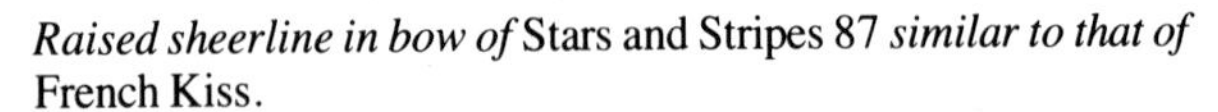

Raised sheerline in bow of Stars and Stripes 87 *similar to that of* French Kiss.

Stars and Stripes 87 *on arrival in Australia. Dubbed the ''Upside Down Concorde'' for sheerline that rises dramatically from the mast to the bow.*

national stardom, but for the wrong reasons. The tank had lied; *Mariner* was hopelessly slow. Scientific testing in 12-Metre design was halted for a decade and the Cup career of Chance almost finished, until 1984.

Marshall, Pedrick and the man being given another chance were joined by a designer with a completely new approach to 12-Metre design – Bruce Nelson, a successful designer of ocean racing IOR yachts.

But Conner was not going to leave it all to them. Experts in aerodynamics, hydrodynamics, aircraft design and computers were called on to lend their specialist expertise to the designers. To the fore was the biggest Pentagon design ''think-tank'' – Science Applications International Corporation (SAIC). Aircraft giants Grumman and Boeing also assisted. A key individual in the 35-strong team was Peter Lissiman, the aerodynamicist who had created the Gossamer ultra-light aircraft which was creating new long distance records in the skies over North America.

Although Conner announced his intentions later than the New York Yacht Club, he still attracted strong support for his challenge. In the eyes of many, he was still the best 12-Metre operator in the world and they were prepared to back him in his bid to ''right the wrong of 1983''.

Conner also had a strong team. Six of the men who had sailed with him on *Liberty* signed up again, while Marshall headed the design process. Again the Maritime College of Fort Schuyler backed him, supplying veteran organisers including Fritz Jewett, the chairman of the America's Cup Defence in 1980/83, and Ed du Moulin, who had managed campaigns in 1977/80/83. In addition, the College supplied the 1983 defender *Liberty* and *Spirit*, which had been passed up in 1982.

Conner and his key men had already been busy studying the conditions in Fremantle. But they did not want to prepare in the defenders' territory. ''In Australia we are the enemy, in Hawaii we are among friends,'' Conner concluded. After considering weather patterns around America, Hawaii appeared closest to Fremantle in its winds and waves. It was a controversial move. In their favour, Conner's team would have not only strong winds, but also total secrecy to keep the rest of the world guessing at their progress. On the negative side, they would run the risk of being out of touch. The other advantage was that, while secluded, they were still close to mainland USA and the design team.

While Hawaii appeared the best alternative, Conner was not

prepared to take its conditions as final. Arrangements were made to develop a complete computer model of the conditions in Fremantle over summer.

Every fortnight a package containing complete readouts of wind strengths and wave patterns in Fremantle was mailed to the syndicate's new base in Honolulu. The information was supplied by the Bureau of Meteorology and a private oceanographic company, Ray Steedman Ltd. In all, seven measurement stations were placed around and on the new America's Cup course. Every minute, 24 hours a day, each would measure wind strength and direction and send the information to central recording points. Three buoys at sea also measured wave heights. All major syndicates purchased the information for their meteorologists and designers.

Conner's key shore man, Robert Hopkins, passed the information on to the design team, which analysed the weather thoroughly. While they knew the weather in Hawaii was close to that of Fremantle, they were always conscious of what would be needed in the summer of 1986/87 when their final boat would have to race for four months in a wide variety of conditions to qualify for the Cup itself.

Conner planned a US$15 million budget and a program that called for two new boats, both to be called *Stars and Stripes*. His syndicate became the Sail America Foundation for International Understanding. But there was to be no output of information from the new syndicate, as it prepared to lock itself away behind security fences at the University of Hawaii's Marine Research facility at Snug Harbour, just outside Honolulu. Conner meant business: "There was a belief in the initial stages that in Perth the Cup would not be competitive. But when I realised that it would be competitive and retain its stature my juices got going again. I had to win it back."

The syndicate was confident that it knew how good the new benchmark of design, *Australia II*, was and how *Liberty* measured up against her, in order to evaluate progress. The designers were briefed to develop not just the winged keel, but to look at any other possible breakthrough keels as well. Their first new boat, *Stars and Stripes 85*, was to test size parameters as well as keels. It was to be a big boat for the big winds of Fremantle. Pedrick says they designed it to see just how big they could go without losing out totally in lighter conditions.

A massive amount of design prediction work went ahead on the computers at SAIC and Grumman before their best ideas

All Conner's boats were painted identically to deceive "spies".

were turned into one-third scale models for testing at Offshore Technology Corporation in California, the new research centre that was also used by the New York Yacht Club, the Eagle syndicate and Canada's Bruce Kirby to check his redesign of *Canada II*.

The designers welcomed their new ability to have virtually unlimited use of massive research. "Nineteen-eighty-three was very frustrating for all American designers and we went through some pretty rough, unfair treatment," Pedrick recalled. "We argued that to develop we needed time and research, which meant money, but the syndicates kept saying we had been good boys and done our work and to leave it to them. It took Ben Lexcen to wake everyone up."

Stars and Stripes 85 was the star of the show in Honolulu in October 1985, when the syndicate began its intense campaign. The new boat with its winged keel promptly began to outpace the benchmark *Liberty* in strong winds so the designers were asked to come up with another trial horse for *85*, quickly. Their answer was to put a new hull and keel under the former reject *Spirit*, renamed *Stars and Stripes 83*.

Again Conner was spending as much time as possible on the water. More than 200 yachtsmen tried out for his two crews while he notched up almost as many sailing days testing the boats.

Jack Sutphen, who had stuck with Conner through thick and thin, was on the receiving end of Conner's competitiveness as he steered the trial horses. "At times you feel – God he's going overboard on this, there's more in life. A perfect example was the testing. He always wanted to do one more. He has this strong will. He feels if you are in this campaign, you're in it for the America's Cup, nothing else."

Largely absent from the scene of the action were the designers. They were deliberately kept away from their boats, instead meeting regularly and staying in their mainland US offices while being kept up to date by daily reports facsimilied from Honolulu by Robert Hopkins, the former US Olympic coach who was in charge of full size testing.

With all the research and brain power at their beck and call, it was inevitable that the designers would develop radical ideas that demanded full size testing. *Stars and Stripes 86* was added to the program to allow them to do so. She was a big boat, full of radical ideas. In some ways she was like another 1986 radical, the second British Twelve, with a big bustle for'ard.

High-tech 12-Metre with a very low-tech spinnaker pole.

Another idea to be tried, although no-one will discuss the tests even now, was a bulbous bow.

According to Pedrick the new boat was only a partial success. "We had a number of ideas which held real potential. Some risked pushing the extremes of design too far, but we had to try them. At times in Hawaii she reached the speeds we expected, but there were other times when the environment of the real world hampered her."

Social day on arrival in Perth.

Designers from other syndicates were amazed when they saw pictures of the big boat. "If they're right, we're wrong," was the typical reaction. Some followed Conner's lead, others worried. Members of the Australian syndicates crowed that Conner had gone the wrong way and elevated the New York Yacht Club to the status of favourites to challenge.

Outwardly at least, Conner couldn't give a damn. He was happy to be out of the limelight and was keeping the lowest possible profile. Visitors were discouraged, particularly Australian photographers and journalists who were accused of "being spies for Alan Bond". Inevitably rumours spread: the boats were "dogs"; there was vicious infighting within the camp; Conner was rattled. Even when they arrived in Perth a year later, the insiders would say nothing.

Unlike 1983, Conner was content to stay out of the initial design process, preferring to test what the designers gave him and then give them his thoughts via Robert Hopkins. ''I'm very impressed by the results of their forecasting programs, the boats turn out just as they predict so I have complete confidence in what they tell me. These boats float better than any in the past, too. The old boats from Sparkman & Stephens and Johan (Valentijn) had problems with their helm and balance, but these have come out just as the design team said they would.''

The designers, too, were happy with their progress, and with the fact that for the first time they had almost completely unrestricted research facilities to try their ideas and theories. Pedrick: ''It was fascinating to work with such a large team of extremely intelligent people. The amount of creative thought and sheer work far exceeds anything done before. What we have done would be impossible for a single designer on his own.''

Pedrick was not exaggerating about their workload. In just 12 months they had designed and delivered three new Twelves. Conner was in the process of notching up 300 days sailing them. The data from the testing formed a never-ending stream of information back to the designers for assessment as they deliberated over their full size experiments and the final boat that would carry their flag into battle after its launch in May 1986.

Conners' solitude was emphasised over the summer of 1985/86 when most syndicates gathered in Perth for the World championships. Conner never intended to be there – as well as being too busy working up his new boats, he was determined to keep the others guessing about his own progress. That did not mean he was staying out of touch, as he sent key men including Robert Hopkins to Fremantle to watch the racing and weigh up the opposition.

Most foreign syndicates were surprised by the wide range of winds that prevailed during the championships that were sailed exactly 12 months before the Cup itself. A number who had not researched the weather thoroughly found themselves uncompetitive with boats that were big and heavy with small sail areas, intended for strong winds which did not predominate.

Like others who had been ''doing their homework'', Hopkins was not overly surprised by the moderate conditions. He considered it an atypical year, but there was still a lesson in the experience as the design team finalised its plans for the new *Stars and Stripes 87*.

It was a tight program but one which the designers were happy with, as they had always planned to peak with a last minute boat. As well as their own thoughts and what they had learned over the previous two years, they had a unique computer program which they felt gave them an edge. It was a version of a Star Wars video game, a computer simulation of the race course into which they could enter a design and study its performance around a course in any conditions they wished to choose.

Just how much help it provided remains open to conjecture. Pedrick said it was sophisticated enough to allow for the effects of another boat in a tight situtation such as a mark rounding. Hopkins laughed it off as a ''crude program''.

Computer games aside, Pedrick and his colleagues were happy with the new boat. ''It is not a breakthrough; it is a darned good development. We have not done a single brilliant thing like *Australia II*, rather we have taken a number of very good developments and combined them. It is not designed for a particular breeze; it is designed to win as many races as possible over the summer. It was a very exciting peak to the program. When it came time to decide we were unanimous. Sure we all had little things we disagreed about, say ten per cent of the boat. But on 90 per cent we totally agreed.''

Though Pedrick believes in tank testing ''as long as you go for one per cent improvements, not five per cent leaps'', he was very impressed by the computer prediction programs developed by their research team. ''The research back-up we had was fantastic. We originated the concepts and then used the science to check it out, measuring everything thoroughly and quickly and then comparing it with what had gone before. It's a bit like being back at school. You do the work, and then the computer gives you a report on the work you've been doing. But then it is still up to the designers to assess the results of the computer and relate them to reality.''

Conner was equally positive. ''*Stars and Stripes 85* is very fast in heavy airs and with this new boat we are looking for a boat that will hold that performance and also be better in moderate airs as well. Only time will tell, but we are confident.''

Before leaving for Australia, Conner divided his crewmen into ''A'' and ''B'' teams. One relative newcomer went into the A team afterguard as navigator for the Cup king. He was Peter Isler, who had been skipper of *Courageous* until leaving the syndicate after the 1986 World championships, when it was announced that they would not build a new boat.

Conner finally broke camp in Hawaii to ship *Stars and Stripes 85* and *87* to Fremantle in August, after a month of racing between the two boats. In Perth his syndicate had facilities waiting in a prime position right next to Alan Bond's dock. Ironically, as the tender towed the two Twelves to their new home for the first time, it ran aground, and it was up to members of Bond's team to tow them off.

Straight edges find the tiniest blemishes in hulls which sap speed unless filled and faired.

Conner's latest in Perth.

As for Conner himself, when he arrived at the new home of the America's Cup three days later he was all smiles and bonhomie. As well as planning to host an open public day at the dock, he would be taking a number of young sailors out to sail on his yachts. Yes, he told reporters at a news conference on his arrival, he was looking forward to an exciting regatta and winning it. No, it would not be the end of the world if he was beaten again; after all, he had survived 1983. Yes, he expected the Australians to be tough – both Parry and Bond – but first he would have to beat the other challengers, particularly the New Zealanders, the *America IIs* and *French Kiss*.

After the public relations offensive – another ironic twist because it was managed by Lesleigh Green, who had held down the job for Alan Bond in 1983 in Newport – the smiles gradually became more wan as the afternoon sea breeze known as the Fremantle Doctor refused to appear. "Looking at the conditions here," commented Conner as a lazy five knot breeze from the desert prevailed, "I'm glad we spent so much time in Hawaii. The others must be worried."

Hopkins conceded their frustrations. "It was a little disappointing. We wanted good conditions to race against other good boats. When you have high ambitions as we do it's hard having to sit back and hope the weather settles."

It must have been at least as frustrating for their designers who, in line with syndicate policy, were kept away from the action. While Hopkins kept sending them memos at the end of each day he explained the reasoning behind keeping them away, unlike most syndicates. "If they were here they would be too close to it all. It's hard to maintain an overall picture when you are dealing with yachties who are getting off the boat and grumbling about this and that. It's better to leave them in their own environment and keep them fully informed. Besides, it would be mighty expensive bringing 30 people over here."

Conner took the new boat *87* into the preliminary series but kept *Stars and Stripes 85* "up his sleeve", in case drastic alterations were needed if another challenger had succeeded in designing a breakthrough. According to Hopkins, they would be able to change both boats considerably between each series to suit the weather they expected. "Each is riddled with holes for changes, including keels. If the weather goes strange again then maybe we will just have to sit it out, waiting for what history shows us will happen eventually.

There is no doubt that Conner will be less than happy if he has to sit anything out. Four years is a long time for anybody, but particularly for the man determined to reinstate himself in the eyes of everyone who noted his "transgression" in 1983.

AMERICA II

Hungry For Revenge

12
Newsweek
THE INTERNATIONAL NEWSMAGAZINE

After the shockwaves of *Australia II's* win in 1983 began to dissipate, 10 American syndicates were formed to challenge for the Cup. For 132 years no American clubs had been able to send representatives to win the Cup away from the New York Yacht Club. Under the Deed of Gift, participating American yachts could only represent the club which held the Cup. However, while excited yachtsmen, businessmen and local governments discussed the gains to be won by successfully challenging Australia for the Cup, the club with 132 years of experience in Cup campaigning was quietly and efficiently going about its business of trying to get the Cup back.

Before the Cup was even lost a syndicate had been formed to either challenge or defend it. It was made up of some of the key men who had been in other American syndicates eliminated by Conner in the trials to select the 25th defender. Helmsman/skipper would be John Kolius, the newcomer who in 1983 had shaken the American 12-Metre establishment to its foundations. Kolius had arrived on the scene like a breath of fresh air. His yachting credentials included a class win in the prestigious Bermuda ocean race, two wins in World J24 championships, a silver medal in the Soling class at the 1976 Olympic Games and the 1980 USA Champion of Champions. But it was his laid back approach to the traditionally stuffy scene that made people sit up and take notice.

As skipper of the 10-year-old *Courageous*, trial horse for the new *Defender* skippered by Tom Blackaller, he had faced none of the pressures of the big two – Blackaller and Dennis Conner. But Kolius soon found himself thrust into the limelight when *Defender*, despite two major modifications, failed to live up to expectations and was eliminated, leaving Kolius to push Conner. Conner's *Liberty* proved superior, but Kolius was hooked on the Cup scene.

When he thinks back to the racing of 1983, Kolius' comments are typical of his relaxed approach to the sport he thoroughly enjoys. "We had a good time sailing together. We had some awesome races ... it was like going into a heavyweight championship. You can't just rough up the champ, you have to knock him out and we weren't able to so we lost. That's the game. You know how it's going to end so that's life."

With Kolius came his 1983 tactician, he of the same name as the winning Australian skipper, John Bertrand. The Bertrand from San Francisco and Kolius had formed a formidable team aboard *Courageous* and enjoyed mutual respect that few other afterguards enjoy. Like Kolius, the younger (then 26) Bertrand had sailed since boyhood and made his reputation in international one-design, in his case the singlehanded dinghy Finn class in which he won a silver medal at the 1984 Olympics, and the Laser class in which he won the World titles.

The new syndicate quickly decided to stay with the yacht design company that had served America so well, providing five successful defenders including the last successful American defender, *Freedom*. In 1983 this venerable company,

Sparkman & Stephens, had found itself in unusual controversy. Dennis Conner's syndicate had commissioned S&S to design one boat and Johan Valentijn another, each seeking to break new ground at either end of the size scale. Neither worked, and Conner asked the two design groups to join forces, something unheard of in the top secret world of 12-Metre design. After some half-hearted attempts the planned partnership failed to get off the ground and Conner went to Valentijn for the design of *Liberty*.

Sparkman & Stephens, through chief designer Bill Langan, then concentrated their attentions on *Courageous*, modifying her for the role of *Defender's* trial horse before she eventually vanquished the new yacht. It was the beginning of a close partnership between Langan, Kolius and Bertrand, so there was no hesitation in naming him designer of their new boats.

For Langan it was a quick rise to fame. An experienced yachtsman in his own right, he had long been interested in yacht design and after meeting Rod Stephens in 1975 he began spending his school holidays in the S&S design office. After qualifying at the Webb Institute, one of America's three schools of naval architecture, Langan joined a ship design firm where it took just "six months to work out that it was boring work". It was an appropriate time for Olin Stephens to call Langan and offer him the all-important job of chief draftsman for S&S, with the tacit understanding that if he worked out he would take over as chief designer on Stephens' retirement. It was a great honour for Langan, exceeding his wildest dreams. Quickly he found himself involved in 12-Metre design with his mentor, the legendary Olin Stephens, and in 1980 he was project manager for Dennis Conner's S&S designed *Freedom*, directing the day-to-day design projects for the boat.

At the end of 1983, the new syndicate's three key people totalled just 85 years between them, an average age of a very tender 28. But backing them were some considerably older heads, members of previous America's Cup syndicates who were also leaders in America's high-powered business world centred on New York. In addition, largely through their personal support of Kolius, a number of wealthy Texans were key members of the syndicate, promising further extensive bankrolling.

Quick to add its support was the United States Merchant Marine Academy, a college established before World War II to train young maritime leaders. It had been involved in the America's Cup since the days of *Intrepid*. The Academy provided the new syndicate with a fundraising platform so necessary to America's Cup campaigning, as donations to the Academy for "international amateur sports competitions" were tax-deductible.

The syndicate's offer to represent the New York Yacht Club was quickly snapped up and a formidable organisation went to work while other syndicates were still in the embryonic stages. One of the syndicate's first decisions was that their new boats would all be named *America II*, a symbolic gesture that gave

Three Twelves from the wealthiest syndicate representing the New York Yacht Club.

America II, US46, *being unloaded in Fremantle.*

their fundraisers the opportunity to make a patriotic plea to potential supporters – *America* had been the first and last US yacht to win the Cup from a foreign country back in 1851.

Quickly they began to lead their American rivals, establishing a track record others could only envy – first American group to enter an official challenge, first to build a new Twelve, first to set up headquarters in Fremantle, first to obtain major corporate sponsorship, first challenger to sail the America's Cup course off Fremantle and first American boat to race a potential challenger (Italy's *Azzurra*) and a potential defender (*Kookaburra I*).

With the support of the Academy and influential business leaders holding important positions within the syndicate, budget limitations did not threaten any part of the NYYC's campaign to regain the Cup, which for so long had given it worldwide prestige, and in the eyes of many its reason for simply existing. Without the Cup, its members felt naked. The loss had been a bitter experience. Some members resigned, furious that the club's America's Cup Committee had not refused to race against *Australia II* which, to their dying days, they will consider cheated the Rule. Long friendships were shattered overnight in bitter arguments over whether the 1983 Cup should have been allowed to take place.

That was of no interest to the new syndicate, which sent its members out into the corporate world with enticing packages to encourage support for a patriotic mission to win back the Cup that bore their country's name. It was a powerful approach to a new world in which the Cup was not protected by home-made rules, tradition and experience. This was a crusade: America out to regain its position as leader in the prestigious sport of yachting. For the first time, the Club had to go along with the argument that the Cup was not just a "friendly competition between friendly countries". As Alan Bond had been saying for so long and had finally proved, this was "a war", which meant the campaign would only be as good as its people, planning, funding and boats.

The designer's brief was "to prepare a program to develop a boat as sophisticated as possible with all the new technology that could be offered in the United States". For Langan, it was the opportunity to prove he was not "establishment", with ideas restricted by preconceived notions within a 50-year-old company. He was given the go-ahead to try everything in search of a breakthrough like Lexcen's winged keel. He also had approval to hire the best technological brains and

Bill Langan: *''If being conservative means having the benefit of 50 years of experience then that's fine with me. We've actually been very innovative.''*

John Bertrand – tactician and potential helmsman of the future who may put the second name ''John Bertrand'' on the Cup.

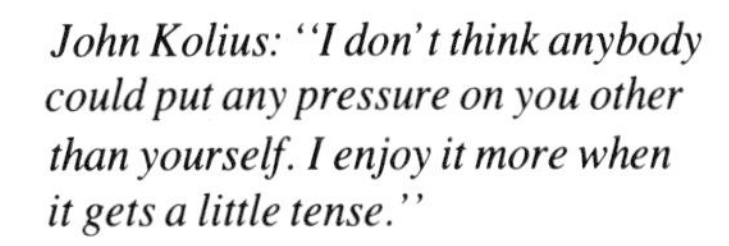

John Kolius: ''I don't think anybody could put any pressure on you other than yourself. I enjoy it more when it gets a little tense.''

US46 *shows trend of syndicate's sailmakers towards all Kevlar mainsails. White patches are dacron for reinforcement in high load and chaff areas.*

equipment he would need to test ideas. ''When they said to do everything, even if it would take three new boats, I naturally took that to mean we could build three boats.'' In 1986 three Twelves bearing the name *America II* would carve through the waters of Fremantle on the other side of the world.

The early start enabled Langan to get a jump on other syndicates and attract the people and facilities he wanted for his team. ''Before developing my design ideas I looked for people who could work in tight situations, contributing to a free exchange of ideas. Having people from different disciplines is hard, some cannot get on with others, others are academics who cannot apply themselves to reality. By starting first we had the pick of the crop, we talked to everybody before the other syndicates began moving in.''

With a design brief and budget most designers only dream of, Langan nonetheless began carefully. He cast his net wide and within months had a highly qualified team consisting of some of America's top technologists in science, engineering, naval architecture, space and defence development, hydrodynamics and aerodynamics.

The more people Langan talked to, the clearer became the magnitude of his task. ''At the time we didn't really realise what we were getting into, it was a nice thought. The task was more formidable than we had ever imagined. There is so much information available and so many well-intentioned people with ideas you have to sit through before you decide whether they will flip or flop.'' Sorting out the available information reinforced Langan's belief that he would have to make maximum use of all the tools available to him, and have them developed as much as possible to improve their accuracy and usefulness.

Sparkman & Stephens had long led the way with tank testing and had developed a considerable bank of knowledge through use of the tanks at the Stevens Institute of Technology. Langan knew he would need the best possible information from the tanks to come up with the quantum leap demanded by the success of *Australia II* and the massive design programs beginning around the world.

He also knew that there was not the time or money available to put all their ideas through the test tanks, so from the outset he began recruiting the right people to develop computer design programs with new standards of accuracy.

An early recruit was John Hess who had been part of the team that developed the original design program for aircraft

Conventional hull lines of the syndicate's yachts are vehicles for an array of keels/displacement/sail area configurations.

giants McDonnell Douglas 20 years earlier. In following years Hess had applied the program to the problems of other aircraft companies, the US Navy and the space agency NASA.

"Obviously he was valuable in our fine tuning of the method to our specific problem," Langan recalls. "It was interesting for him, too, because he was used to dealing with aircraft which operate in a single medium of air alone. With us he found himself dealing with the dual medium of air and water."

Others included two experts in aero and hydrodynamics from Massachusetts Institute of Technology, Nick Newman and Jake Kirwin, and a number of technologists and engineers at the NASA Research Centre at Langley.

Like all American designers, Langan was wary of using a computer in design development. "Very early we decided that while computational programs were a fantastic tool, they were not the answer to the problem. The technique had weaknesses but fortunately they were the opposite of the weaknesses of the towing tanks."

The syndicate's early start put the designer a step ahead of the others in his search for the best tank. Finally he picked a new company, the Offshore Technology Corporation in California. One of its principals was Karl Kirkman, who had spent considerable time testing earlier S&S Twelves including *Enterprise* and *Freedom*. Another attraction was that Langan had a say in the development of their new testing equipment. "Being new to the game, they had no preconceived notions about their equipment or anything else. Another reason was that they had done a lot of study of seakeeping abilities of oil rigs. There was a lot of debate at the time about hull shapes, whether wings would work and what shapes would work. So we did a rigorous study of seakeeping of our boats in the tanks and on the computer as well.

"The basic problem with towing tanks is that the boat is always sailing into a head sea. We were able to do a fairly rigorous seakeeping program, towing one-third sized models down their tanks in waves. To tow a boat across the entire spectrum of waves would be extremely expensive, so we did it in waves in 10 knots of breeze and waves in 25 knots, using the computational technique to fill in the gaps."

Although Olin Stephens had retired as chief designer of the firm, he was still actively involved in Langan's design process. While Langan was comparatively the "new boy on the block", looking over his shoulder was the man who had

All three America II *yachts have additional winch power: the pedestal is behind the helmsman and can be linked to mainsheet and runner winches.*

been successfully drawing 12-Metre yachts since the 1930s. Langan describes the pairing as a "good combination". Many of his ideas had been tested by Stephens during his years at the drawing board and often Langan would not waste time on an idea because it had already been tried and proved incorrect by Stephens. But some discarded ideas that had been tested over the years by Stephens on one-tenth and one-third models, they believed were worth looking at again in the one-third models in the new tank. Langan found that with thorough testing the initial findings of Stephens with his much smaller research program had been incorrect.

Langan looked hard at many different ideas before committing himself to definite design paths. "We looked at lots of experimental keels and various hull shapes, but once we eliminated the basic questions we concentrated on the good points. There was no need to waste time on the others."

Langan's first boat was christened in New York in August 1984 and after a short work up became the first foreign Twelve to sail in Australian waters since *Vim*. The boat, the first of three to be named *America II*, was dubbed US42 after her sail number. Little work went into her design: she was a conservative Twelve aimed at getting her crew and instruments to work in Fremantle to measure local conditions and test the equipment then available.

The boat was also the first of a new breed of America's Cup yachts, a "Lego" boat, built so that with a minimum of effort her shore party and yachtsmen could change her complete configuration almost overnight. Three keels were aboard the ship carrying her to Australia, as well as a number of rudders. Everything about the boat could be changed – displacement, rig and sail area as well as keels and rudders – all while maintaining the yacht as a 12-Metre. Her special mast step and chainplate attachments meant the mast could be moved fore and aft to suit new configurations. Her deck layout put tactician and navigator behind the helmsman, but with a new idea for the Twelves in the form of a winch pedestal that could be linked up to the mainsheet to back up the normal grinder or the runner winches.

The sleek white yacht was to be the ultimate test bed for the ideas of her test team. Not only could they try different design ideas, they could measure their effect on the yacht's computers and relate them back to the predictions of the computer programs and the wind and towing tanks so they could determine just how accurate their design tools were.

In Fremantle the yacht's new home was a well-equipped dock just 100 metres from the first Australian syndicate to establish its base in Fremantle, that of Alan Bond. Tourists were amused to turn from the boxing kangaroo flying over the defence headquarters of the West Australian business tycoon to the nearby American dock, where a flag with the international symbol for "prohibited" was printed over another boxing kangaroo. While *Australia II* hung from her crane with her winged keel uncovered, the New York yacht was swallowed up in the latest in security, a completely enclosed concrete and steel pen.

The new, untraditional approach of the syndicate was graphically illustrated when the New York Yacht Club's colours flew aboard the yacht during two series against the 1983 Italian yacht *Azzurra*. While it defended the Cup the Club had always insisted that potential defenders should not race against foreign boats. In Fremantle, with the shoe on the other foot, tradition was not going to restrict the new syndicate.

As well as racing the Italians, with Kolius at the wheel and Langan either aboard or watching from the tender, the Americans sailed whenever the winds blew. It became common to see the yacht leave its dock at the first indication of the "Fremantle Doctor", as locals refer to the afternoon sea breeze.

At the same time, work was underway at Manchester and Williams in Newport, Rhode Island, on the second "Lego" boat. At the same time contributions continued to pour in, with many important companies and individuals contributing towards the syndicate's budget of $15 million, among them Cadillac, Newsweek and Amway.

After the launch of the second boat, the summer of 1985/86 was to be decision time for the design team, using both boats to test their ideas full size before committing themselves to a final boat to be launched mid-1986. Langan knew that despite the growing sophistication of his research and scale-testing equipment, none were as accurate or definitive as testing one boat alongside another.

Soon after the mid-1985 launch of the second yacht, trouble broke out. Kolius resigned, blaming politics ashore for keeping him from concentrating on his task as skipper. The syndicate was stunned. Bertrand and crew-training boss Tom McLaughlin were named as helmsmen, but within weeks Kolius was back aboard, while there was a shake-up at the top of the syndicate. McLaughlin had forcefully pointed out to syndicate heads that the crew wanted Kolius and no-one else, while the Texas backers also used their influence. It was sorted out just in time for Kolius to join the rest of the 70-strong team in Fremantle for their two boat testing phase.

Over the summer of 1985/86 the crews sailed more than 3,500 kilometres in 51 days in their "Lego" boats, *US42* and the new *US44*. They tested as many as 17 different configurations. Both boats were constructed so that the keels could either be changed entirely, or the lower section with the wings could simply be replaced. As both boats informally raced others, opponents commented on the different range of wings the Americans were trying out. One set was so wide that it appeared to almost break the surface of the water when the yacht was well heeled. In the *America II Log*, the syndicate's official publication, Kolius described the second yacht *US46* as "simply awesome. If the America's Cup was held today we would be very difficult to beat."

Like the first boat, *US44* was easily altered. Kolius was to comment: "We have so much lead here in so many keels that if the Australian Government decided to put a special tax on lead we'd go broke, it would be the end of us."

Langan says they were looking for big results with their changes to the two boats. "You can trial two boats in two ways. The first leaves one boat constant throughout and you change the other boat against that which is great if you are looking for small changes. The second method is the leapfrog technique which we used – keeping one boat constant while we got the other one going faster, then changing the slower boat to make it the faster of the two. The danger is going off on a tangent and not being able to get back. We did that a few times but having *US42* made it easy to get back to the starting point. That technique paid big dividends for us."

Langan says that no matter how good the research programs, designers still have to know their boats, watching and sailing on them as much as possible. Langan's approach often saw him joining the afterguard of the yachts, returning to shore to study the data from the yachts' computers before relaying information back to his consultants to compare against the predictions of tanks and computers. "There is no way you can design one of these boats without sailing on them. It's very easy not to believe the guys on the boat, to say they weren't sailing it right or the sails were not right. Every designer is guilty of it. You get an idea you firmly believe in and it's awfully hard to convince yourself that you are not right. There are a lot of guys who in my experience have pursued things way beyond their limit and wasted a great deal of time."

The busy summer of testing, changing and testing yet again had a brief respite for the World Championships, in which the Americans entered *US42*. It turned out to be a forgettable regatta for them. After getting off to a great start by being first to finish in both invitation races the series became a nightmare. In one race they wrapped a spinnaker around the forestay and spent an embarrassing 20 minutes cutting it free while the fleet sailed past. In another race, a mistake saw the spinnaker topping lift released while the bowman clung to the outboard end preparing the sail for a takedown. Of course gravity took over, dumping him in the sea and the crew were virtually out of the race as they returned to pick him up. Finally, in the last race they appeared to have it all together when they led around the last mark. But on the previous leg a boom vang fitting had broken, allowing the boom to sky and the mainsail to wrap around a spreader. A small tear resulted which grew as the yacht sailed towards the finish, her crew helpless to do anything about the faster *French Kiss* which went on to take the gun. It was a depressing experience for Kolius and crew. As their skipper said later: "It was like hitting your head with a hammer, nice when you stop."

As Langan had feared when he started, he was collecting unbelievable amounts of information. Kolius said he could not understand how Langan got through it all. "We've been doing an incredible amount of boat testing," Kolius said. "Keels, appendages, masts, we've been all over the place. We've tried to have a methodical improvement. We've looked from a technical viewpoint at a lot of fringe boats but haven't been convinced enough to build them so we have taken a methodical approach to improve our existing designs. We've definitely made a lot of improvement to our boats since we started, so if everyone hangs in we are in good shape."

While *US42* was sailing in the Worlds, the syndicate's new boat was being lofted back in Newport. *US46* was to be the pièce de resistance from the design team, taking all the good points from the first two yachts and putting them into an unbeatable package. The yacht was launched in May for a month's racing before shipment to Fremantle. At the same time a team of builders flew to Australia to modify the hulls of *US42* and *44*.

The new boat was not as changeable as the first two, reflecting the designer's conviction that the experimenting had given him enough answers. But he could still alter the configuration to cope with different wind strengths over the long summer.

"To win you need a boat you can change between each series of races. There are obviously two goals. The ultimate is to win the Cup, but that is in February and you have to get there first. There are substantial differences in wind speeds across the summer and it was amusing for us in the World Championships when everyone arrived and said they were surprised that there was not as much wind as they'd been told. We knew that because we'd been here for a while. The key to winning is having a boat that has the ability to get through December which requires a substantially different boat to what will be necessary in February. Sure, on the law of averages you have to have a very good heavy air boat, but you can design a heavy air boat and sit there for a week without any wind. A lot of our work has been figuring out how we can make constant changes to play the averages while not giving away the odd chance that you might have wind conditions that are totally different to what you expect."

According to Langan, the measurers are going to be very busy remeasuring altered boats between each series. Certainly he will be first in the queue with his boat, with its range of displacement, waterline and sail area.

Above the water there is little difference between the three boats carrying the New York Yacht Club's flag. The third boat is slightly smaller than the first, with her forefoot shallower but the same fine bow and a powerful stern with easy chines leading to the flat underbody. It's what is camouflaged below that sets them apart. Langan gives no clues except to say that all boats in Fremantle will have some kind of winged keel. He goes further. "What Ben Lexcen did not have last time was the time to get the hull shape right. There were a lot of problems with *Australia II* and he would be the first to admit that the relationship between hull and keel needed more work. The keel shape is critical but you can have a great keel on an awful boat so that is the key to winning this time. The boat that wins will have done the best job of tying things together."

Hard running conditions make downwind steering an art form to prevent the big yachts from nose-diving and halving boat speed.

Kolius adds further light when asked if he is worried about someone else having an *Australia II* type breakthrough. "You have to make sure you are adaptable so that if someone comes along with something really spectacular, you can adjust to it."

Comfortable is a word that is used a lot in the New York dock. The laid back Kolius is "comfortable" with his boats and his people. Langan is "comfortable" about the boats he has created. "Sure I'd have liked more time. Another year would have been nice, but because we started early we managed to cover a lot of bases the others were not able to."

Langan laughs when he points out that after the 1987 America's Cup he will know whether he has been right or wrong. He's looking forward to the moment of truth. On a personal note it's important too. The "master's apprentice" will know whether he has proved to be a worthy successor to the man who dominated 12-Metre design from the 1930s until Ben Lexcen's winged keel revitalised the old class and laid down the challenge to all yacht designers to cast away their preconceptions.

EAGLE

Talons Drawn

The new: Johan Valentijn (left) and "Hot" Rod Davis.

The old advising ashore: from left Jerry Driscoll, Lowell North and Bill Ficker.

"I will win the Cup before I drop dead. We're going to give it a good shot this time, although it's too early to tell at this stage."

The "stage" referred to was the final days before the 1986 October preliminary challengers' trials. The man uttering the words was one of the young tyros of the America's Cup, Rod Davis, 31-year-old skipper of California's Newport Harbour Yacht Club Twelve *Eagle*. Despite his lack of years, the young sailmaker was well qualified to make such statements. In 1977 he was bowman of *Enterprise*, which was defeated for the right to defend by the legendary *Courageous*. In 1980 he was coach to the crew of challenger *Australia* led by Jim Hardy. In 1983 he sailed as mainsheet trimmer for Tom Blackaller aboard the ill-named *Defender*, which proved slower than the 10-year-old *Courageous* and Conner's new *Liberty*.

His sentiments would readily be seconded by the other key young man in the Newport Harbour group, designer Johan Valentijn. The Dutch-born naval architect is the only man to have designed unsuccessful challengers and an unsuccessful defender. The former were *Australia*, which he co-designed with Ben Lexcen, and *France III* for Baron Bich's swansong in 1980. The latter was *Liberty* which was no match for the revolutionary *Australia II*.

For the 1983 campaign Valentijn adopted an American passport to design two Twelves for Dennis Conner. First he was briefed to produce the lightest 12-Metre of all time and the resulting *Magic* weighed in at 46,000 lbs (20,860 kg). *Magic* was even lighter than *Australia II*, but while Lexcen had dreamed up the inverted keel with wings, Valentijn had not progressed beyond the conventional long low aspect keel. The yacht was hopelessly unstable and slow in strong breezes and it took Conner only six weeks to scrap it. As the ultimate insult it became a tourist attraction in Newport, Rhode Island.

Valentijn himself was not scrapped by Conner, who asked him to join forces with Sparkman & Stephens after pronouncing himself unhappy with their design *Spirit*. However, the union was never consummated and Conner went ahead with Valentijn for his third new boat *Liberty*.

Valentijn had little say in the new boat. Disillusioned by the failure of designers to produce a boat that was faster than his 1980 winner *Freedom*, Conner included him in a committee of the syndicate's key people. Together they worked out performance figures which they were confident could be reached and Valentijn went away for a week of thought and drawing before he began lofting the boat. It's history now that *Liberty* was beaten, but if Lexcen had not made his revolutionary discovery it should have been good enough to successfully defend the Cup.

Failure of such magnitude was bound to result in casualties but Valentijn survived, largely because most of the criticism was directed at Conner for taking over the design process himself. Valentijn was soon at work again, this time for the Newport Harbour Yacht Club.

The group got off to an impressive start with strong local financial support. First it purchased and restored *Magic* for use as a full-sized test bed and then as a trial horse for two new Twelves commissioned from the former Dutchman. Another cheque went to the Netherlands Aerospace Laboratories for the design of a winged keel based on that of *Australia II*, to be fitted to *Magic*.

Eagle *and* Magic *obscured to windward while trialling on Newport Harbour.*

12
US-60
12
US-38

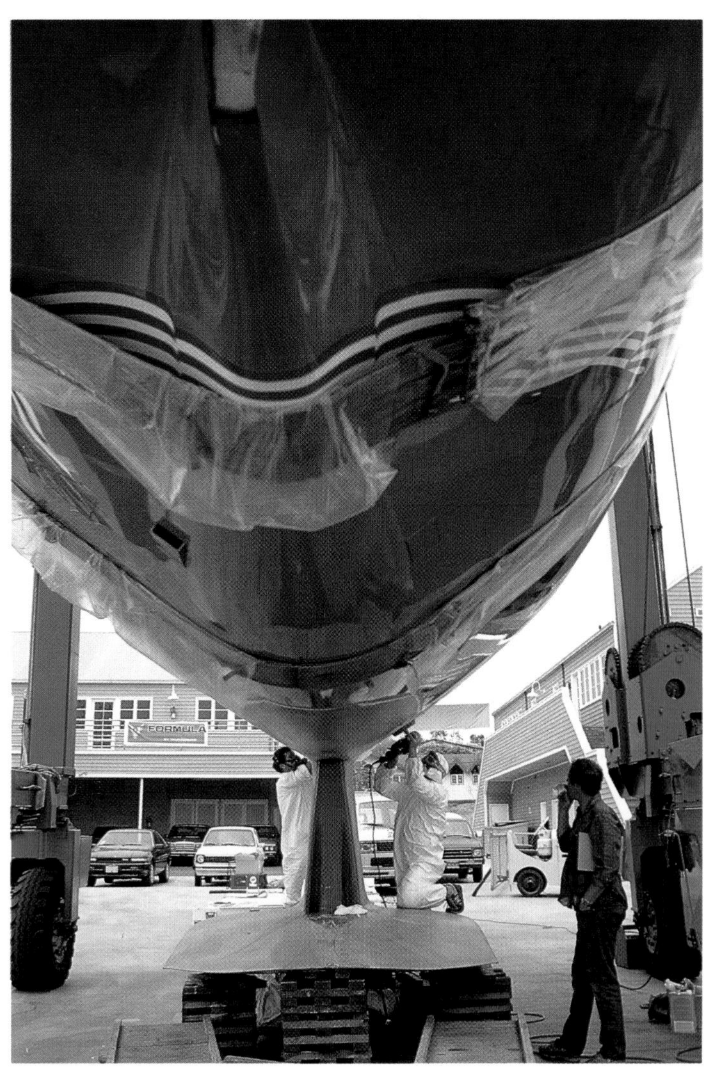

Join between inverted keel is high stress area demanding fine engineering.

At the same time a strong line-up of talent was being assembled. Davis, who had resigned himself to going back to life as a sailmaker after *Defender*, won the job of helmsman ahead of several other yachtsmen. His response to this new display of confidence in him was to get on with the job of beating others on the water. He was the tactician aboard *Victory 83* when it won the 1984 World 12-Metre championships in Sardinia. In the Olympic Games of the same year he won a gold medal as crewman in the Soling class. In 1985 he defeated other America's Cup skippers including Conner and Kolius, Britain's Cudmore and New Zealand's Dickson in the Congressional Cup.

Ashore, the team obtained support and advice from former Cup skippers Bill Ficker and Lowell North, who added the weight of their not inconsiderable experience to the growing team.

The group quickly began testing *Magic* to build up their data base. First the yacht was turned into a floating laboratory with instruments recording and comparing everything possible as the yacht sailed with the conventional keel and then with the new *Australia II* lookalike. Later the yacht's rig was removed and the boat was pushed and pulled around on flat waters with special devices recording drag and resistance.

The original plan was to build two yachts, the first a winged keel development and the second the most promising radical boat that Valentijn could conceive. But the syndicate ran into funding difficulties, like all others mounting their first challenges. The second boat was shelved and the date of construction of the first was put back from August to October

Close-up view of the Eagle's *wings.*

1985. The reluctant decision to go for just one boat meant Valentijn had to be given as much time as possible to get that boat right. There was no room for error.

The responsibility never worried Valentijn. While his former employer Dennis Conner and other groups had abandoned the principal of using one designer and formed committees, Valentijn preferred to design alone. ''If you have a committee you end up with a camel, each designing different parts. Also, my way I can't blame anybody else. If there is a fault it's my fault.''

Always a believer in making technology work for him, Valentijn was determined to use it to its limit in the wake of the 1983 embarrassment. For computer design power he turned to McDonnell Douglas, the aircraft giant which adapted its aircraft design programs for his hull configurations. Boeing provided the computer technology for analysis of pressure distribution on the hulls, similar to the work done by the Netherlands Aerospace Laboratory which had ''crunched the numbers'' for Ben Lexcen in 1982.

For tank testing, to take the computer analysis further and fill in the gaps, he turned to the Offshore Technology Corporation of Escandido in California, which had also tested the ideas of the *America II, Canada II* and *Stars and Stripes* syndicates.

Valentijn also decided to take the radical step of building the hull from fibreglass, convinced that he could develop a method of construction that would be stiffer than aluminium, which flexes between the hull support beams and changes shape slightly when the enormous loads are hydraulically pumped into the rig. The problem he faced was to get Lloyds, the British company which supervises 12-Metre construction, to accept his construction method.

After a considerable amount of work with a high-tech construction company he was satisfied that he could build the stiffest 12-Metre of all time from fibreglass. But, as he had feared, Lloyds rejected his method and in frustration he dropped the plan to build in ''plastic''. Several other syndicates also investigated the approach with all but the New Zealanders dropping the idea. Valentijn was angered by what he perceived as a hindrance to development in a so-called development class. ''I know the Kiwis did a lot of studies and went ahead, but while Lloyds are there it is no good, they hurt the construction system.''

Meanwhile Valentijn persisted in looking beyond the

winged keel for another breakthrough. As well as testing bulb bows he tried twin keels – high aspect fins side by side, each with a big bulb at their base. Another idea to be tank tested and discarded used horizontal wings mounted at waterline level on both stern quarters in an attempt to keep the quarter wave down.

In all Valentijn tested six models, 24 keels and 12 rudders, supervising all the runs in the tank himself. In an article published in the magazine *Yachting* in May 1986 he wrote: "Model testing is very valuable, but it is also a very dangerous area. Results, good or bad, are subject to interpretation; test tank accuracy is always questionable. We're all trying to squeeze a mere one-quarter per cent speed improvement out of our designs, but if you get only one-quarter per cent gain from a model throw it away – the measurement error is probably larger than the gain!

"Finally I learned so much from test observations that our boat *Eagle* is actually none of the boats we tested. It may sound strange that after all the money we spent on testing, we'd build a boat "on spec", but it's true. Testing gives you only the basic numbers, but a designer's instinct has to put its two cents in.

"When it came time to loft and build ... I took a year's worth of work and let it all sink in. That's the way I operate. I just sit at my desk, or walk, or drive my car. I just mull it all over at odd times of day or night. I give in to my instincts and let the numbers take care of themselves. I remember the tank tests and what the waves told me."

While the designer kept looking at large and small ways of making a Twelve go faster, the yachtsmen were reaping the benefits of close co-operation with the new Italian syndicate representing the Yacht Club Italiano. While they developed their new *Italia* they sent their former British boat *Victory 83* to Newport in the spring of 1985 for racing against *Magic*. When it became obvious to the Americans that they could not afford to send a boat to Australia for the World championships, they arranged with the Italians to have the use of *Victory 83* for a month before the series, in which Davis would sail as tactician. Though *Italia* did not figure highly in the series, Davis was able to obtain valuable experience in the Fremantle conditions and the move saved the struggling syndicate at least $US 1 million.

The new yacht was finally launched in May 1986 amid great fanfare. The syndicate's logo was "*Eagle* – bringing the America's Cup to a New Port". Guests were amazed when she was unveiled – on either side of the big grey hull was emblazoned a long, multi-coloured eagle with its wings and talons reaching down the keel. Davis joked to the crowd: "I said to Johan when he told me about it that we'd better be fast because, if everyone is going to see us, we won't be able to hide in the pack."

Valentijn described *Eagle* as a good medium boat with a small but heavy keel, which would accelerate and turn easily. "It's a medium and light air boat, not a heavy weather boat. I'm pretty confident the breeze will average 16-18 knots. If it does blow 25 knots every day we'll be going home early."

Davis agreed. "We're shooting for 18 knots and we'll hang in under that. No-one will be dramatically quicker than others except perhaps in one condition. But then they will be slower in others. I remember Johan had one that blew the doors off in six knots of breeze but at 16 it was slow."

Measuring in at 66 ft (20.1 m) overall, 47 ft (14.3 m) on the waterline, 62,000 lb (28,100 kg) in displacement and carrying 1,615 sq ft (150 sq m) in sail area, the boat showed a keel that had a big trim tab, making up about one-third of the entire keel area.

Soon after the launch the crew stopped covering the keel, which had thick, aerodynamic delta wings extending aft beyond the trailing edge of the trim tab to form a flat endplate. There was nothing radical in the hull shape and Davis said this fitted perfectly with what he had asked for. "I don't believe there will be any breakthrough boats in Perth; no-one will be

10 per cent faster although guys like the "Hippo", *Italia* and Blackaller are trying. I kept saying to Johan to give us a boat that was one or two per cent faster and then it is up to us to do the rest."

On revealing the keel: "We don't feel like playing paranoia. For the amount of trouble and expense, what the heck. If we change keels we might then." Valentijn was equally laid back. "There's more to this than a keel, there are the people, sails, rig, and money. In 1983 it was not just the keel that won the Cup."

At last the crew was able to go to work on the new boat with three months of sailing against *Magic* before moving to Perth. Davis was not concerned about the late start. "Sailing is not a sport where you have to practise manoeuvres forever. I'm not like Dennis Conner. I don't have to baby-sit my crew, they've all sailed Twelves and they're self-motivated, so I don't expect to have to kick butts every day."

Comparisons between the different approaches of the two men are something both have to live with in the high profile world of the America's Cup. Davis is the young, relaxed natural, while the older Conner is the man who made long-term campaigning an integral part of the Cup and whose philosophy is the title of his book "No Excuse To Lose". Davis is quick to point out the differences between himself and the man who once wore the crown he covets.

"I've sailed with Dennis a couple of times and we got along great. We just have different styles, maybe because I started crewing while he started in the afterguard. I basically like to keep the team a unity, not like Dennis who likes to keep his afterguard separate from the crew. There is no way he would let himself be sandwiched between the two, he likes to be saluted. He also worries a lot more about security while we're more open."

Davis gets along well with his crew, some of whom opted out of programs with Conner. Calling the tactics is Douglas Rastello who has been tactician for Davis in all of his five Congressional Cups. Navigator is Jim Allsop, who sailed on *Clipper* and *Enterprise*. Mainsheet hand is Kimo Worthington from *Clipper* and the sail trimmers are also the sailmakers, Mike Topa and Mark Wilson.

Davis says: "Because we have been able to prepare against the Italian crews we have been able to keep our own crew down to 16 which is good. I don't want the logistics of running two full crews; that's a financial headache. We're one team of 16, we're not trying to have an A and a B team. We'll have to rotate over the summer and like a baseball team will probably be putting our top guys on when we race the top boats."

On his arrival in Fremantle a month before the October preliminaries, Davis was amused to see the lack of preparedness of others. "Sure, we could have used another month in California but no-one else is ready either. Dennis isn't even here yet. His campaigning in Hawaii is a bit like working in a closet and popping out at the end to see how you go. I'm already here.

"There will be a lot of experimenting in October because nobody is ready. In November the pressure goes right on. No boat is going to be way faster than the rest, and don't forget 1983 showed that no-one can win in a slow boat, no matter how good their guys are."

Davis also sees weight of numbers taking the Cup away from Australia. "The battle between Bond and Parry will be good, and tipping the scales to Australia is local knowledge. But the winner of the challenge trials will beat Australia. The only reason will be because there are 13 or 14 boats all working on the problems of making a 12-Metre go faster, while Australia only has four teams working on that."

If Davis is right and the Cup does leave Australia, Valentijn believes the winged keel could become a concept of the past. "It's pretty good for Perth because of the additional stability. But there are other concepts which may be very fast. If it goes elsewhere with lighter winds you may see something else completely different."

As for the present challenge facing Davis, the man who has the motivation of establishing himself as an America's Cup skipper in his own right: "I'm psyching myself up for a real fight, a cut-throat and dirty battle. The pride of countries is riding on these boats and it will be a really close yacht race."

USA

Shooting For The Stars

We have really taken a step off the deep end; it is a significant breakthrough.'' That is designer Gary Mull's description of the 12-Metre *USA* representing the Golden Gate challenge by San Francisco's St Francis Yacht Club. ''It is a design that everyone will have to copy for the next Cup as they copied Lexcen's fantastic winged keel for this one. I won't say how much faster it is, but it is significant.''

Brave words, but Gary Mull has never been afraid to lay it on the line, nor does he ever lose his sense of humour. ''The last two years have been very, very interesting. Not much fun, nor economically rewarding. You have to learn to deal with all sorts of strange attitudes. Everyone in the 12-Metre world has an enormous ego. I know I have an enormous ego, but I manage to get it under control, occasionally. Everyone has their area roped off and if you intrude, watch out. They all take it too seriously, some are not loose enough to even do their jobs right. They see you smiling and they think you're having the day off.''

Mull put his head into the lion's mouth when he left Dennis Conner's design team during its embryonic stage to design two Twelves for the Golden Gate Challenge. He was running the gauntlet of the syndicate's skipper Tom Blackaller, renowned for having made egotism an art form.

It is perhaps a tribute to Mull's sense of humour that Blackaller was still speaking to him when he left for Australia to begin battle. ''It hasn't been easy but I think he's still talking to me. I'm not sure at the moment, I'm not going to Fremantle until I have to. I can't think of a worse place in the world for any 12-Metre designer to be right now. But seriously, I've sailed with Tom for 20 years and I've never seen such pressure on a man. It would be alright if he just had to skipper the boat, but everything is his responsibility. He's like a chief operations officer and it's too much for any man.''

In fact, the problems encountered by the syndicate would have been sufficient to eliminate all but the strongest. As well as the inevitable difficulties in establishing credibility and raising the money to pay the bills, their program suffered a major setback when the first of two new boats had to be almost completely rebuilt, after the Lloyds Registry inspector rejected the welding on the boat.

In Gary Mull, the new syndicate turned to a widely respected designer, another Sparkman & Stephens graduate who also had considerable influence in high places by being US Representative to the Ocean Racing Club and a member

Cloud cover in Fremantle helps camouflage the radical keels/rudders on USA RI *which continued policy of carrying names of major sponsors when not racing.*

12
US-49
duraflame

of the Technical Committee of the International Yacht Racing Union, the sport's ultimate controlling body. The west coast naval architect had always been a free-thinker, not letting himself become bogged down by tradition.

Refusing to accept that lack of money should hamper their first attempt to win the America's Cup, the syndicate gave Mull the go ahead to design two boats, the first a development of the winged keel and the second a radical yacht that would hopefully "blow them all away in Australia".

In addition to his own skills, Mull was to have the best technology that nearby Silicon Valley could provide. "I had so many researchers coming up with ideas that I never even met some of them," Mull recalls. "Aerodynamicists like Peter Lissiman and Bob Liebeck, both crazy but brilliant, smarter than the next 10 people you will ever meet. And so good to work with. I could ask them anything and they would never treat me like a dummy who should have known the answer."

Mull's consultants included some of the top brains in the US defence system. At Hercules Aerospace he was only their second civilian client in 10 years. In-house physicist Heinrich Mellner had done much of the work on President Reagan's Star Wars program. Leading researcher and NASA consultant Alberto Calderon was another who answered the call to arms. "It has ceased to be a sporting event. We are seeking the frontiers of technology to answer a specific scientific challenge that today we regard as one of the most important."

McDonnell Douglas helped with computer programming, as did the civilian giant Tandy Electronics. Cray Computers, which manufactures the world's most powerful computers, gave him virtually unlimited time on the world's biggest computer. The United States Air Force Composite Materials Laboratory tested materials for Mull, all of course in the greatest secrecy.

Mull began the design process on his own computer, doing a lot of line drawings and comparing their performance on his own velocity prediction program. For three months he concentrated on hulls and winged keels. As soon as he was satisfied with the hull design, he froze that program to concentrate full time on appendages. For tank testing of the hull he towed one-third scale models through the tanks of Offshore Technology Corporation, the new Californian facility favoured by most American syndicates. As tanks were still not absolutely accurate in the testing of keels, Mull turned to the largest civilian wind tunnel in the USA, at the University of

Tom Blackaller – still shooting from the lip.

Designer Gary Mull and friend: "Everyone has these enormous egos. If they see you smile they think you're taking the day off."

USA EI *trialling with* Clipper *nee* Heart of America *on San Francisco Bay.*

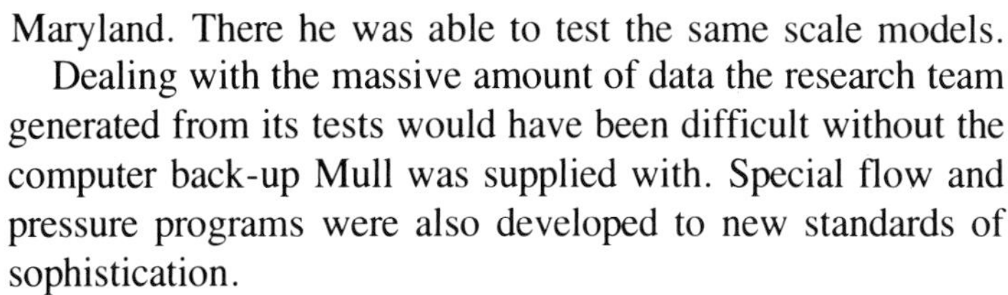

Maryland. There he was able to test the same scale models.

Dealing with the massive amount of data the research team generated from its tests would have been difficult without the computer back-up Mull was supplied with. Special flow and pressure programs were also developed to new standards of sophistication.

One program divided the hull surface into 1,000 small squares and measured pressure over them. Any difference in the interface between each square meant a problem of drag, and the super Cray XMP 48 computer kept modifying the shapes of the micro-chip hull at a rate of 24,000 instructions per second. As Mull put it: "You could do it with a scratch pad and a calculator, if you had 30 years to spare. Having the computer meant we could make our mistakes that much faster."

While Mull looked ahead to his breakthrough boat he also went back to basics, visiting the aerodynamics library at the nearby University of California every night for three months to read up on the subject. "They had literally every paper that had been published in the world. They even had German papers carefully bound together, dating back to before the First World War. Some were printed in black and red and were embossed with the swastika. Amazing."

Complete secrecy was the keyword for the syndicate. The affable designer found dozens of polite ways to say no to repeated questions about what he was up to, while he frantically re-educated himself in search of his breakthrough.

Making lots of noise was skipper and manager Tom Blackaller as he put together the rest of the campaign. As in all American syndicates, the skipper was the selling point – and Blackaller loved the role. A former World champion in the Olympic Star class, as were his rivals Dennis Conner and Buddy Melges, Blackaller was renowned for the speed of his speech, which at times seemed to almost equal that of the racing cars he loved to drive.

The silver-maned extrovert enjoyed fierce loyalty from his crews and several from his unsuccessful 1983 bid to defend the Cup in *Defender* agreed to have another go in Australia. Among them was his right-hand man, Paul Cayard, a sailmaker at Blackaller's North Loft in San Francisco and crew for him in the Stars, as well as being a successful helmsman in his own right.

Despite problems between the syndicate and the St Francis Yacht Club, they enjoyed good funding for their US$10 million budget. Local companies including Coca Cola and the telecommunications business Telefix provided cash and kind support.

Both boats were to be called *USA*: the first nicknamed *E1* for evolutionary; the second *R1* for revolutionary. *USA E1* was to be launched in August 1985 and worked up on San Francisco Bay, but her launch was delayed drastically when the Lloyds inspector insisted that the boat be rewelded. This was a body blow to the syndicate, keen to get the new boat on the water for testing, sail and crew development and to revitalise flagging fund-raising.

''Boy did we have problems,'' Mull says, shuddering at the memory. ''Sure, some of the earlier welding wasn't as good as it might have been, but it was OK for a Twelve. The real problem was that we had a Lloyds inspector who was used to working with big ships, he wasn't used to yachts. Once a Lloyds inspector gets away from you then there's no turning him around. It cost us months.''

Finally, in February 1986, the new yacht sailed for the first time on San Francisco Bay, the spectacular waterway rivalling Sydney Harbour that provides yachtsmen with strong winds and choppy seas similar to Fremantle. The new yacht was kept covered but had a winged keel similar to that of *Australia II*. It differed by having less angle forward on the leading edge, more angle aft on the trailing edge, and the tail end of a torpedo bulb filling out to the trailing edge. The yacht had suffered cruelly through distortion during the rewelding, and when she began racing *Canada II* and the former *Clipper*, renamed *Heart of America* by her Chicago crew, she was beaten convincingly.

The syndicate was saying little, except that they were happy with their progress, despite their late start. That certainly was not worrying Blackaller whose main criticism of Conner had always been that he had turned the Cup into a grind with his long campaigns. ''Many people over-react to the America's Cup; they spend too much time at it. I thought sailing was meant to be fun.''

While Blackaller and crew practised aboard *USA EI*, a handful of them interrupted their program to secretly sail a very special boat, one that was a quarter the size of a 12-Metre yacht which had been fitted with a version of Mull's underbody for his new, radical Twelve.

''I wasn't even sure if we could put this thing under a boat. We needed a big working model to see if it would work. I didn't know if the crew could control the yacht with it,'' Mull says. ''When the tests went well I went to the builder Paul Derektor in Newport and showed him the sketches. He couldn't quite believe what I was showing him, he just kept muttering 'wierd, wierd', and went to work.''

As they waited for the new boat, the crew began to get the first *USA* performing, to the stage where they were happy with its speed and handling in stronger winds which it had been designed for. *Canada II* was still faster in light winds but Mull says that did not concern them.

For information on the weather in Fremantle he had been supplied with complete records of the winds on the new America's Cup course by the Australian Bureau of Meteorology. When Mull began studying the figures he realised that the stories about the big winds of Fremantle were not quite true. ''How those people turned up for the World championships with such big boats is beyond me. Anyone could get the weather statistics and it was obvious that you had to shoot for 14-18 knot winds and slightly higher, not 25-30 knots.''

The evolutionary *USA* was a small boat measuring in at about 65 ft (20 m) overall and about 44 ft 7 in (13.6 m) on the waterline. The yacht carried its maximum beam well aft giving the yacht slab sides. On deck the only surprises were twin hatches either side of the mast for easier spinnaker setting and dropping, and pump outlets set into the topsides midships.

When the revolutionary *USA* was launched three months later she was obviously the most radical Twelve built for the 1987 America's Cup. Although the hull was almost identical to the first boat, beneath the waterline appeared to be a second rudder, fixed well ahead of the keel. With the new smaller America's Cup course, manoeuverability would obviously be almost as important as straight line speed. The boat getting in front at the start would be very hard to pass providing it was well sailed.

Arguments about what exactly was under *USA RI* raged. Some said it was a canard keel as had been fitted to the second British Twelve by its creator, renowned model designer David Hollom. ''Wrong,'' replied Mull. ''That's old hat, just a heavy slug of lead with wings hung from twin foils. We've gone way past that.''

But as to what was there, no-one who knew was going to say. ''Keep asking me and I will happily lie through my teeth; I'm not going to tell you,'' was Mull's usual reaction. According to Cayard, who was sharing the helm and tactics with Blackaller ''I've never seen anything like it. All the tests say her VMG (velocity made good) is four-tenths faster than anything that's been designed. If it's half of that it will be enough.'' Blackaller for once was muted: ''This boat is far beyond the state of the art Twelves.''

Mull may not have had much fun during the design process, but he was certainly enjoying the controversy. ''It doesn't matter how long you look at it in the water, you are not seeing what is really there. It is not what it seems. I've been told it is a rudder that is the same size that a 40 footer IOR racer would be carrying. That's rubbish.''

''Out of the water it just looks like any other Twelve. Below, it is not, but you will have to wait until we pull it out at the end of the races to see what we have. It's going to be a lot of fun.''

Mull conceeded that for Blackaller, like John Bertrand on *Australia II* in 1983, the radical design was difficult to handle. ''Tom had to learn it all again. The configuration is quite different so he had to keep that in mind continually while he was steering.''

Before leaving for Australia the new boat was spirited away into a shed for modifications to lengthen her. Ask Mull anything specific and the joker comes out. ''It's white with a

Blackaller enjoys confidence of a fiercely loyal crew.

light grey deck. Yes, it does have a waterline length, every boat should have one, they're really helpful.''

Blackaller was not having as good a time as his designer as he tried to cope with the pressures of preparing a campaign which would succeed or die on the other side of the world, well away from the sponsors he needed to keep them operating. ''No, we don't have enough money to see us through to the end. I don't know where it will come from. I'm not worried about it at this stage. I know that if it's needed then it will turn up from somewhere, somehow.''

After raising the hackles of all Australians in Newport in 1983 by saying he hoped the Cup did not go to Australia ''because there is nothing there but Aborigines and flies'', he was still shooting from the lip. ''We don't just want the Cup, we want the whole damned Island,'' was one quote that was turned into a fund raising bumper sticker for cars.

The Blackaller team that arrived in Australia in September 1986 was lean by American standards, reflecting the shortage of cash threatening to hamper their last minute development as the yachtsmen discovered whether they had been wasting the past two years because their designer had been deceived.

''It will work,'' Mull insists. ''The computer programs, the tank tests and the wind tunnels all agree. I am sure it is a significant development in sailboat design. I just hope it is not applied to other classes. It's too expensive and difficult. I would have put nearly 400 hours into structural analysis, working out how to build it and have it stay in one piece. Normally that job would take me about 45 minutes. And the materials we had to use to make it work are very rare and cost about 50 times the normal. If it goes into other classes it will be a disaster.''

''Superboats'' have been around before, but some have been beaten in the America's Cup because the rest of the campaign has not been in place. Even with a fast boat the crew needs to be well honed, the sails need to be state of the art, the support must be smooth and efficient, and the money must be behind it all. So, even if *USA* is the boat her owners claim, that does not mean they will automatically win the America's Cup.

Other designers merely raise their eyebrows when asked about *USA*. Most are derisive, saying they do not believe there will be a breakthrough such as Mull believes he has.

And of course designers have been misled by the tanks and wind tunnels before. But if all the money that has been poured into updating the research since 1983 has failed to make scale testing of 12-Metre yachts considerably more accurate, then designers such as Gary Mull could be forgiven for throwing their computers away and pulling out their old pencils and erasers.

HEART OF AMERICA

From The Heartlands

Most people who have had anything to do with 12-Metres in the America's Cup would agree that it is a sport for the young, people who are physically tough enough to endure the rigours of long and difficult campaigns. But in Perth this year, one man is out to prove that a fallacy.

Buddy Melges, skipper of the Chicago Yacht Club's *Heart of America*, qualifies as the grandfather of the fleet at 56 years of age. Only one other man rivals him in the "age stakes": South Australia's Sir James Hardy. But these days yachting's "Gentleman Jim" is content to step off the yacht to watch from the tender and later offer the "young Turks" the benefit of his long Cup experience.

Not so Buddy Melges. He's thrown himself into his first America's Cup campaign with the dedication of a Dennis Conner and the energy of a Marc Pajot. But when it comes to attitude he stands alone. Totally undisturbed by the hype surrounding the Cup, Melges is as refreshing as "Captain Outrageous" Ted Turner was when he successfully defended the Cup in 1977. Both men are "skippers of the people", determined to bring the Cup and its followers back to earth. Melges promises more than did the egotistical Turner. While he does not recognise the superiority of other yachtsmen, he still shows no delusions of grandeur. It is a compliment that he is widely recognised as the man who "keeps the others honest", on and off the water.

Melges is the linchpin of the first campaign by the Chicago Yacht Club, located on the fresh water Lake Michigan in the Great Lakes. To gain approval to challenge, the Club had to go to court to overturn a 100-year-old ruling that barred challenges from clubs on the Lakes. The ruling had been made by the New York Yacht Club after two Cup challenges by Canadian clubs on the Lakes turned into embarrassing debacles in the late 1800s.

In 1984 the Chicago Yacht Club succeeded in convincing the New York State Supreme Court that it was located on "an arm of the sea", as the Lakes were linked to the Atlantic Ocean by the St Lawrence River. "There is international navigation on the Great Lakes, Chicago is an international port, and marine life comes into the Lakes from the ocean", the syndicate's attorney successfully argued. It was a long, drawn out affair, but concluded in time for businessmen to dig into their corporate accounts to back Chicago's first crack at the America's Cup.

To design their first 12-Metre the Club cast its net wide. One of its initial approaches was to an Argentinian, German Frers, renowned for his fast IOR offshore racers. However, more legal problems loomed when the Royal Perth Yacht Club would not rule on his eligibility to design an American Twelve, and Chicago YC dropped the idea.

Instead, at Melges' suggestion, the Club turned to the young, local team of Scott Graham and Eric Schlageter who had become a force to be reckoned with in yachts that were quite unlike the bulky, old-fashioned Twelves. Graham and Schlageter had first made their names in the MORC class, lightweight

Spinnaker set in Santa Cruz.

Designer Scott Graham

Buddy Melges

"midget" ocean racers guaranteed to provide excitement, thrills and spills by the nautical mile. They were also a power in the IOR racing fleet including the North American One Ton champion *Slip Sliding Away* among their credits.

When they began talking about the America's Cup they called on outside talent. One man brought in was Jim Gretsky, a designer heading the strangely named Obscure Boats Inc. in Rhode Island who was fully conversant with the 12-Metre Rule after working with David Pedrick on *Clipper* in 1980 and *Defender* in 1983.The fourth member to join the team was naval architect Duncan MacLane, who specialised in sailing craft that were not only the total opposite of the Twelves, but which raced for an international trophy known as the Little America's Cup. MacLane was America's most successful designer of C Class catamarans, the 25 ft (6.52 m) multihulls of almost totally unrestricted design that are among the fastest sailing craft in the world today. His series of *Patient Lady* designs had successfully defended the International Catamaran Challenge Trophy against Australian and Italian challengers from the mid-1970s until 1984. Then the technologically superior Australian C Class *Victoria*, designed by specialist Lindsay Cunningham, returned the Cup to Australia to make it a yachting quinella over the USA.

Nineteen-eighty-four proved a tough time for the new syndicate from the Great Lakes, where local yachtsmen race ice yachts in winter and normal yachts in summer. The legal challenge absorbed most of the syndicate's time while it struggled to raise money. It purchased the 1980 yacht *Clipper* for crew training and use as a trial horse for their future yacht. While other American syndicates were well into three and four boat programs, Chicago struggled to put into train a one boat program, with the young design team having to learn as much as possible from *Clipper* before putting everything into the one boat.

Fundraising revolved around Melges and his tactician Gary Jobson who had leapt into America's Cup prominence when he was tactician for Ted Turner aboard *Courageous* in 1977. His star had been tarnished when he was tactician on unsuccessful boats in 1980 and 1983, but the Melges/Jobson team promised to be a force to be reckoned with.

Though a newcomer to the Cup, Melges was already a legend for his exploits over many years in small boats. He had won numerous national and world championships in the most competitive classes, as well as a bronze medal in the two-handed Flying Dutchman class at the 1968 Olympics and a

gold medal in the Soling class in 1972. In international yachting folklore, Melges is remembered as the man who enters new classes, casts a critical eye at how others prepare themselves and their boats, and then proves them all wrong – with a minimum of fuss and a maximum amount of humour.

First it was in the Soling class in 1971, when he arrived at the CORK Olympic regatta in Canada and won every race by more than five minutes. Seven years later it was in the equally competitive Star class, when he set up his boat totally differently from everyone else and thrashed them. Among his surprised victims was Dennis Conner, who was then putting into effect the practice of spending as much time on the water as possible before a series. "Dennis told me I didn't have a hope because I hadn't been out on the water. But I had been busy cutting a new set of sails and I had the faster boat. If you have a fast boat it cuts a lot of corners." To prove that win was no fluke, Melges won the Worlds the following year as well.

Melges is known as the "Wizard of Zenda" after the tiny town on Lake Geneva, Wisconsin where he lives and works. Zenda virtually exists because of Melges. He has a sail loft and boat building and spar manufacturing factories. His scow designs race on lakes all over the USA. During winter he races ice yachts.

Despite several approaches in the past he was never interested in the America's Cup. "I didn't want to be the one to lose the Cup and I didn't want to represent the New York Yacht Club," was the standard reply.

Early in 1985, with legal approval and growing support for their campaign, the Chicago syndicate saw its way clear to go ahead. In March the design team went to work, with construction to begin in December and the launching scheduled for April 1986. It was a late start which, according to Graham, forced them to concentrate on developing the winged keel. "We looked briefly at some pretty way-out appendages but because of the shortage of time we concentrated on taking the winged keel and developing it as much as possible. *Australia II's* keel was a brilliant stroke and we knew if we were close to it then it would work."

Design began with their own velocity prediction program, testing hull shapes and assessing directions. Tank testing of hull shapes was carried out with one-third and one-eighth scale models at the biggest tanks in the USA, the US Navy's David Taylor Ship Research Centre in Washington DC. Graham says they tested the smaller models to "get a feel for the differences in the more accurate one-third tests''. In six weeks of testing the team put six models through the tanks. Two models were modular, capable of having entire sections and appendages changed. Twenty keel shapes were tested in a special tunnel at the Massachusetts Institute of Technology ocean engineering laboratory. In the laboratory the team hung their keels from a portion of the hull and towed them through a tunnel filled with water, which guaranteed it was completely free of interference.

Graham says the fifth model was modified and after extensive testing became their final design. Recalling their first intensive experience with the test tank still makes Graham groan at the memory: ''Someone once said it was as much fun as a case of the measles. They were right.''

Undaunted was tank testing supervisor Pierre de Saix, a noted engineer in the field of yacht research who had been involved with the testing of Twelves since 1964. He reported that he had never seen an improvement such as he found when comparing models of the benchmark *Clipper* and what was to become the new *Heart of America*.

While the designers were lofting the boat, the crew was participating in the first 12-Metre regatta ever held in Canada. When they purchased *Clipper* from the *Canada I* syndicate it was on the understanding that they would co-operate with them in their tuning up. The first occasion was a month of sparring early in winter off Victoria, British Columbia. It was an unforgettable regatta for the participants, as sub-zero temperatures froze the spray on the decks and lashed them with cold. It was also unforgettable for Melges and his crew, including Jobson, who were soundly thrashed by the rebuilt *Canada I*.

Melges and Jobson visited Australia for the 1986 World championships to watch and act as television commentators. Ashore, Melges took some of the limelight away from the participants. On his comparatively small $8 million budget: ''Sure I'd like another million dollars. I'd build a sail loft on the dock and bring in more people, but we will just have to hire a truck and take the sails to a loft elsewhere. So what?''

On racing for the Cup on his home waters: ''There are no thermals on the Lake, it's a funnel system, the wind doesn't blow – it sucks.''

On his home town, Zenda: ''It's not the end of the world but you can see it from there.''

On the high-powered America's Cup scene: ''It's all blood and guts, politics and international war. I like to sail competitively at a high level, but some of what I've seen disturbs me.''

On the security of some syndicates: ''It's disgusting, we won't be hiding our boats.''

On the fact that he had never match raced before: ''It doesn't worry me. You know where your bow-plate is and you can butt it up against another boat's ... transom. All you have to know is what your turning capabilities are and what your stop and go are and let the rest take the Cup.''

On the potential of the new *Heart of America*: ''I've always said that a fast boat makes Melges a smart skipper and we have reason to believe that our new boat will make me a genius.''

Back in the United States, Melges in *Clipper* raced Tom Blackaller aboard his first Gary Mull design *USA*. The racing was hardly conclusive, as the 1980 design was faster than Blackaller's new Twelve. Of more note at the time was Jobson's resignation to accept an offer as commentator on the Cup for a US television network. Melges was undaunted and looked forward to the launch of the new *Heart of America*.

That day arrived in April 1986 when the new yacht left its yard in Newport on the east coast for a long haul across the continent to California where it was to race *Canada II, Eagle* and *USA*. It was an unusual trip, as the yacht's journey was delayed in Chicago for her official christening. The stopover lasted only hours, as the people of the Midwest proudly set eyes on their new 12-Metre yacht before it resumed its journey to California, without even getting its keel wet in the formerly controversial waters of the Great Lakes.

Throughout, Melges kept his word and left the yacht's underbody uncovered for all to study. The keel was, as promised, very like that of *Australia II*, upside down with a well angled leading edge, wings running to the trailing edge and a big trim tab. Obvious to any onlooker was a horizontal join 18 inches (45 cm) above the keel base, allowing the wings to be removed after about two hours work. Like all other designers, the creators of *Heart of America* knew they needed a full-sized model for accurate testing of such things as angle of attack and size of the wings.

The stern was typically American with broad, powerful shoulders and a cut-off transom, quite different to the Australian breed of Twelve with finely chiselled stern overhangs leading to fine transoms. In front of the rudder the new Twelve had no skeg, but a wide and shallow bustle with a crease. *Heart's* transom proudly bore a map of the Great Lakes surrounded by the names of everyone who had donated funds towards the campaign. The Midwest theme was carried along the topsides, too, with an ear of wheat heading a gold stripe around the sheer.

The deck layout was largely left to Melges by the designers, at his insistence. They were happy to bow to the ''Wizard's''

Heart of America's *transom carries name of financial supporters.*

The master's touch.

experience. The result was a standard US layout with small differences in detail.

According to Graham the yacht measured in at 67 ft (20.4 m) length overall, 45 ft 6 in (13.9 m) on the waterline, 12 ft 5 in (3.8 m) in beam and weighed 58,000 lbs (26,300 kg).

On Californian waters in Santa Cruz, the yacht began extensive trialling with *Canada II*, by then the chosen boat of the amalgamated Canadian syndicates at the expense of *True North*, which had promised so much but delivered so little in Australia the previous summer. Early in the trials the Chicago crew found they were better than the Canadians in heavy airs but slower in light breezes. Graham felt that both boats were orientated too far in opposite directions, but both improved their overall performance with tuning.

At one stage *Heart of America* was removed from the water for minor surgery to her transom. Graham says they finished up beating the Canadians in the light weather as well as heavy after the changes.

The designers worked closely with the crew and Melges during the trialling, the skipper often joining them on their accompanying tender to see the yacht's movement through the water with his own eyes. As for her performance, he was happy: "She tracks really well, I can leave the helm to itself for minutes at a time. Maybe they won't need me."

The designers reciprocated his feelings. Graham recalls only one occasion when they were in trouble with "the boss". "We had a design problem and at the end of the day Buddy took us aside and said quietly 'You designers had better sharpen your pencils'. That was all he had to say. We worked all night to solve the problem."

Graham's first experience with the Twelves was in itself an eye-opener after years of designing fast, light displacement racers. "If it's blowing they are a lot of fun. If the wind strength is 10 knots, they are boring. If it is 30 knots it is terrifying." How did he find working with such big boats? "It is a misconception that the hulls are too heavy. Under the 12-Metre Rule certain things are underweight, just as they are underwinched and undermanned."

While the late start to the design process restricted the avenues they could explore, *Heart's* designers believe they have prepared their program thoroughly to handle the different conditions of Fremantle. Graham says they have four configurations for different conditions. "As well as changing the wings at the bottom of the keel, we can change the flotation, draft and displacement. We can change the ballast, the sail area and move the mast step anywhere along a 2 ft (0.6 m) track.

"We have tried for an allrounder which we will alter during the elimination series to suit the weather. We expect moderate winds early in the series, then heavy winds in November and moderate breezes again in the finals."

Heart of America was one of several late starters after her arrival in Australia in September. Before the yacht even touched the Indian Ocean she was whisked away for modifications to her stern under the watchful eye of Jerry Gretsky. Like all other syndicates, Chicago would have liked more time. But that is not the sort of thing that would concern Melges.

The grandfather of the 1987 America's Cup is not one to worry too much about the details and the number crunching on computers that has become such an important part of the America's Cup. He has developed his skills through sailing by the seat of his pants and having a natural affinity with the wind, water, his boat and crew.

Melges will not be among the flotilla of skippers leaving their yachts after each race to be sped back to the dock in a high speed runabout to study the data records from the day. He is a natural sailor, preferring to harness all around him by feel and instinct.

Although the Melges style differs greatly from that of the former "Cup King" Dennis Conner, the two enjoy a rare position in the battle for the 1987 America's Cup. All other syndicates put them among candidates to watch, simply because they are who they are. Conner has the edge with his experience, his budget and his massive campaign. And he still attracts the attention because he is Dennis Conner. Melges enjoys few of the benefits of a big campaign. He's happy to stand tall in his own right.

NEW ZEALAND

Tough Trans-Tasman Trio

Until recently in the history of the America's Cup, all newcomers to the scene had been humiliated when making their first attempts to reach the pinnacle of the sport. Over the years the British, French, Italians, Canadians, Swedes and Australians proved time and time again that it took repeated efforts to even begin to match the experience of the Americans in key areas:

- Technology in boat, sail and rig design
- People in the form of tactics, boathandling and ability to perform under pressure
- Fundraising to support all activities
- Support at sea and on land to ensure that the crew would not be distracted and their craft not disadvantaged by breakdowns.

Achieving maximum efficiency in all facets proved beyond most challengers. Even Sir Thomas Lipton who challenged a record five times never succeeded.

The man who went closest to perfection was Alan Bond. Back in the 1970s, after two humiliating defeats, he realised that unless he got together all of the ingredients for success he was wasting his time. He also knew that he would need a design edge on the defenders to overcome their advantages of Cup experience, being in their own environment, and having their crew honed to a superior standard following an exhaustive selection series. In what he declared would be his final attempt in 1983, he did have his technological edge with the winged keel and despite some lapses in other vital areas it was just enough to make the difference.

When New Zealand announced its first challenge the following year the news barely raised comment. After all, what hope would such a small country have of taking on such a technological challenge? History alone should rule them out at their first attempt.

As it turned out, the New Zealanders hit the America's Cup scene with a broadside that Lipton and Bond would have envied. On 7 February 1986, one of New Zealand's two

New Zealand KZ5

Near plumb sides of KZ7, result of wide waterline.

ZEALAND

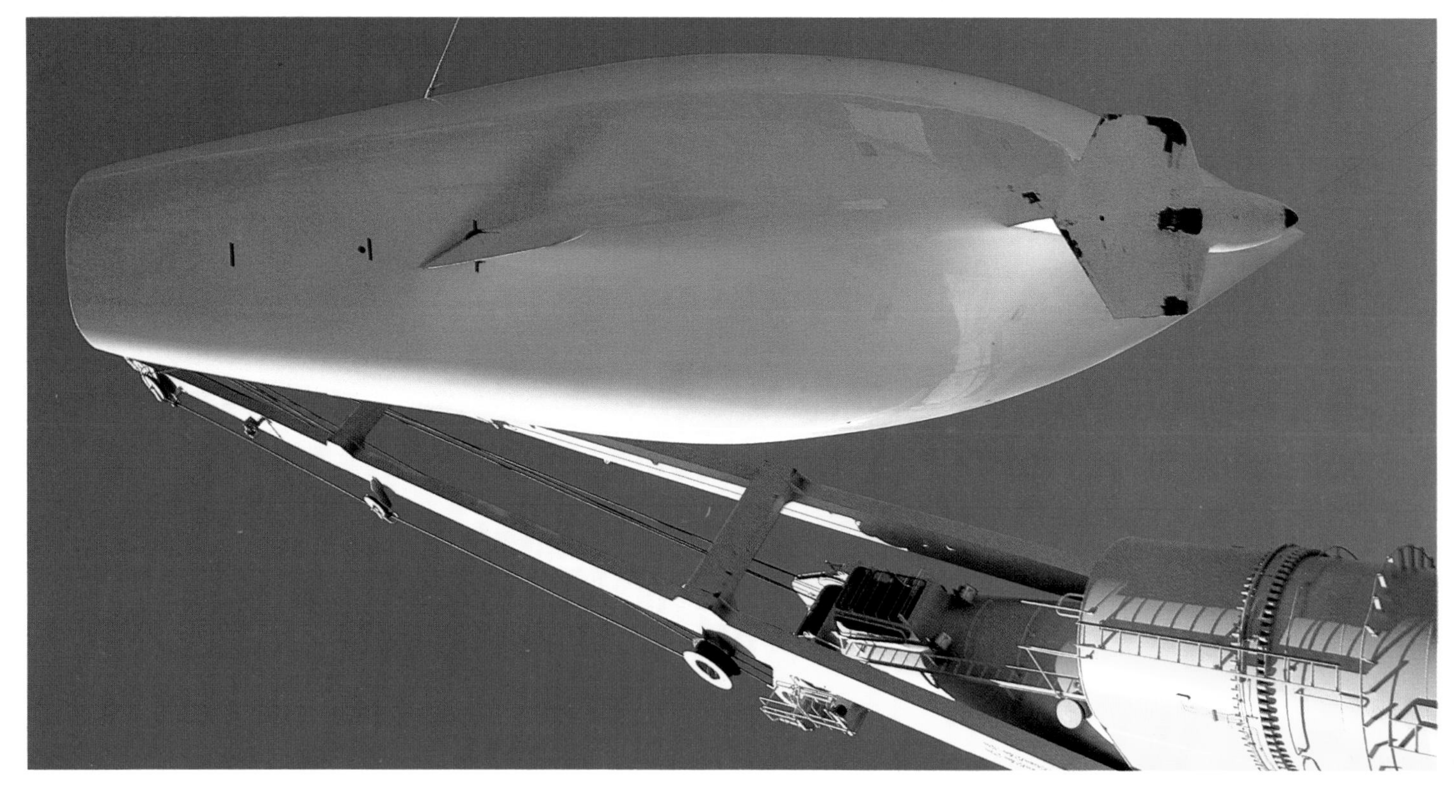

Keel bulb and first delta wings of first boats. Stern sections show soft chines running to transom. Wide waterline beam and "slab" sides show designers' emphasis of stability.

Michael Fay and family "on holiday" from merchant banking.

identical 12-Metre yachts won the first race of the 1986 World championships. Not only was it the first time a New Zealand 12-Metre had raced; the yacht was the first fibreglass Twelve ever built, and the first to carry a rig with triple spreaders. It was also the first time any syndicate had built two identical Twelves and it was the first yacht to win a formal 12-Metre race on Australian waters.

The yacht, simply named *New Zealand KZ5*, went on to finish the regatta in second place behind the latest yacht of the Alan Bond syndicate, the Ben Lexcen designed *Australia III*. In the process *KZ5* defeated other yachts from the United States, Great Britain, Italy, France and Australia. The fact that it was only the ninth time the Kiwis had sailed their boat silenced even their sternest critics. Instead, they found themselves elevated to sharing favouritism with the New York Yacht Club and Dennis Conner to challenge for the Cup.

Put in perspective, their success was really a comeback. Less than a year earlier their challenge had been foundering, on the brink of sinking without trace.

When *Australia II* won the Cup in 1983, the applause in New Zealand was almost as great as it was in Australia, but for a very different reason. Australia, the New Zealanders argued, had done them a favour by bringing the Cup close enough to make a challenge possible. Quickly the New Zealand Yacht Squadron notified the Royal Perth Yacht Club of its intentions and expatriate designer Ron Holland was commissioned to design his first 12-Metre. Like so many other designers around the world, he was caught up in the new fever to win the Cup.

However Holland soon found himself almost alone. Like several other challenges around the world, once the initial enthusiasm wore off the effort began to run out of steam. No-one, it seemed, was prepared to pick up the reins. In frustration Holland turned to a man with a minor interest in yachting but a major interest in making risky ventures succeed. He was Michael Fay, then a 37 year old mercurial businessman who in partnership headed the merchant bank Fay Richwhite which, by the time of Holland's approach, had quickly grown to be the biggest in New Zealand.

Fay was immediately interested. Already he had dealt with finance in the sport, having sponsored two New Zealand teams to the AWA Southern Cross Cup, the premier ocean racing series in Australia which had become a grudge match between the two countries. In addition he had put together the finance behind round-the-world racers *Ceramco* and *Lion New Zealand*.

Fay applied a business approach to the possibilities of mounting a challenge. In March 1985 he gathered together the

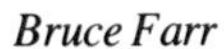

Bruce Farr

Laurie Davidson

Ron Holland

Chris Dickson

Twin cockpit and almost watertight deck of KZ7 *with trimmers moved from their own "pits" to the main cockpit.*

country's top yachtsmen and sporting administrators for a concentrated think-tank to answer four vital questions – did they have the design talent, the yachting talent, the time and the money? The answer to all four was yes, and Fay pledged to underwrite the challenge and personally manage it by taking twelve months away from his business.

The biggest problems were lack of time and America's Cup experience. Fay convinced everyone that they had to compete in the 12-Metre World championships in Perth in just ten months time. That series, he reasoned, should be approached as if it were their first America's Cup.

One of Fay's first moves was to recruit two more New Zealand designers who joined Holland to form a team that included three of the most successful yacht designers in the world. They were Bruce Farr, the brilliant designer who had revolutionised the offshore racing scene in the 1970s with his lightweight yachts and who, in the early 1980s, had successfully moved from Auckland to the USA to conquer that market. The other newcomer was Laurie Davidson who had also applied the lightweight approach to yacht design with great success and who, like others including Australia's Ben Lexcen and Canada's Bruce Kirby, made it appear that formal training in naval architecture was almost a handicap.

None of the three had designed a Twelve before and with Fay's support their approach was original. Although they were short of time they would not slavishly imitate others – they were to be their own men going into battle carrying their country's colours. Designers are notorious for jealously guarding their own secrets. But the three quickly got off to an amicable start. Based in Ireland, Holland was able to oversee the tank testing. With his large American design office, Farr was able to concentrate on the detailed research and planning. In New Zealand, Holland was able to personally oversee the construction.

While Fay was busy raising the money and signing up yachtsmen, the designers went to work. As well as using their own computer evaluation programs, time was booked on the computers at the Maritime Testing Institute in the Netherlands. But a tight budget meant they could not afford the Dutch test tanks. Instead they arranged to test one-tenth and one-quarter sized models at the Woolfson Institute in England.

The first subject for discussion was the winged keel that had revolutionised 12-Metre design. Like so many other designers they took the *Australia II* keel as their benchmark, studying how it worked before trying to improve it.

All three acknowledged the creativity of Lexcen. Davidson said: "Our first model was our best bet at what *Australia II's* was like and then we tried to beat it. In light airs we were

First keels were left uncovered but not that of the third yacht.

possibly slower but in heavy airs ours was much faster. Winged keels are not perfect. They are slow downwind but fast upwind and everyone will have them next year.''

Farr says: ''Our program was really orientated towards understanding what was going on, rather than rushing around looking at different keels. We got a good understanding of winged keels and were then able to massage the program along. We included keels of all types. Some we thought would be very fast were real dogs, we couldn't believe they were so slow. Amazingly, some turned up on other boats in Fremantle, so someone wasn't doing their homework.''

Another item high on the agenda was choice of hull material. The three designers knew they had no time for mistakes if they were to have a yacht ready for the World championships. They were also concerned that there would be insufficient time to improve the boat as they continued their research and development.

Like others, including Lexcen before them, they looked closely at the possibility of building from fibreglass. The construction method meant they would need less time to build the boat. And, according to Farr, they believed fibreglass would offer them ''fairer boats with high panel stiffness giving a boat with less drag and higher loading capabilities''.

It was a strategy with problems. Lloyds Registry of Shipping, the British company that approves construction of Twelves, had only agreed to the use of fibreglass in hulls late in the 1970s. However, no-one had asked them to draw up the rules of construction. The New Zealanders went to work with Lloyds, defining the construction method and paying to have an inspector present during the entire construction process in Auckland.

Meanwhile Fay was not letting the grass grow beneath his feet. Having put the budget at about $15 million, he used all his contacts within the Wellington finance world to attract support. His approach struck the right chord with his audiences. According to Fay: ''The America's Cup is not a sporting event, it's an industry. This is bigger than individuals like the Alan Bonds and Peter de Savarys; it's big business and that is how we are going about it.''

New Zealand, with a population of three million, has always been very proud of its sportsmen and women, particularly in the 1980s when their victories took peoples' minds off their economic woes as the country slumped through a downturn in its primary produce exports. Fay added that to

Emblem of main sponsor Bank of New Zealand emblazoned on the stern of all three yachts.

The best possible means of testing sails and keel changes – two identical yachts – another Kiwi first.

his arguments: ''New Zealand's standard of living is lower than Libya's. Part of our company's activities over the years has been to concentrate on the entrepreneurial areas – what we call the development and high risk areas. We see the America's Cup in the same light – with a huge economic impact resulting from an investment. For New Zealand, the Cup is a very good investment which could have a huge economic impact. An investment of $10-20 million in the Cup will result in an economic boost of two to three billion dollars if we win.''

''Don't call us, we'll call you'' is a line well known to syndicate fundraisers around the world. Not to Fay. Shipping lines offered to carry the yachts to and from New Zealand, marine supply companies donated their products, cars were donated, complete computer packages were placed at their beck and call. Cold cash also went into the syndicate's coffers with the biggest injection being $5 million from the Bank of New Zealand.

Fay was living up to his promise. ''I'm a lawyer by trade and a banker by profession so while I might not know a lot about yachts, I do know a lot about numbers. I'd love to sit down and have a contest over which is the best financed syndicate. I'd win, end of story.''

Yachtsmen also rallied to the call of the man who was leading the effort with the energy and perception of a Bond and de Savary rolled into one. One nominated helmsman was Chris Dickson, a 24-year-old yachting whizz-kid who had been winning world championships and international match racing regattas from a tender age. Another was 40-year-old Graeme Woodroffe, a vastly experienced ocean racing helmsman with 30 years of competitive racing in all types of sailing craft behind him. For the role of tactician three men were originally named, one of them Dickson's father. At the time there was a shortage of big boat racers available owing to their absence aboard two yachts taking part in the Whitbread Round the World Race, but the syndicate knew they would be available and eager to start after the Race ended early in 1986.

Midway through 1985 the project was beginning to fall into place with Fay spearheading the effort in New Zealand and the three designers meeting in some strange places around the world as they fitted the crash 12-Metre design program into time between other commitments and liased continually by telephone and facsimile.

It was not until October 1985 that they finally won approval to build in fibreglass. But the delays in the building program did not mean the thinking of the principal people had slowed. While the designers extensively tested keels, they also decided that two identical boats should be built. Had they been building in aluminium they would not have had the time. But because the same mould for laying up the "plastic" hull would be used, it would be simple to turn out two hulls within weeks of each other. This, they argued, would not only allow them to train more people, but would give them full-sized test beds for design and sail evaluation. It was to be a master stroke.

New Zealand's two major boatbuilding yards created new records with the building of the two boats. McMullen and Wing built the mould from which the hulls would be taken and the aluminium space frames that would fit inside the hulls to absorb the extreme rig loads. Marten Marine then laid up the hulls, using a standard method of laying the fibreglass on both sides of a balsa wood core.

With the World championships looming, other problems inevitably arose. The major setback was in the casting of the keels. Two moulds broke during the process and the first yacht finally went on public show for the christening without its appendage. After two hours of sailing on Auckland Harbour the yacht was packed up for Australia.

The two identical yachts arrived in Perth in January in time for just a few days' sailing. But disaster struck when *New Zealand KZ3* with Woodroffe at the helm broke its mast. New spars with triple spreader rigs had been ordered for the yachts in Australia, but they had not been completed, so the syndicate was forced to borrow an old cast-off from an Italian syndicate.

The New Zealanders were so busy they did not have time to bask in some of the praise being directed their way. Americans and Australians alike, Alan Bond and Dennis Conner among them, had dubbed them the dark horses of the Cup, the ones to watch for surprises.

Michael Fay, leading his troops from the front, mounted the most successful public relations campaign of the championships. His first targets were other syndicates who came in for friendly criticism for their paranoia over security. Before the racing, Fay opened the gates to the New Zealand dock for an open day, with everyone invited to look at the yachts, without their keels covered. "Kiwis don't wear skirts" became the catch-cry.

The boats were nicknamed the "Plastic Fantastics", as anyone even resembling a New Zealander seized any opportunity to extol the virtues of fibreglass. The arguments that they were stiffer than aluminium and easier to repair in the event of collision were ridiculed by other designers and syndicates. Undaunted, the Kiwis stuck to their guns and quickly notched up a psychological edge over the rest of the world, almost approaching that of Ben Lexcen with his winged keel in 1983.

In shape, the boats were different from most others in that their waterline lengths were close to their overall lengths. Instead of relying on long overhangs at either end, the New Zealand designers had gone for boats which were to be sailed upright and so did not need overhangs to add waterline length when heeled. Keeping the waterline length short at about 45 ft (13.8 m) allowed sail area to be large at approximately 1,730 sq ft (160 sq m). Farr said they wanted to keep the overhangs down in size to keep weight out of the ends of the boats. In beam they differed as well, being wide at the waterline for additional stability, and carried the maximum beam well aft.

Later Farr revealed that the final design of the boats had been completed before they had the results of their tank tests. "We didn't have time to use more than our computer velocity prediction program results. We were confident we had good hull shapes because we were being conservative, we weren't rushing off into corners."

Beneath each boat for the World championships was an inverted *Australia II*-type keel with a considerable bulb along the base and wider wings than those of *Australia II*, but shorter in length and slightly fatter. A small skeg led to the rudder. Above the water the designers had given the yachts a standard layout with tactician and navigator behind the helmsman, adding an additional winch pedestal linked to the mainsheet for fast sheeting before the start and around the buoys when they needed to accelerate quickly in tight situations.

Throughout the championships the two boats had mixed successes; *New Zealand KZ5* with Dickson at the helm finished second, while *New Zealand KZ3* with Woodroffe skippering suffered equipment failures and other accidents, including a man overboard, to manage just seventh place.

As *Australia II's* winged keel had dominated 1983, the "Plastic Fantastics" of the New Zealanders were the talking point of Fremantle three years later. The New Zealanders admitted they had never realised what a psychological advantage fibreglass would turn out to be, but they exploited their edge for all it was worth, with other syndicate principals constantly asked whether they were considering building in fibreglass and designers publicly debating its advantages and disadvantages. The Kiwis loved every minute of it.

The designers met again in Fremantle during the series to finalise the design of their third boat. Farr says they were satisfied with their first efforts. "They turned out to be pretty good all round boats with no significant weaknesses. We were concentrating on the whole range of wind strengths, from 8 knots to 30 knots."

After the championships the New Zealand campaign was able to step into top gear, taking advantage of the fact that they had the best possible method of testing modifications. Like other designers, Farr, Davidson and Holland needed to test their keels full-size to confirm or deny the tanks, wind tunnels and computer prediction programs. At least three different keels were tested beneath the boats, one with wings that trailed well aft of the trailing keel edge to form an endplate. The sailmakers were also able to increase their testing. Farr considered the twin-boat policy more successful than anyone in Perth realised. "There are so many variables that even with the best telemetry sending back data on the boats, you still cannot accurately measure them as well as having two boats

Removing trimmers' cockpits allowed wider range of headsail sheet tracks.

you know exactly racing against each other. It's ideal for testing different keels. It's great for the sailmakers too: they're not stabbing in the dark. Quickly we can find out whether A is faster than B. It also enhances the confidence of the sailors; they know they are not shooting the breeze."

One vital area in which no-one enjoyed confidence was masts. Like everything else about the boats, 12-Metre masts were previously unknown in the "Land of the Long White Cloud" and when the initial plan called for one boat for the summer of 1985/86 two masts were ordered from Britain, one as a back-up.

While other syndicates had the time to thoroughly analyse what was available commercially and go to work to make sure that what they had would survive the rough conditions of Fremantle, the New Zealand designers were too busy with the rest of their program to look at the question until almost the last minute. As in much of the engineering design work the analysis of the spars fell to Farr who, with his larger design office, was able to plan in detail. When it came to the masts ordered from Britain his findings were discouraging, indicating that they were suited more for the lighter winds and smoother water of Newport, Rhode Island than Fremantle, Australia.

First he ordered spare masts for each boat from the Australian company Zapspar which, along with the Lexcen spar designs for the Bond syndicate, were the only single section spars available for 12-Metre yachts. Masts for Twelves were traditionally made from two lengths of aluminium tube, sleeved together. Zapspar believed that by using a single length they would eliminate a weak point in the mast and provide a section with uniform bend.

Farr went further. Determined to avoid more delays in their already late sailing program, he agreed to the suggestion that the masts be rigged with triple spreaders with standard hydraulically adjustable jumper struts supporting the upper section. The additional spreaders would, he argued, provide greater support for the towering 90 ft (27 m) masts.

Once again the Kiwi propaganda machine went into action, claiming another breakthrough. Triple spreader rigs, they claimed, would be stronger, safer and easier to control. In addition, the argument went, they would give narrower sheeting angles for the headsails to allow the yachts to sail closer to the wind when sailing to windward. Added to the fibreglass hulls, it was something else for other syndicates to think about.

Like some other things, the New Zealanders' mast program "came unstuck" owing to their rush to meet the deadline of the World championships. The new Australian masts were not ready when the yachts arrived in Perth and, as feared, the British masts were not up to the job. When the yachts began sailing their tuning was constantly interrupted by the need to make running repairs.

On one of her first outings *New Zealand KZ3's* mast buckled under compression. To replace it they were forced to borrow an old section from an Italian syndicate. It constantly gave trouble and was described by Woodroffe as "an old piece of rubbish''. Finally a new Australian mast with triple spreaders was fitted during the championships.

At the same time the three designers were in Fremantle analysing their first boats and finalising the plans for their next creation. On the question of masts they concluded that conventional double spreader spars could be built that would do the job. ''The problem with the triple spreaders were more weight aloft, more windage, and the fact that there were ten more rigging joins that multiplied your chances of failure accordingly,'' Farr concluded. ''As for the sheeting angles, we found they were too damn narrow anyway, we were sheeting outboard all the time.''

Consequently bare aluminium sections were purchased for the masts to be built by the syndicate's sparmakers themselves. The decisison to use conventional double spreaders surprised no-one, but other syndicates were prompted to examine the question of triple spreaders. From Hawaii, Dennis Conner ordered Australian-made masts for his *Stars and Stripes* stable but later changed his mind because he was ''happy with what we have got''. Ben Lexcen went ahead and designed triple spreader spars for his new *Australia IV*, testing the first for a month beforehand on *Australia II* before his new boat was launched. ''You would be mad not to do it now that the rule includes spreaders in the overall weight, they give you so much more control over the rig,'' he concluded. As for the Kiwis: ''If their fibreglass is so good for the hulls, why don't they build their masts from the stuff? It is not as stiff as aluminium, it is harder to alter and repair. I know, I've checked it out twice for Twelves.''

Another area to receive close scrutiny from the NZ designers was the deck layout for the crew. Two cockpit mock-ups were built and then modified as the yachtsmen explained their problems to the designers.

The 12-Metre Rule allows only 11 crewmen on the yachts, five fewer than a similarly sized ocean racer. To compensate for the lack of manpower, some of the yachtsmen have a number of jobs. For example, after a spinnaker set, the navigator must race from the aft cockpit to the bow to help the foredeck crew gather the headsail as it is lowered, before bounding back to resume his role in the afterguard.

As well as determining the most efficient layout for their third boat, the New Zealanders were looking for ways to reduce the amount of water finding its way below. Most of the boats racing in the championships were slowed when going to windward by having growing amounts of water sloshing around in the bilges.

While they worked on making the boats easier to sail and the crew more efficient, Fay and his lieutenants were also working on who would make up the crew. The yachtsmen had been contracted only until the end of the championships. Then, they were told, the whole situation would be reviewed. The resulting competition was too much for some, particularly with new talent becoming available as members of the two Whitbread Round the World Ocean Racers began arriving in Perth after the end of their race. Some crewmen were sacked, others quit, more had ongoing arguments with Fay.

The syndicate decided against returning home to Auckland for winter, preferring to stay in Fremantle. As the third boat was built, the first two continued their program of testing and tuning. The designers continued to talk frequently and meet regularly to analyse the data and information from Fremantle and the test tanks in Britain.

In August the third yacht was launched in a spectacular occasion masterminded by chairman Michael Fay. To mark the occasion he organised a gala dinner and invited the 1983 protagonists John Bertrand and Dennis Conner to be special guests. They could only watch in amazement as Fay auctioned seven silver-plated Cup replicas to the cream of Auckland society. The guests, who had paid $500 each to attend, went overboard. Each replica went under the hammer for $105,000. Fay then had the owner of New Zealand's leading racing sire Sir Tristram auction a service to the sire with live foal guaranteed. In one hour, more than $1 million went into the syndicate coffers.

When the new boat went on show it was wearing ''a skirt'' to keep its keel covered. The boat was longer than its two predecessors but showed the same U shaped bow sections and maximum beam run well aft.

On deck was its biggest surprise. As well as having a smaller cockpit, it was a total departure from the standard 12-Metre layout. The headsail trimmers were not accommodated in the usual personal cockpits known as ''pits''. They had been moved into the main cockpit behind the grinders operating the new Lewmar winches. Instead of the normal walk-way fore and aft through the cockpit, the helmsman was separated from the rest of the cockpit by a transverse beam.

Farr explained that the extra time had allowed them to concentrate on using the characteristics of fibreglass to their best advantage. ''For the first boats our thinking was very conventional because you cannot ignore what others before have succeeded with. In fact that was the story of our early program, being very orientated towards the existing technology. With that experience behind us we wanted to exploit our own technology. We reduced deck weight through less surface cockpit area. It's also more efficient for the crew, maybe not perfect for everyone but pretty good for all. We changed the layout to incorporate better hull structure. For example, the beam separating the two cockpits is part of the overall structure. Moving the trimmers back into the main cockpit meant doing away with separate structurals there and it also made the boat more watertight. There were some boats carrying a lot of water around last summer and that's slow, real slow.''

Again Farr stressed they were looking for all round performance. ''It takes all the good points of the first boats and hopefully improves on them, particularly in heavy airs. We've really concentrated on upwind speed in moderate and heavy winds. It's pretty hard to make Twelves faster downwind, you really just need big sails and a slippery hull, which we have. But when you go upwind there are a whole lot more forces at

One keel tried on first two identical boats had sweeping endplate.

work to complicate things so there is a lot of scope for getting more performance. There is no doubt that the new boat is better.''

The test was to be off Fremantle in early August. Fay says they knew within hours that their new boat was the best of the three. But the prevailing light airs of the West Australian winter kept a question mark over the new yacht's supposedly better heavy air performance.

At least before the launch of the new yacht *New Zealand KZ7*, with the sub-title on her transom *Kiwi Magic*, the question mark over the crew was lifted as the syndicate nominated ''A'' and ''B'' teams. Dickson was to lead the A team aboard the new boat while the B team under Woodroffe stayed aboard *KZ5*. Personal disappointments were largely overcome by the arrival of the new boat and the commencement of the final campaign towards the Cup.

For the designers it was time to concentrate on making the new boat realise their ambitions. It was designed to have four different configurations of displacement/sail area/waterline length so that it could be changed between series to suit different wind strengths.

As far as the syndicate chairman was concerned, the launch of the third boat meant standing back and taking a lesser role in the day-to-day running of the program, leaving the details to the managers.

''We have the infrastructure now, we can keep challenging for the America's Cup as long as it takes to win. My role is much smaller, they won't even really need me after this challenge. But I will say that even if we don't win it this time, we will eventually. There is no doubt of that in my mind.''

Farr was more positive during his final visit to Fremantle before the preliminary races. ''I put us a one in three chance of challenging the Australians. The New York Yacht Club has to be the toughest to beat. Then there is Dennis Conner because he is Dennis Conner, but I would put us above him at this stage. He's way behind. He got here too late, he won't know the conditions at sea while ashore the Australians certainly will not go out of their way to help him. He's certainly had problems too. *Stars and Stripes 86* was a 'dog', an extreme boat in shape. Presumably it was tested in the tank, but it must have been a long shot, looking to be extra fast. When you see boats like her and the second British boat it's a bit of a worry. You have to ask yourself: 'If those guys tested it and it looked fast, maybe we should be trying it'. Believe me, it's a relief when you hear they are no good.''

One of the big topics of conversation before the Cup racing began was whether there would be another breakthrough like *Intrepid* and *Australia II*. Farr had definite ideas. ''Look at the amount of money that's being spent. There has to be a chance of someone arriving with something magic like *Australia II*. It was the magic of the thing that was the big deal in 1983. It wasn't that much faster, it was a new and wonderful story. We will have another one here this summer.''

Press any of the New Zealand designers and you will get chuckles and statements such as ''Not 10 per cent faster it's 20 per cent, a real breakthrough''. To outsiders they enjoy a joke, but it's a very serious matter to these men from the smallest nation to challenge for the America's Cup. Time will tell whether they have the boat that will fulfil Farr's prediction of a ''magic'' boat sweeping all before it in February 1987. They are certainly not putting their heads on the block. Instead they simply point to the transom of *KZ7*, emblazoned with the sub-title *Kiwi Magic*.

The yacht's sail number *KZ7* is the only visible part of their campaign that is not the result of careful, reasoned logic. It exists because of the superstitions of two men. The youngest skipper in Fremantle, Chris Dickson, will not sail a yacht with even sail numbers. Michael Fay, a keen racehorse owner, admits he ''can't get to the tote quickly enough to put my money down'' to back a horse he owns if it carries the number seven saddlecloth. ''They win every time.''

The lawyer/entrepreneur/merchant banker/America's Cup syndicate chairman has put much behind his latest ''steed'' to carry the number seven. He is counting on his business instincts and approach to carry them through the treacherous waters of the America's Cup on their first attempt. If the New Zealanders succeed, they will complete what the Australians began in 1983 – the transformation of the America's Cup into a truly international competition that will be the world's greatest sporting event.

While they realise that fact themselves, they don't bother having such wide horizons. New Zealand sportsmen like nothing more than beating Australians. Yachtsmen from other nations are merely stepping stones.

CRUSADER

British Crusades

Lady Diana, Princess of Wales, at the christening of Crusader.

While Britain is the home of the International Rule which gave birth to the 12-Metre yacht, the record of her yachtsmen in 12-Metre racing and the America's Cup in general is nothing short of abysmal. Since 15 British racing yachts were beaten by the New York Yacht Club's schooner *America* in 1851, yachts representing Great Britain have unsuccessfully challenged for the America's Cup no fewer than 16 times.

After the Twelves were introduced to the Cup in 1958, British challengers *Sceptre* (1958) and *Sovereign* (1964) were thrashed by Olin Stephens designed yachts. In 1980 *Lionheart* was beaten by *Australia* for the right to challenge. In 1983 things looked more hopeful after a newcomer in the mould of Sir Thomas Lipton, financier Peter de Savary, did everything but buy the Cup as he bankrolled another British challenge. His *Victory 83* proved better than other yachts from France, Italy, Canada and Australia but was no match for *Australia II* which went on to win the Cup.

De Savary's determination to encourage competition within his syndicate led to several of the best yachtsmen leaving the group before the racing began in earnest. Probably the most damaging loss was that of leading match racing skipper, Harold Cudmore. Cudmore has always been a man only interested in doing it "his way". De Savary was equally determined to do it his way and it was inevitable that they should part company.

While de Savary was much criticised, he did revitalise feelings of creativity towards the Cup that existed in his country's yachting circles. Responding to the massive energy de Savary threw into the project, designers, sail and sparmakers, and yachtsmen were encouraged to take new approaches to the problem of winning the America's Cup. De Savary encouraged competition between the designers to try to come up with results. His first yacht from IOR designer Ed Dubois was scrapped after she could not beat *Australia*, which had been purchased from Alan Bond. Ian Howlett, who had designed *Lionheart*, was commissioned to design *Victory 83*. The result was a a good conventional Twelve, but Howlett had almost "done a Lexcen" by experimenting with a winged keel. Without the accurate forecasting facilities Lexcen enjoyed in Holland, Howlett's experiment was a real gamble, and after mixed results he stopped pursuing the breakthrough which helped win the Cup for Australia.

Involved to a lesser extent in de Savary's grand plan was model yacht designer David Hollom, an innovative designer with thousands of radio controlled model yachts of his design sailing on inland waterways around the world. De Savary asked Hollom for a completely radical design and got it with what was known as Project Acorn. Hollom's design incorporated a long torpedo bulb and winglets at the base of a canard or double keel. It was as radical as the winged keel, but was stillborn as de Savary decided to put his trust in the

Crusader's *stern overhang rides above wave as she dips into choppy seas of Fremantle in 20 knots of wind.*

conventional course taken by Howlett.

After his 1983 defeat de Savary vowed to try again and immediately sent Howlett back to the test tanks to pursue the winged keel concept. After some months de Savary decided to quit the Cup scene and while that was very bad news for the financial well-being of a new British challenge, he still left a legacy of renewed interest in 12-Metre design and development. Researchers in the aircraft and maritime industries suddenly found themselves in demand as designers and yachtsmen began to talk to them about another campaign.

To fill the breach left by de Savary, the Royal Thames Yacht Club agreed to put its name on a challenge headed by Defence Department "heavy" Admiral Sir John Easton and Graham Walker, a successful offshore yachtsman who had managed British teams at major offshore regattas. British Aerospace came to the party by paying the entry fee of $20,000 for the challenge and offering its research facilities and aircraft design computer programs. Three boats were to be designed and built.

Both Howlett and Hollom were retained by the syndicate and Harold Cudmore was put in charge of the sailing program with complete control over the selection of the crew. Cudmore quickly put together a top team including 1983 skipper Phil

David Hollom

Ian Howlett

Conventional lines of wing-keeled Crusader.

Sailing director and tactician Harold Cudmore with syndicate director Graham Walker.

Crebbin as technical and design co-ordinator and Angus Melrose of North Sails as sail designer.

As well as the facilities of British Aerospace and British Airways, the designers had plenty of support. Facilities included the Woolfson Unit of Southampton University where Howlett had once worked as a consultant and had tested models for both *Lionheart* and *Victory 83*, and the National Maritime Institute where one-third scale models were tested in a quarter mile long tunnel angled to allow for curvature in the earth's surface.

While Walker sought financial support for the new syndicate, he personally underwrote the most diversified design process for any British challenge. Late in 1984 Howlett was commissioned to design a development of *Australia's II's* winged keel concept, with building to commence in May 1985. His brief was to use the knowledge he had at the time, and the schedule did not give him long to create a boat that could win the America's Cup in 1987. Meanwhile, Hollom was given a free rein to come up with a revolutionary boat which would hopefully be a breakthrough.

Howlett's was the first boat to be built, but the shortage of funds saw the building of the boat put off until August 1985. The setback enabled the designer to continue testing one-quarter scale models at Southampton and one-tenth sized models in wave testing tanks at the Admiralty Research Establishment in Portsmouth.

Howlett worked in isolation from the second design team. He had always been a "loner" in his design work, which included not only the two earlier Twelves but also a number of successful 6-Metres. The test tanks and computer programs enabled him to complete his work on the wings he had designed in 1982 for *Victory 83*. At that time, with unsophisticated test facilities, he had only been able to pursue his ideas to a limited extent. He had put aircraft type wings on a conventional keel, but did not redesign the keel shape as well.

Howlett recalls: "Unfortunately I didn't have the equipment then for testing the wings properly. I had to use a wind tunnel which was hard to relate to reality. It was bizzare when we tried to develop it full size. When we bolted the wings onto *Australia's* keel they improved her performance immediately. But on *Victory* there was not the same performance improvement. I knew the effects and the scope for improvement and had lots of arguments to keep persisting, but maybe I wasn't strong enough."

In 1984/85 he did have the facilities, as well as the proof that he had been on the right track. Thinking of Fremantle, he again concentrated on keels. "I've adopted the philosophy that this is a keel game. First I had to decide what size of boat I wanted but I got that out of the way quickly so that I could concentrate on the keel. Other things come into that too, such as the size of the bustle. In straight line sailing *Victory 83* and *Australia II* were pretty close, but when it came to

The most unusual looking Twelve in Fremantle, Britain's second yacht dubbed "the Hippo."

manoeuvrability and speed out of tacks we were blown away by *Australia II*."

The British syndicate knew they could rely on Howlett for one good boat. Lack of money meant that a third yacht could not be built. But their wild card was the team led by Hollom to design a second yacht. For advice on translating his thoughts into his first full-sized yacht, Hollom was teamed up with leading aerodynamicist Herbert Pearcey and naval architect Stephen Wallace, the head of the Laurent Giles design office who also had 12-Metre experience. The innovative Hollom appreciated Lexcen's originality in 1983, commenting: "It was a very bold step that was successful; he was really thinking along the right lines and we are now trying to think beyond the winged keel."

To do so, the 45-year-old salesman handed in his resignation to turn his successful hobby into a full-time profession and attempt to prove what he had been saying for so long – that yacht designers had been wrong to ignore model yachts for testing purposes. While he turned to various computer design programs and the test tanks that Lexcen had returned to favour in international yacht design, he refused to turn his back on his beloved radio controlled yachts, sailing one-tenth scale models of his Twelves for hundreds of hours on his favourite lakes and waterways.

Said Hollom: "You have to be more objective with models because you cannot measure data; you have to rely on your eyes and brain. But they are good for designers to learn from. After all, model yachts have been racing since the 1890s."

Hollom went all out for a breakthrough boat that would be considerably faster. He says he always wanted a boat that was biassed to succeed in wind strengths above 15 knots while hoping it would retain its performance in lighter airs. With the rest of his design team he tested "30 to 40" design variations on the computers before settling on the best 14 for conversion to one-third sized models for tank testing.

While financial difficulties delayed the building of both boats, technical director Phil Crebbin, who was responsible for overseeing the progress of the two design teams, said the value of the extra time this gave the designers would outweigh the lost sailing time.

To inject the capital needed to build the boats, Graham Walker finally turned the syndicate into a public company and three million one dollar shares were issued on the London stock exchange. Surprisingly, considering Britain's history in the America's Cup, all the shares were snapped up by people willing to take a big risk on future profits if Britain won in Perth in 1987.

Titular head of the Royal Thames Yacht Club was Prince Charles, and in another move to fill syndicate coffers, the Prince's wife Lady Diana was invited to launch the first yacht to take shape, Howlett's *Crusader*.

Like other struggling syndicates, the British believed that

when they had something concrete to show for their efforts, i.e. a boat, fundraising would become easier. Due to the delays in the building program, they would not be ready for the World championships in Perth in February 1986. So the syndicate decided to keep the first yacht in England a little longer to help raise money. Princess Diana christened the uncompleted yacht in December 1985 before it went on to be the star attraction at the London Boat Show at Earl's Court.

Cudmore and a number of his crew were in Perth to watch the World championships and catch up on what everyone else was doing. When the second French syndicate withdrew their Lexcen-designed *Challenge 12* due to financial difficulties, Cudmore quickly chartered the boat for the series. *Challenge 12* was totally outclassed by the new generation of winged keel Twelves, but still gave the British yachtsmen valuable practice, not only in the art of sailing a 12-Metre, but also in experiencing the conditions off Perth.

To sail the British Twelves, Cudmore had recruited the best big boat yachtsmen he could find. For himself he reserved the position of starting helmsman and tactician. As race helmsmen he attracted two of his adopted country's top helmsmen, Olympians Chris Law and Eddie Warden Owen. When the team finally arrived in Fremantle Cudmore was full of confidence, as ever tempering his more serious statements with humour. "We are the best qualified team in the Cup. We have five invitees to the match racing circuit in our team. When we sat down to draw up a crew list we decided who we wanted and simply went out and got them. It's a very intelligent group, everyone has an honours degree. You even have to have a degree to sweep the compound. No, the real reason we need a team with honours is to understand what the designers are trying to tell us."

The British team's presence in Fremantle was very different in style to that in Newport in 1983, when the British had had more of everything, from people to boats and money. In 1983 more than 100 people had rushed around at de Savary's bidding. In 1986 a lean group of less than 40 arrived to conduct their campaign on a budget of $5 million. While waiting for their first boat to arrive they joined local builders in putting together their dockside facilities including a sail loft.

In March the Howlett-designed *Crusader* was unloaded in Fremantle. Members of the Bond syndicate commented that she looked like the old *Australia I*. The British followed the lead of the New Zealanders and left the keel uncovered for all to see, commenting that they would be changing it anyway. They had little need to worry about anyone copying it; in most aspects it looked just like the one that was uncovered by the victorious Bond team three years earlier in Newport, Rhode Island. Besides, the boat the British hoped would be the breakthrough in 1987 was still on a ship bound for Australia.

Crusader was described by Howlett as a "medium boat" with length overall about 65 ft (19.8 m), displacement of 55,000 lbs (24,950 kg), sail area of 1,750 sq ft (162.5 sq m) and waterline length at 45 ft (13.7 m); "the same as Sparkman & Stephens have been doing since 1946", according to Howlett. "I've tried to hit the middle of the wind range at 16-18 knots and hopefully cover conditions above and below that. Hence a medium boat."

There was nothing "medium" about the second British Twelve to be launched in Australian waters. Hollom's unnamed boat was dubbed "*The Hippo*" by the Australian news media the day it arrived. The model yacht designer had created an extraordinary Twelve, about five feet (1.5 m) longer overall than Howlett's version but with the same short waterline length. Largely responsible for her nickname was an extremely long stern overhang to increase her overall length by approximately 20 ft (6 m). In front of the covered keel there was a big bulge, added by Hollom, to keep as much displacement as possible around the mid-sections of the boat and out of the ends, particularly the fine bow.

A few days later the yacht set sail and her keel was revealed to all observers in the shallow waters of Gage Roads. It was a canard keel, with twin keels running along the centreline of the yacht joined at their base, and winglets either side emerging from a torpedo shaped bulb. Canard keels are popular in model yachts and are fitted to the hulls of the small keelboat "Fighter" class in Britain. Hollom agrees it appears there should be more drag and resistance through having two leading edges but says the advantages outweigh the disadvantages. "The front keel smooths the flow of water over the rear keel which is consequently less likely to stall and become inefficient. It's particularly good coming out of a tack. When a boat is moving slowly the flow of water separates very easily and a conventional keel stalls. But the canard keel reduces that considerably."

The deck layout of both yachts was identical to avoid problems for crewmen when they were switching boats. In the American style the tactician and navigator were behind the helmsman, with their computer pedestal between them.

While they waited for the new boat the British put in a lot of miles racing *Crusader* against *South Australia*. Unlike the syndicates which had summered in Perth before returning home for the northern summer, the British elected to stay in Fremantle, concentrating on getting their infrastructure in Perth absolutely right. They hoped the usually light winds of Perth's winter would stay away so they could assess both boats in the fresh conditions they could expect when the summer's racing began. Windy days proved rare.

In the light to moderate airs the Lexcen-designed *South Australia* appeared to have a slight edge in speed upwind and down. But the South Australians had been sailing their boat on those waters for more than a year, while the British were on a steep learning curve.

As Hollom's boat began to be tuned, Cudmore was hopeful, although still sceptical. "With *Crusader I* am happy that we have a boat we can succeed with. If the second boat proves to be the breakthrough we are hoping for then we are obviously looking even better."

After watching his "Hippo" for a fortnight, Hollom returned to Britain, where his design team had been working

Night falls on 22 crewmen during close quarters duelling on Gage Roads.

on new keel concepts. *Crusader* was fitted with a new keel and later Hollom's boat also went into the shed for surgery. The syndicate was keeping quiet about the modifications, except one. Four feet (approx. one metre) were removed from the transom. Cudmore said they had anticipated the truncation of the longest overhang in Perth by fitting a special bulkhead that would become the new transom and by having the backstay pulley mounted inside it. "We weren't surprised," Cudmore laughed. "All 12-Metre designers want to cut length off the sterns of their boats."

Cudmore would not laugh when Hollom's boat was referred to by its nickname. "That is not a name we recognise here," was always the gentle rebuke. Also taboo was comparison of performance of the two boats. "We do not discuss that. Obviously we will use the best of the two, which we will decide at the last minute." As had been the case throughout the long campaign, the two designers had little to do with each other professionally. The decision of which boat to use was to be made by Cudmore.

Howlett returned to Fremantle in mid-September to participate in the syndicate's preparations for October – the month of truth for all. Not for the Englishman the mad rushes planned by some designers between each series to change the keel and configuration for the next round of races. "Changing keels is a pretty big deal and we will have to see how we go before we make any decisions like that. Anyone completely changing their boat will need meteorologists at work 24 hours a day, seven days a week, and they might still get it wrong. The big danger with the America's Cup is that you get confused and make mistakes. That was always a big problem with the challengers in Newport. I believe you need an all-rounder like *Australia III* and *Crusader*. I believe in a conservative boat and I'm pretty certain I know what I am doing."

CANADA II

Joint Venture

Amidst all the high technology that has been poured into the new crop of 12-Metres is one yacht that not only raced in 1983, but is also completely untested on the computer programs that have flourished in the wake of *Australia II's* win. The yacht is *Canada II* and like Ben Lexcen her creator is not a qualified architect. For Canada's Bruce Kirby, drawing successful boats is a natural talent and an occupation he enjoys.

Canada II carried the maple leaf into battle in 1983 under the title of *Canada I*. Today the yacht bears little resemblance to what was a fast conventional Twelve in Newport. It has been lengthened and carries an *Australia II*-type winged keel. While it is remarkable that *Canada II* is one of only two 1983 triallists to be in Perth along with *Courageous*, also remarkable is the story of how she came to be Canada's representative Downunder.

Yachting is not a mainstream sport in Canada where the climate is more conducive to ice hockey and other indoor sports. Consequently there was never great support for an America's Cup challenge, after two half-hearted efforts in the late 19th century failed dismally. But when international interest grew and more countries started challenging, a group of businessmen in Canada's west, headed by Marvin McDill, decided in 1980 to challenge for the Cup, using the traditional rivalry between Canada and the US as a spur to bring Canada together.

The idea was fine in principle, but the public yawned loudly when the syndicate's publicists tried to enthuse them to donate to the coffers. Several times the syndicate faced bankruptcy, only to stage miraculous recoveries.

In Newport finance continued to be thin and often the group could not afford new sails. When new sails did go on *Canada I* she proved competitive and made her way into the semi-finals. But *Australia II* lay in wait to crush the hopes of all competitors in 1983.

Like other designers, Kirby was bursting to see Lexcen's keel. He was shown sketches which turned out to be very accurate, but he wanted to see the real thing so that he could use that knowledge for his next boat. As *Australia II* continued to mow down the other challengers, Kirby became worried that Alan Bond would insist on keeping the keel secret even after the racing. He knew other syndicates had underwater photographs of the keel taken by frogmen while the yacht was at sea, and asked some of his own people to take photos of the keel while the yacht was "in international waters so there wouldn't be a fuss".

Kirby says he was horrified when he learned that police had arrested a Canadian trying to take photographs of the yacht in her dock. The Australians had spotted the man and dragged him from the water, seizing his camera before turning him over to the law.

Kirby need not have worried. Alan Bond allowed all to be

A refreshing approach to say the least.

revealed after *Australia II* won the Cup and Kirby, like all other yacht designers, faced a new challenge to master the winged keel. He quickly began testing it on new boats. The 8-Metre yacht *Octavia* was the only yacht in the 1984 world class championships with a winged keel and she won. The 6-Metre *Capriccio* carried a winged keel to third place in the European championships the next year.

Another Canadian grappling with the winged keel was a young designer Steve Killing who had worked for Kirby when he designed *Canada I*. The country which had failed to adequately support one challenge in 1983 was this time to have two challenges competing for support. While McDill planned to try again, one of his helpers who had quit in frustration in 1983 also intended to mount a challenge. The newcomer was successful yachtsman and businessman Don Green. The question of finance did not bother Green, who ignored advice that he should merge with the established syndicate.

While the *Canada I* syndicate took its time to recover from the financial mauling and regain strength for another try, the new syndicate based in Ontario and named True North began getting on with the job. Steve Killing was recruited as designer. Olympic gold medallist Hans Fogh, who headed Canada's biggest sail loft for North Sails, was put in charge of sail design and also was nominated skipper of the boat. The skipper of *Canada I* in 1983 was sought by both syndicates but Terry McLaughlin would not commit himself to either.

Launch date for the new *True North* was scheduled for mid-1985. Then the yacht would go to Perth for the summer and the 1986 World 12-Metre Championships. Another Killing design, said to be radical, was then to be built for the Cup.

Back in the west, McDill asked designer Bruce Kirby to assess whether *Canada I* could be revamped as an effective trial horse for a new boat. Kirby was glad to oblige. In 1983 he had been frustrated by the lack of cash that prevented his yacht from realising its potential. In fact, the Australians believed *Canada I* would have been their biggest threat if the Canadians had campaigned more strongly.

Kirby went to work in May 1985. His approach was very different from that of most other designers, who had turned to their colleagues in universities and research centres around the world in an endeavour to catch up with and pass the Australians. Kirby had never liked the idea of computers designing boats. In his view they would never be accurate enough to measure the small differences he was always pursuing. The same applied to a lesser extent to tank testing. He commented: "I'm not anti-computer; it's just that I love drawing boats with my eyes. I guess the boffins are trying to take the element of luck out of yacht design but I don't know if they will ever succeed."

Kirby was well known for his good eye for lines. A journalist by professión, he designed his first boat – an International 14-foot dinghy – during time off from his duties with the Montreal *Star* at the age of 29. More boats followed, from dinghies to Metre boats and keelboats, until in 1969 he hit the financial jackpot when he designed the Laser.

Designer Bruce Kirby

Skipper Terry Neilson

True North – *the first Canadian Twelve to sail in Australia and the first to be discarded by the new syndicate.*

The one-design, singlehanded dinghy was a runaway success, becoming an international class sailed in large numbers around the world. Some 140,000 have been built. Royalties from the project and accompanying stardom led Kirby to toss in journalism in 1974 to design boats full time. More than 30 IOR offshore racers have since left his drawing board, along with several production and cruising boats.

When he turned his attention back to his first 12-Metre, Kirby decided the yacht could be considerably improved. Unlike some others, he decided against automatically going for a very big boat to handle the strong winds of Perth. He had been thinking long and hard about the winged keel with its dramatically improved stability factor. As well as designing a winged keel packing a punchy 47,000 lbs (21,320 kg) of lead, he decided eventually to add 3 ft (0.9 m) to her overall length, lengthen her waterline, incorporate a new higher bow, more freeboard and a new stern. The result would be, he said, "virtually a new boat".

Her new measurements saw her length overall at 65 ft (19.8 m), 57,000 lb (17,370 kg) in displacement and sail area of 1,800 sq ft (167.2 sq m). On the waterline she measured about 45 ft (13.7 m). Kirby concentrated on changing displacement

Bow angle during spinnaker drop shows raised bow modification for rougher waters of Fremantle. Sponsors' names painted into topsides.

rather than changing the hull shape. He said the lines altered little from the 1983 version, although if the two measurement certificates were placed alongside each other no-one would guess they were for the same boat.

Rebuilding began in Victoria B.C. in mid-1985 and *Canada II* was sailing in October. The syndicate was far more low-key than the new True North group and limited funds kept them from going to Australia for the World championships. Instead they arranged local competition with other American groups who also were in no shape for the expensive Australian excursion.

McDill had sold their 1983 trial horse *Clipper* to the Heart of America syndicate from Chicago. Part of the deal was that the Americans, led by Buddy Melges, would race against *Canada II*. In November the two yachts raced off the west coast as winter closed in. This Maple Leaf Cup was a 12-Metre event unparallelled in history as the crews battled the elements in sub zero temperatures, the spray freezing on the decks. *Canada II* won three of four races, losing the other through equipment failure. She was clearly superior, winning by margins ranging up to two minutes in strong winds. On every windward leg she would open a margin of 20-30 seconds every mile to windward. The regatta proved that Kirby had been on the right track and the syndicate stopped worrying about financing a new boat. Both Melges and his tactician Gary Jobson predicted that *Canada II* could be right in there at the end in 1987.

Although *Clipper* was a pre-winged keel era boat, the Canadians and Americans knew she had provided a good test. She had been defeated for the right to defend the Cup by Dennis Conner's *Freedom* in 1980, but many people had thought *Clipper* faster but not as well sailed. According to Kirby, that argument was backed up by the fact that Conner tried to buy *Clipper* from them in the summer of 1983, during which it proved to be on a par with *Canada I,* when he knew *Liberty* might not be fast enough to beat the radical *Australia II*.

Kirby was amazed at the difference the winged keel configuration made to his boat. "It made less leeway and pointed higher and was faster. It was a quantum leap, even better than I hoped." Like Lexcen, Kirby had elected an upside down keel with the base of the keel longer than the root where it met the hull. In front of the keel the yacht's sections were U-shaped, while behind the keel the beamy stern provided a long flat run aft for downwind speed and a deep skeg running to the rudder. On deck she was similar to American boats in layout. Kirby believed having the helmsman in front of the navigator and tactician, because this positioned him closer to his all-important sail trimmers which made communication easier. In addition, Kirby had put a lot of thought into the layout in order to keep the deck as watertight as possible in the rough waters off Fremantle.

Then, working on an opposite schedule to other designers, Kirby went to the test tank. Using a model of *Canada II* he wanted to try ways of improving the boat. As there was then no testing facility in Canada capable of testing one-third scale models, the Royal Perth Yacht Club gave Kirby permission to use the tanks of Offshore Technology Corporation in the USA, which were also used by the America II, Eagle and San Diego syndicates. He says he was pleased to find no advancements, but tried five widely different keel configurations to answer some questions.

Meanwhile *True North* was shaping up against other Twelves in Fremantle. Terry McLaughlin had finally decided to join the syndicate and had been appointed helmsman in place of Hans Fogh, who was relegated to sail trim.

Performance against other yachts in straight line sailing was encouraging. But in the championships *True North* finished a disappointing sixth, after many problems. McLaughlin found himself off the boat after four races, with Fogh back in charge. Changes to the boat to improve balance and helm did not help, and a dispirited team returned to Canada, where Killing's second boat was already being built. Worse was to come. Green, who had put an estimated $4 million of his own money into the effort, announced that the syndicate had run out of funds and would only be able to keep going with a major and immediate injection of cash. Work on the second boat stopped as did pay cheques to the crew.

At this time *Canada II* was racing in San Francisco, continuing to encourage her supporters by beating *Clipper* again, as well as the first of two new *USA's* of Tom Blackaller. Skipper was Terry Neilsen, a newcomer to keelboat racing with an impeccable record in small boats including a silver Olympic medal and a world championship win in the highly competitive Laser class. Tactician was friend and Laser rival, Andy Roy, a two-time North American Laser champion. From San Francisco they moved to Santa Cruz, where they continued racing the new *Heart of America* skippered by Melges.

While Green was trying to work out how to pay *True North's* bills, so too were the *Canada II* organisers. It was obvious that they had to amalgamate to survive. One man who had stepped in back in 1983 to settle outstanding accounts was wealthy Toronto businessman and successful yachtsman Paul Phelan. He had put money into both Canadian groups and when the call went out for help it was Phelan who persuaded both parties to join forces, with McDill and Green as vice-chairmen.

The new administration decided to hold exhaustive trials to pick the best yacht to send to Australia. Phelan was determined not to throw good money after bad. He wanted the best possible crew and boat to go to Perth, with the best possible sails and support. The mistakes of 1983 and 1985/86 were not to be repeated.

So ended an inglorious career for *True North*, when she quickly proved to be slower than *Canada II*. Just as the rebuilt boat had beaten *Clipper* and *USA*, she was clearly superior to *True North* – faster in a straight line, faster out of tacks and more manoeuvrable. Kirby found that despite general opinion, *True North* was a boat too big to perform in all but the strongest winds; in fact in measurement specifications she was close enough for *Canada II* to use her sails with only minor alterations.

Besides choosing which boat to send to Australia, there was also the task of cutting the two crews down to one. Among those to miss out were Terry McLaughlin and *True North* crew boss Geoff Boyd. Terry Neilson and Andy Roy maintained charge of *Canada II* with Hans Fogh joining them in the afterguard with responsibility for boat speed and some downwind steering. In Perth he was also in charge of sailmaking, while design was the principal responsibility of another sailmaker, Phil Leitch, once a classmate at the University of British Columbia of Tom Schnackenberg, sailmaker to Alan Bond's syndicate.

With Phelan underwriting the program, the financial shortcomings of 1983 would not be repeated. The sail development program was well underway when they yacht began racing in Fremantle in October, and crew morale was high with Neilsen enjoying respect from his men.

While Kirby had eschewed the use of computers in the design process he was keen to use all that technology had to offer when it came to assessing the boat on the water. Like other syndicates he had access on the yacht's tender via telemetry to the readouts of all instruments aboard the yacht. He was able to "eyeball" wind readouts as well as boat settings like trim tab and rudder angles to know when *Canada II* was going well. In addition, he spent considerable time sailing aboard the yacht; a successful yachtsman in his own right, he still refused to put his faith blindly in the microchip.

In the final run-up to the elimination series the Canadians

Stern counter lengthened during rebuild.

Canada II *duelling with* Heart of America *before leaving for Australia.*

spent a week refaring the hull before getting it measured. It was typical of their thorough approach. Kirby knew the measurers would be extremely strict on the rule that there must be no hollows in the yachts' topsides anywhere above the waterline. They would run a straight edge over the hull looking for the finest dent in the surface. The preparation was worth it, allowing the Canadians to spend more time on the water than some others who wasted valuable days bringing their boats up to scratch. Kirby was also pleased that the measurer found the yacht weighed in at just 88 lbs (27 kg) over the minimum weight for his 12-Metre, remarkably close for a boat weighing 57,000 lbs (17,370 kg).

Kirby did not have a host of new tricks up his sleeve in case they ran into trouble. He did have a new keel standing by, the last he had tank tested, but said it had tested no faster and no slower.

He said: "If, say, two other boats beat us badly in heavy weather then I would change the keel, certainly. The only other thing we can do is reballast the boat. I aimed for a boat that would do its best in 18-20 knots and also perform well either side of that. I think I have such a boat. Some will beat us in 10 knots of breeze, some will beat us in 25 knot winds. But they will not be the same boats."

The jaunty 57-year-old journalist turned yacht designer who lives in Connecticut but keeps his Canadian passport, bubbles with confidence when he discusses their chances. "One of the best things was getting Paul Phelan in. That saw a businessman take over and the dreamers go. His approach was that we should do everything we possibly could to win the Cup, but not to worry about the money, he was underwriting us.

"I don't have any excuses if we fail. Sure I could have used another six months to look for something quite different but I'm comfortable. Everyone here has an *Australia II* type keel. Most of the boats are pretty similar, it's the whole effort that will count. I'm comfortable."

If Kirby is right he will make a mockery of the huge sums that have been pumped into other syndicates. Certainly his boat did everything he'd promised before the first warning signal was fired off Fremantle.

If he's wrong he will not be crushed and go into hiding. He'll get himself a job as a commentator so that he can watch the Cup. Then he will have a good look around at what the other designers and their researchers have cooked up and go back to doing what he enjoys most, drawing boats.

AZZURRA

Flair And Flamboyance

Mario Pelaschier – typical stance at helm of Azzurra *with headphones.*

In 1983, when the 12-Metre yacht *Azzurra* finished third behind the Australians and the British in Italy's first America's Cup campaign, a new nation was welcomed with open arms to the pinnacle of the sport. Not only had they charmed their way into the hearts of Cup regulars ashore; at sea they had shown they were credible competitors, a force to be reckoned with in the future.

When the Yacht Club Costa Smeralda became the first formal challenger to the Royal Perth Yacht Club for the 1987 America's Cup, the outlook for their second Cup campaign appeared assured. However, 14 months later their campaign was in tatters and in serious danger of collapse. The emergence of another Italian syndicate had taken some of the glamour and support from them. Then the new *Azzurra* they raced in the 1986 World championships in Fremantle was trounced. At sea and ashore, they were a team in theory only, their numbers divided into quarrelling factions, with high turnover in personnel.

If ever a 12-Metre syndicate appeared to have a chance of success it was the Azzurra syndicate. While others around the world struggled to raise the money for their campaigns, the Italians from the outset had guarantees from some of their country's leading companies. At the head of the syndicate was one of the world's wealthiest men, His Royal Highness the Aga Khan, the spiritual leader of more than 16 million Moslems around the world. Based in Paris but with extensive interests in Italy, the Aga Khan had given Italian keelboat racing a much needed boost with his development of a resort for the rich at Porto Cervo in Sardinia. At the same time the Yacht Club Costa Smeralda was formed and became host to a new international ocean racing regatta, Sardinia Week. Next they took on the America's Cup and what they admitted was an initial learning experience in Newport, Rhode Island.

Sharing the chairmanship of the syndicate with the Aga Khan were two men who had been planning to get Italy into the America's Cup since 1960. Gianni Agnelli brought the same management skills to the syndicate that he applied to the automotive giant Fiat, of which he was President. Beppe Croce was also well versed in the America's Cup. The former Olympic yachtsman had been President of the International Yacht Racing Union for 17 years and had been a member of the America's Cup Jury, which adjudicates protests against rule breaches.

Azzurra IV

Duelling with Stars and Stripes 87.

In 1984 the YCCS was riding high on the 12-Metre wave. It was to host the World 12-Metre championships in Porto Cervo, most of the key people from its 1983 campaign had rejoined and, despite the emergence of two new Italian syndicates (one was later withdrawn), its fundraising was progressing well. Plans were made for the original *Azzurra* to be sent to Australia to spend the southern summer sailing the new America's Cup course and learning the conditions while designer Andrea Valicelli drew a new Twelve. In addition they were appointed the Challenger of Record for the 1987 Cup, a prestigious honour placing them in charge of the challengers' elimination series, formally known as the Louis Vuitton Cup.

Their syndicates confidence received an unexpected setback in the 1984 World championships when *Azzurra* was beaten by *Victory 83*, the former British Twelve that had been purchased by the new syndicate representing the Yacht Club Italiano. Suddenly the syndicate found it was not having it all its own way at home.

In January 1985, the renamed *Azzurra 83* became the first European 12-Metre yacht to sail in Australian waters. For three months the yacht sailed alone and then against the first *Kookaburra* of the Australian Taskforce syndicate and the first

Launch of Azzurra III.

America II of the New York Yacht Club. It was a valuable experience as the syndicate learned the conditions of the new home of the America's Cup.

While they were busy in Australia, the designer of the first *Azzurra*, Andrea Vallicelli, was finalising his new boat to be named *Azzurra 2*. Vallicelli had produced a string of successful ocean racing yachts since opening his own office in Rome in 1975 at the age of 24. Fifteen of his IOR racers had won all major events in Italy and several European championships before he turned his attention to the 12-Metre Rule for the new syndicate. His second Twelve was launched in Venice with her winged keel covered in the new 12-Metre tradition of secrecy. What could not be kept secret was the fact that this was a big boat aimed at providing results in the strong winds that Fremantle was renowned for over the summer months. Specifications supplied by the syndicate showed her to be longer overall but shorter on the waterline and lighter than the first *Azzurra*.

AZZURRA 83
LOA .... 65 ft 3 in (19.90 m)
LWL .... 44 ft 7 in (14.20 m)
Beam .... 12 ft 5 in (3.80 m)
Disp .... 61,700 lb (28,000 kg)
Sail area .... 1,800 sq ft (168 sq m)

AZZURRA 2
LOA .... 65 ft 9 in (20.05 m)
LWL .... 45 ft 7 in (13.90 m)
Beam .... 12 ft 8 in (3.85 m)
Disp .... 57,320 lb (26,000 kg)
Sail area .... 1,800 sq ft (168 sq m)

Two months later the first indication that all was not well within the syndicate came with the announcement that Lorenzo Bortolotti had left the rival Italian syndicate and been appointed the new skipper of *Azzurra* in place of Cino Ricci, who had been skipper in 1983. The disgruntled Ricci was given the title of "Sport Manager", with responsibility for running the program ashore. The upheaval came after *Azzurra's* 1983 helmsman, Mauro Pelaschier, had shocked the group by his departure. Stefano Roberti had switched from mainsheet trim to helming. The crew changes were upsetting

Franco Schiomachen
Designer brought in for final boat.

The Aga Khan –
the power behind the force.

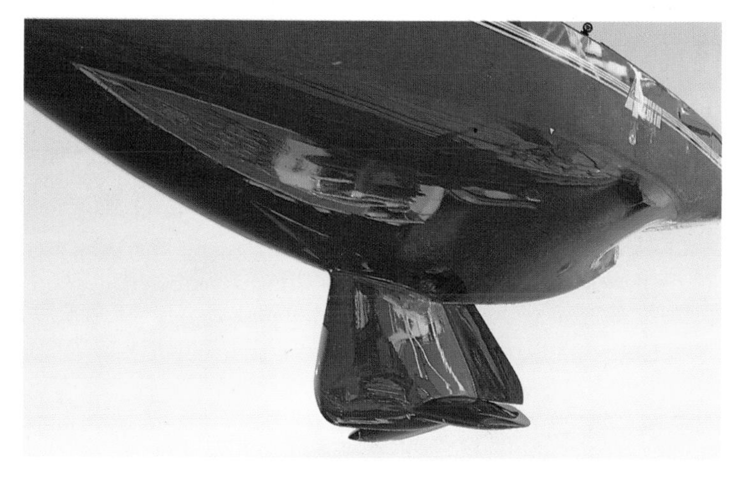

Australia II *type winged keel on reject* Azzurra II.

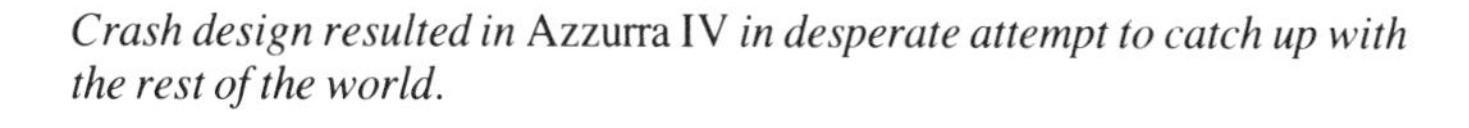

Crash design resulted in Azzurra IV *in desperate attempt to catch up with the rest of the world.*

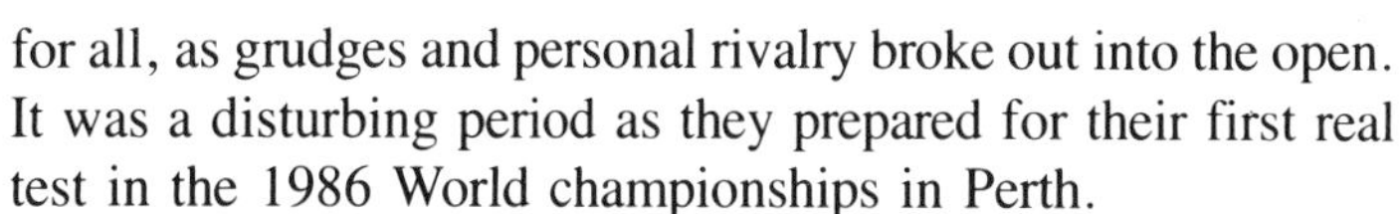

for all, as grudges and personal rivalry broke out into the open. It was a disturbing period as they prepared for their first real test in the 1986 World championships in Perth.

Outwardly at least, in Australia, there was no indication of the internal troubles as the slick marketing team began to repeat its first class job of selling *Azzurra*. With the rival *Italia* syndicate they led the fashion stakes with their stylish clothing created by sponsors Fila and Porto Fino. All who had seen them in action in Newport three years earlier remarked that they looked just as good again. Such comments could not have been further from the truth.

When the championships began, the results indicated that they had learned nothing since 1983, while the rest of the world had forged ahead. In the fleet of 14 yachts from six nations, *Azzurra* finished an embarrassing tenth, with only the old yachts *Victory 83*, *Challenge 12*, *Courageous* and *Gretel II* behind her.

It was a humiliating result that demanded action. The new boat was obviously too big for the mixed conditions of Perth. Despite having sailed in Fremantle the summer before, the lesson that the strong afternoon Fremantle Doctor was not as reliable as commonly believed had obviously not registered.

Work on the the second new *Azzurra* had already started, but it was frozen for a month as arguments raged over what was needed to get back into the race for the America's Cup. Vallicelli's design was to be simply an ''evolution'' of *Azzurra 2*. With the lessons of Fremantle in mind it was to be a shorter, lighter and more stable boat, which Vallicelli promised would handle the chop of the seas better, with less hobbyhorsing. In addition, he said, his continuing studies with winglets had led to a new solution which would be kept top secret.

But Vallicelli had lost some of his supporters following the failure of *Azzurra 2* in the championships, including the chairman of the syndicate's executive committee, Riccardo Bonadeo, who commented: ''The designer was a little confused, I suppose. It was the wrong type of boat, long and heavy, with too small a sail area.''

Cinno Ricci was another who argued for a whole new approach to design. After the championships he had suggested to Vallicelli that he design a smaller boat quite different to what he had originally planned. When he was unsuccessful Ricci took his argument straight to the syndicate chairmen. He also discussed it with the Sciomachen design studio in Bologna, a group with several successful ocean racing boats of all sizes but no 12-Metre experience.

Ricci managed to convince the Aga Khan and Agnelli of the need to come up with completely different type of boat. In desperation, the syndicate briefed Sciomachen to design a Twelve. They had just four weeks to design their first 12-Metre, leaving no time for tank testing of the boat, but only for computer evaluation, with help in keel design from the Hydraulics Institute of Engineering Faculty at the University of Bologna.

With all this frenzied activity going on, the 12-Metre industry in Italy was flourishing. While their rivals' new *Italia* was built and then rebuilt after a dockside accident soon after its launching, the two new *Azzurras* of Vallicelli and Sciomachen were crash built at the same yard, S.A.I. Ambrosini, under the supervision of engineer Carlo Bertorello, a member of the syndicate. With typical extravagance, the Italians were going for broke to try to catch up. The other syndicates to build three new boats, Australia's Taskforce syndicate, the New York Yacht Club, Dennis Conner's Sail America and the New Zealanders, had all completed them in time to be optimised, but the YCCS was still building its second and designing its third.

Crew training continued on the second *Azzurra* at Sete in France, where they raced against *French Kiss* before she was taken from the water for modifications. Then it was back to Italy in late July for the launch of Vallicelli's new Twelve. After just three weeks of sailing the yacht was shipped to Australia. Meanwhile, the new Sciomachen *Azzurra 4* was built in a record six weeks. There was no time to even christen the new yacht, let alone sail it, before it was shipped.

As well as having two brand new boats from two different designers, crew problems continued to add to the Italians' worries. Stefano Roberti, who had helmed *Azzurra 85* in the 1986 World championships after Pelaschier had left, suddenly found himself out of a job with the return of Pelaschier.

The on-off Pelaschier saga was closely watched by Italy's Cup followers. Pelaschier was their best known yachtsmen, a sporting hero whose face adorned T-shirts around Italy following his meteoric rise to stardom in 1983. He had resigned from the syndicate in 1985; "tired of arguing about the mistakes that were being made." In 1986 he said he was glad they had been sorted out so that he could return.

But the official version of Pelaschier's return to favour was that he had never really left. According to Bonadeo: "He just needed five months to reflect and think about it a little bit before he decided to come back to us. There is no problem with the crew. On the contrary. Under skipper Lorenzo Bortolotti and Cino Ricci they are settled and involved."

Unfortunately everything was not as settled as they hoped. Soon after the new boats were delivered, Ricci quit, leaving some stinging comments in his wake. It had all become something of a farce, prompting journalists trying to keep up with the changes to write disclaimers into their copy as they knew it would be out of date by the time it appeared in print. Indeed, as well as wet weather clothing the syndicate may have been handing out name tags to the crews so that they knew who they are sailing with.

As promised, Sciomachen had given the syndicate a boat quite different to the latest in the Vallicelli family, despite the familiar colour scheme of azure blue with white stripes along the topsides. In one way it was similar to *French Kiss*, with the bow raised to handle the choppy waters of Fremantle. It was shorter on the waterline than *Azzurra 3*, and also narrower, with longer overhangs and a smaller sail area. The wing keeled newcomer was also to be the lightest Twelve in Australia.

Saved in the nick of time.

Unusual crease behind mid-sections of final Azzurra *show clearly as she races* Stars and Stripes 87.

AZZURRA 3
LOA .... 63 ft 11 in (19.50 m)
LWL .... 44 ft 11 in (13.70 m)
Beam .... 12 ft 8 in (3.85 m)
Disp .... 55,100 lb (25,000 kg)
Sail area .... 1,808 sq ft (168 sq m)

AZZURRA 4
LOA .... 64 ft 10 in (19.77 m)
LWL .... 43 ft 4 in (13.20 m)
Beam .... 12 ft 2 in (3.70 m)
Disp .... 49,100 lb (22,260 kg)
Sail area .... 1,749 sq ft (162.5 sq m)

Understanding only too well the problems of evaluating the two new boats in what would be just a matter of days in Perth before the challengers' trials began, the syndicate's computer programmers developed a new system to compare the performance of the two yachts. Taking data transmitted from the yachts, including wind speed and direction, boatspeed, rig tensions and angles of rudder and trim tab, a computer aboard their accompanying tender would instantaneously compare the performances of the yachts. Another special program was designed to ensure that the yachts' instruments were perfectly calibrated to prevent any distortions in the original data from the yachts' sensors.

But when the yachts began sailing together in Perth just a fortnight before the first race was to start, there was little opportunity to evaluate them. Both had to be removed from the water for modifications.

Running out of time for full preparations was not the exclusive domain of the crews of the *Azzurras*. Other challengers and defenders were also wishing they had more time. But none were in such dire straits as the Italians. While the best prepared groups had developed and tested different configurations for their boats to handle the different weather patterns over the long summer, the Italians would have been happy to have tried their boats in any configuration. After the glory of their first challenge in 1983, their 1987 America's Cup campaign had become a nightmare.

As September drew to a close, with both boats still out of the water the favoured plan was to enter *Azzurra 3* in the preliminary series of the Louis Vuitton Cup from 5-20 October. Under the rules the challengers would then be able to change their yachts, although at the cost of losing all points earned during the first series. If *Azzurra 3* was a failure, but *Azzurra 4* measured up to their hopes, the plan was then to take the latter yacht into the remainder of the series. She would have to be tuned quickly to win sufficient points in November and December to qualify for the semi-finals.

Simple becoming competitive in the 1987 America's Cup races will be a victory for the Yacht Club Costa Smeralda. Winning races along the way will be a triumph. Then it will be back to the drawing board again to put together, from scratch, a 12-Metre campaign for 1991. The battle for the right to design the *Azzurras* of the future should prove interesting. Sciomachen says that, given time, he would build from fibreglass.

ITALIA

First In, Best Dressed

We don't think we will win the Cup this time but we do hope to get a good place. This is our first experience and simply to be there is an historical success for us.''

Rare frankness from a man charged with promoting the image of an America's Cup syndicate. But the man is an unusual find among the America's Cup world. He is Dr Maurizio Gucci, grandson to the founder of one of the world's most famous fashion houses and today, after a bitter family struggle, head of the House of Gucci.

Gucci is one of 13 major Italian companies behind the second Italian group to challenge for the Cup, the Consorzio Italia representing the country's oldest yacht club, the Yacht Club Italiano of Genoa. Their entry into the Cup scene was a result of rivalry, tinged perhaps, with a little jealousy as they had watched the new Yacht Club Costa Smeralda headed by the Aga Khan, grab the nation's imagination and support with its first challenge in 1983.

Soon after the Australians left Newport, Rhode Island with the America's Cup under careful guard, the new syndicate went into action, signing up 10 major sponsors at $600,000 each and grabbing some of the yachtsmen from the Azzurra syndicate. Publicly relations between the two syndicates were cordial, but behind the scenes there was intense competition.

As a design benchmark, the syndicate purchased the boat beaten by *Australia II* for the right to challenge in 1983, the British 12-Metre *Victory 83*. It was important to have a 12-Metre yacht to measure against their own new designs. Performance figures from that boat could be analysed by their computers and used to test changes to the new boats. *Victory 83* was the best possible purchase for the group as it had been the most successful conventional Twelve in Newport.

In mid-1984, crew training began under skipper Lorenzo Bortolotti. While he acted as tactician as well as organising the crew, his helmsman was Flavio Scala who, in 1983, had steered *Azzurra* until the elimination trials when he quit after the syndicate refused to give him complete control over the campaign.

The Consorzio Italia saw the 1984 12-Metre World championships as their first opportunity to show ''the upstarts'' from the young Yacht Club Costa Smeralda a thing or two on their own waters. From a fleet of seven Twelves, the two Italian crews won their trials to make the final an all-Italian affair. As the delighted nation wagered on the outcome, potential backers prepared to decide which group they should put their money and support behind. In the end it was the Italia syndicate which won the day with *Victory 83* easily defeating *Azzurra*.

At the same time the design company of Giorgetti and Magrini was planning a new wing keeled Twelve for the group. For 15 years they had dominated yacht design in Italy, vying with *Azzurra's* designer Andrea Vallicelli for the growing market. More than 70 designs from Giorgio Magrini and Franco Giorgetti were on Italian waters including racing

The two Italias *in light airs off Fremantle at last. The first* (I7) *was an indifferent performer in its summer.*

12
I-7

Concentration by Chieffi in light airs in Fremantle.

Giorgetti Magrini

Tomasso Chieffi

Aldo Migliaccio

Dr Maurizio Gucci

Flavio Scala at the helm of Italia *during 1986 World championships before being one of several to be sacked.*

The first Italia *punching into head seas off Perth.*

and cruising yachts, trawlers and other working craft.

Like all other challenging syndicates they sought as much technological assistance as possible. Among the syndicate's sponsors were two organisations capable of providing major input for the design program. One was Aermacchi, the aircraft design and manufacturing giant which has produced more than 60 prototypes and 7,000 aeroplanes since 1913. The other was Shipyard Intermarine, the country's leader in the research and development of advanced marine propulsion systems and the design of small warships.

The long term program called for two new boats, the first to catch up with the wing keel breakthrough of *Australia II*, and the second to go beyond. The original plan was to modify *Victory 83*, which had already had its conventional low aspect keel fitted with delta wings by designer Ian Howlett when he was experimenting with wings early in 1983. Winglets attached to the British trialhorse *Australia* had been a success, but on *Victory 83* they had not brought the same marked improvement to her performance and the designer had abandoned the idea. After the Italian designers investigated the possibility of fitting a winged keel, they concluded that it would be more constructive to go straight into a new boat.

Computer and wind tunnel testing facilities were supplied by Aermacchi, which had sophisticated flow programs for its aircraft designers. A 12-Metre yacht was no problem for the company's specialists – in addition to aircraft they had already applied their expertise to racing cars and motor cycles.

However, tank testing was a problem, as the only large tank in the country was the Navy's in Rome, which lacked the fine details required for a comparatively small boat. With the Royal Perth Yacht Club's approval, the designers turned to the Maritime Research Institute of the Netherlands where Ben Lexcen had proved in 1983 that technology could help designers break traditional barriers. But that right was removed in 1985 and they were forced to turn to a smaller tank in Trieste to test one tenth sized models and compare those results to what they had learned in Holland.

"We put eight months of research into the first *Italia*," designer Georgetti Magrini recalled. "We used only those solutions we were sure about. If other solutions were at all risky then we did not use them, so *Italia* was a very conventional design. We always planned that the second boat would be more radical."

The syndicate had established a close working relationship

with America's Eagle syndicate after having had their skipper Rod Davis aboard *Victory 83* as tactician in the 1984 World championships. While they waited for the launch of their new boat, the Italian crew spent three months in Newport Beach, California, sailing *Victory 83* against the Americans in their trialhorse *Magic*. In September they returned to the Porto Rotondo Yacht Club in Genoa for the launch of *Italia*.

The elegant gun barrel grey hull was, as promised, a conservative Twelve with most of its volume around the winged keel. A sharply angled trailing edge ended slightly for'ard of the aft edge of flared wings, similar in shape to the tail of a whale. *Italia* was one of the smallest yachts in the first generation of post-*Australia II* wing keeled Twelves. Measuring 64 ft 2 in (19.55 m) overall; on the waterline she was 44 ft 7 in (13.6 m), in beam 12 ft 7 in (3.85 m) and she displaced 60,620 lb (27,500 kg).

For two months the new Twelve worked up in Sardinia against trialhorse *Victory 83*, but the racing was disappointing and inconclusive as the winds stayed unusually light, with the older Twelve winning most of the races.

While the two Italian syndicates refused to race each other, despite the fact that they were sailing within sight of each other, that did not stop the "poaching" of crews. The *Italia* syndicate was rocked by the defection of skipper Lorenzo Bortolotti to *Azzurra*. Bortolotti was frustrated by not having complete control and quit in protest. His was the first of several disturbing switches between the rival syndicates over the next two years. In October 1985, *Victory 83* and *Italia* were shipped to Australia where the syndicate had a very important appointment in the 1986 World championships, not only to race against the rest of the world, but also the new *Azzurra* of their rivals.

In Fremantle the syndicate burst onto the scene in a blaze of fashion. Decked out in specially designed gear by Gucci, *Italia's* yachtsmen were the fashion success of the year. A new currency materialised overnight, with some Cup followers prepared to swap *anything* for a Gucci *Italia* shirt or shoes.

Marketing manager Dr Maurizio Gucci was living up to his promise to promote the syndicate. "The Consorzio has a nose for business and we use the America's Cup to show our new country. Italy is known all over the world for its beautiful countryside and food and that is very important. But there is also our high technology. For example, our marine industry sells military boats and technology to America, to Australia –

all over the world.

"Each sponsor is giving something to create the trade mark *Italia*. Others take the trade mark of the boat in order to sell products, but we don't. Our sponsors give things like aircraft technology, fluid and chemical technology. We at Gucci give the trademark its image. It is important that *Italia* helps show the rest of the world that Italy does not just live on its past history. It is a young country which recognises the times it lives in."

But appearances count for little when sailing aboard a 12-Metre yacht. In the World championships *Italia* did not cover herself with glory. In the seven race series she had a scorecard of fifth, fifth, eighth, tenth, did not finish, disqualified and tenth to finish in the lowly position of ninth overall. It was a traumatic series for the Italians. After their promising positions in the first two races, it was all downhill. In the two windiest races they lost men overboard as their lean hull crashed through the big waves and the chop caused by other boats. *Italia* finished just two places ahead of the syndicate's trialhorse *Victory 83*, which had its own problems including a broken mast. The only redeeming feature of the regatta was beating the other Italian syndicate with its second yacht carrying the name *Azzurra*.

For the syndicate it was a difficult time. To have put so much into their Cup effort, only to find themselves among the backmarkers in the fleet, was traumatic. Heads had to roll and more thought was needed for the second boat.

Helmsman Flavio Scala quit, just as he had from *Azzurra* in 1983. Tomasso Chieffi was promoted to his place. The 25-year-old Chieffi, a world champion in the 470 class, had helmed *Victory 83* in Fremantle and was not suprised to get the number one helming position.

Aldo Migliaccio was promoted to skipper. A Star and Finn class champion who had also sailed at Olympic level, he had skippered *Victory 83* to victory in the first World championships in 1984. In his charge was a comparatively small crew which he kept firmly divided into two, one group to sail the boat, the other to prepare it ashore. "Yes, I am hard on my men. I know what I want and while I talk to everyone about any problem, I usually have the right solution already worked out. When we are racing, the crew returns to the dock, talks to the shore crew preparing the boat and then leaves it to them to go off for a meeting or training."

Fashions in the bow – Gucci style.

The designers of the first *Italia* were not disappointed with their boat, although Magrini conceeded that the results were not as good as they had hoped. "It was still a good result; we were happy with her hull and the performance."

But the America's Cup is a tough world for designers. Before the first *Italia's* potential had even been put to the test in Australia, the worried syndicate had restructured the design team. Intermarine and Aermacchi had earlier provided facilities and input, but for the second *Italia* they were to do more. Intermarine's designer Mike Trimming, a half-British designer famous for a revolutionary minesweeper that had been sold around the world, was put in charge of the program. Aermacchi's Raffaele Marazzi was also to have more say.

Trimming was far from put off by having to direct his skills to a yacht. "It's very different, but I have sailed a lot and I have designed successful warships before. The only difference is in the speeds. I was called to come up with something different to the normal run of Twelves. *Italia* had been a logical development of *Victory 83*; the new boat was to be slightly radical.

We looked at a lot of things including having an IOR type boat which would be a very wide boat with a flat bottom and a powerful stern. In the test tank that gave us very good results over 24 knots. However, it had a lot of wetted surface area which was negative under 18 knots, so we had been wasting our time. After that we came back to a solution which is not a normal Twelve but which is a wide boat at the top, fairly narrow at the waterline and very deep."

Italia II was indeed different, bigger and with topsides that flared out from the waterline to the wide gunwales to set her apart from any other Twelves. Short on the waterline, she had long, fine overhangs for added waterline length when heeled in the strong winds. In addition, the hull had considerable sheer which inevitably prompted comparisons with *French Kiss*. It's sail area was considerably reduced, to the stage where, again unlike any other Twelve, the foot of the headsail was so short that its tack was mounted more than a metre aft of the bow.

"We were designing for Fremantle conditions", Trimming explained. "Of course it had to be a trade-off between waterline length and sail area. We chose to have minimum waterline for less weight, very long overhangs and smaller sail area."

Statistics released by the syndicate showed just some of the differences in approach.

ITALIA

ITALIA
LOA .... 64 ft 2 in (19.55 m)
LWL .... 44 ft 7 in (13.60 m)
Beam .... 12 ft 7 in (3.85 m)
Disp .... 60,620 lb (27,500 kg)

ITALIA II
LOA .... 65 ft 7 in (20.00 m)
LWL .... 47 ft 6 in (14.50 m)
Beam .... 14 ft 9 in (4.53 m)
Disp .... 58,000 lb (26,300 kg)

After the thrill of the launch in June 1986, disaster for the syndicate was not far away. As the crew prepared for their third day's sailing aboard the new boat, the mobile crane lifting it into the water collapsed, dropping the boat onto the edge of the dock and falling onto the yacht as it bounced into the water.

She sank, taking the offending crane with her. When the yacht was recovered the next day, it was extensively damaged around the mast step and chainplates. Several beams had to be replaced, as well as the aluminium plating.

The boat had been booked to leave Italy in July for Australia and its final tune up against the original *Italia*, which had been left in Australia over the southern winter. Having to rebuild the yacht put their plans back a month. It was not until late September that *Italia II* joined its crew in Fremantle, barely giving them time to get to know the yacht, let alone tune it to its optimum before the racing began.

In Australia, more vital time was lost preparing the boat for measurement. The team found the measurers were strictly enforcing the rule outlawing any bumps or hollows above the waterline, and it took days to get the surface absolutely smooth to qualify as a 12-Metre. While other challengers were busy making final preparations, *Italia's* yachtsmen could do little but look forward to the preliminary series in October to really test and tune their boat.

Bad luck is part of any sport; the unforeseen will always be waiting for the unwary. The inexperienced *Italia* syndicate has had more than its share just getting to the 1987 America's Cup. But for the youngest challenging crew in Perth it is all experience, and if they go into the semi-finals they will consider themselves winners. After all, they point out, it took the Australians four attempts to beat the Americans. They will also count it a victory if they beat their fellow Italians aboard *Azzurra*. That is added motivation to overcome the odds and the setbacks.

FRENCH KISS

Vive La France

The headlines in Australian newspapers during February 1986 were seemingly endless as sub-editors strove to outdo each other in their play on words with Cup newcomer *French Kiss*.

"Gate-crashing *French Kiss* almost has the last laugh."

"RPYC will not embrace *French Kiss*."

"*French Kiss*: We are not being rude to anybody."

"A *Kiss* is just a kiss –isn't it?"

"Lip smacking *French Kiss* rides the waves."

"High winds blow *French Kiss* to the victory line."

As if having the first 12-Metre regatta in Australian waters with the Australians as favourites was not enough, added to the mixture was a risque French group cocking its Gallic nose at the establishment.

The fuss was all over the name of the latest 12-Metre group to sail under the French tricolour. The boat's name appeared to be blatantly in breach of Rule 26 of the International Yacht Racing Rules which bans commercial names and advertising on the boats and sails. While a French kiss may have been quite fashionable, *French Kiss* seemed too close to the name of the company which was sponsoring the new yacht on behalf of the La Rochelle Yacht Club, the Kis Instant Service Company.

Flaunting its new name, the yacht won the first battle of the war when it almost won its first race, an invitation event before the 1986 World Championships. The yacht was leading on the last windward leg to the finish, with the New York Yacht Club's *America II US42* and Alan Bond's *Australia III*, when her mast crashed over the side.

The battle of words continued ashore. "This is a problem of Anglo-Saxon attitudes," claimed Paul-Armand Blouzet of Kis Australia. "No it's not," replied the Royal Perth Yacht Club. "It's a problem of the Rules and we must ensure the stature of the Cup is maintained."

While the French gathered a flotilla of lawyers to fight out the battle before the International jury that would adjudicate on the championships, they agreed to tape over the name for the second invitation race.

Other syndicates waited with mixed feelings for the jury to come up with its verdict. Some laughed it off as a foregone conclusion. "If they get away with that I will have to call my next boat *Australia Fourex*," joked Alan Bond, who owned

Trialling with New Zealand *in Fremantle led to one close encounter of a damaging kind.*

the brewery which sold most of its product under the brandname XXXX. "I'm going to be in a lot of trouble at home if they win as I have knocked back a lot of money because I would not risk even the most subtle reference to a backer with our yacht's name," said one of the heads of the New York Yacht Club's syndicate. Others, having problems raising money, began thinking about new colours and names for their boats if the French succeeded.

The French were quite open about the matter. The America's Cup, they claimed, had become so expensive that it had to rely on commercial support if it were to continue. It was only reasonable, they argued, that the company putting up the money for their challenge should receive recognition for doing so.

Privately they were delighted with the fuss. Even if the jury did rule the name illegal, they had received so much publicity that it would have all been worthwhile. The name was firmly in everybody's minds, and if they were forced to abandon it they would simply paint a set of pouting lips on the side of the boat, next to the new name, and not think any more about it.

Much to everybody's surprise, the jury found in their favour. *French Kiss* could remain *French Kiss*, for the time being anyway. The parties went long into the Fremantle night. It was an unlikely ending to a new twist in the long America's Cup story.

That it should come from the land across the Channel from where the America's Cup began was perhaps not so surprising. The French had been trying to win the America's Cup since 1970, when the inventor of the ballpoint pen, Baron Bich, rode into Newport, Rhode Island with style and extravagance that left even New York's wealthy blinking in amazement. Bich fitted neatly into the traditional mould of earlier challengers, full of goodwill and good intentions, with plenty of wealth to back up his Cup bid but no idea of how to go about the task of succeeding.

The Baron tried three times with as many boats to win the Cup. But each time he ran into superior Australian boats in the challengers' trials and never made it into the Cup itself. While he added competition and colour to the scene, he was to be best remembered for taking over the helm of his first boat in a last ditch move to avoid going down 4-0 to the Australians in 1970, only to get lost in the notorious Newport fog and so be

Extreme sheer in bow to reduce nose diving in choppy Fremantle waters.

forced to withdraw.

In 1983 the Baron was missing but his *France III* again carried the tricolour into battle for her new owner Yves Rousset-Rouard, the producer of highly successful soft core pornography films. While he believed in his mission, not enough of his compatriots did, and the boat suffered seriously from lack of finance. After 1983 he quietly slipped from the Cup scene.

But when Australia won the Cup and the world was seized by America's Cup fever, two brothers who were sporting heroes in France decided to leap into the breach. They were Marc and Yves Pajot, renowned dinghy and long distance sailors who were among the country's highest paid sportsmen.

While they planned separately to tackle the new challenge, both were assisted by friends in high places, notably President Mitterand's chief of staff Jean Glavany – a keen yachtsman who was convinced that France had the technology and the people to win the Cup. Carefully arranging support from people and companies in the right places, he convinced the government that it should supply initial funds for both challenges.

It was then up to the brothers Pajot to sell themselves to backers. It was Marc Pajot who hit the jackpot in the form of Serge Crasnianski, like himself a young man in a hurry. It is part of contemporary French corporate history that the nuclear scientist was horrified, on losing his keys in the 1960s, to discover it would take days to have a replacement set made. Seeing an opportunity to make a franc or two, he established Kis – Key Instant Services – selling key cutting machines to shopkeepers around France and eventually all over Europe. Instant shoe repair equipment followed, then engraving tools and colour photocopiers. In 1980 instant photo processing was his next idea, and his company was to become a world leader in this enormously lucrative market. From humble beginnings, Kis became a highly successful multinational corporation, with the Russian-born Crasnianski held up as an example of what the businessmen of France could do when they put their minds to it.

Crasnianski was a marketing wizard, and before Marc Pajot arrived on his doorstep he had been studying the use of sporting sponsorships to trumpet the name Kis internationally. He became convinced that the America's Cup would be exactly the right vehicle and that Marc Pajot would be the right man.

Pajot had spent most of his life sailing racing types of

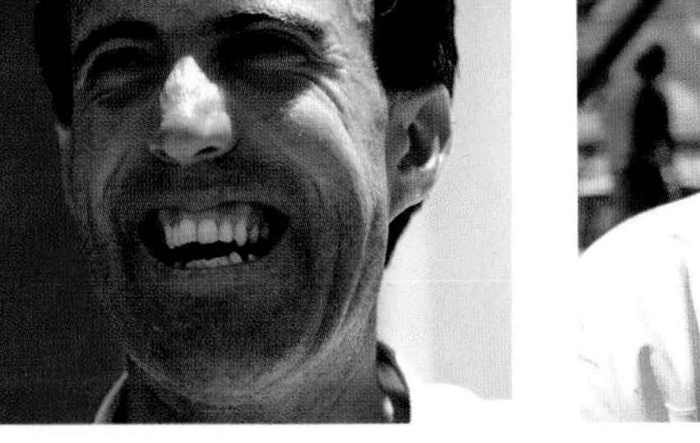

Marc Pajot

Designer Philippe Briand

Transom was to be modified over Australian winter.

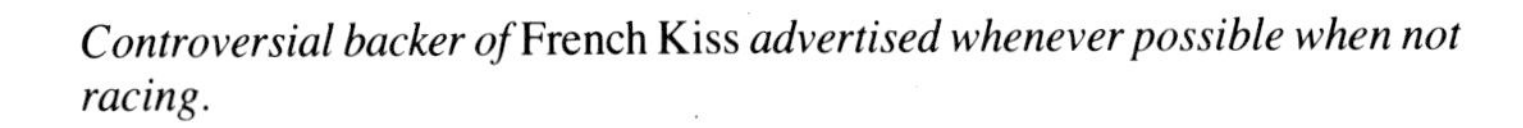

Controversial backer of French Kiss *advertised whenever possible when not racing.*

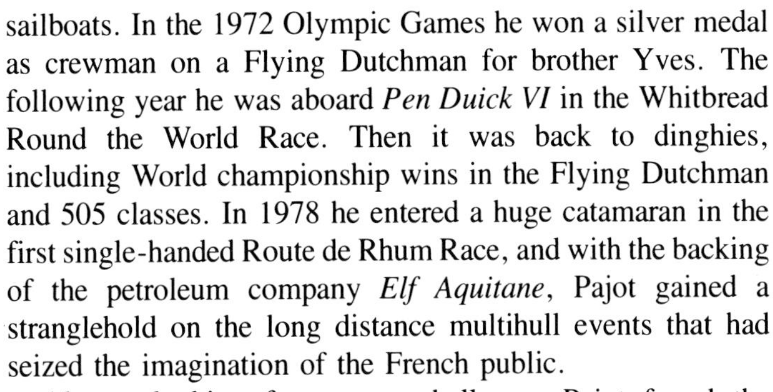

sailboats. In the 1972 Olympic Games he won a silver medal as crewman on a Flying Dutchman for brother Yves. The following year he was aboard *Pen Duick VI* in the Whitbread Round the World Race. Then it was back to dinghies, including World championship wins in the Flying Dutchman and 505 classes. In 1978 he entered a huge catamaran in the first single-handed Route de Rhum Race, and with the backing of the petroleum company *Elf Aquitane*, Pajot gained a stranglehold on the long distance multihull events that had seized the imagination of the French public.

Always looking for a new challenge, Pajot found the America's Cup answered his needs. "I had sailed 10 years in dinghies and 10 years single-handed and I needed a change. The America's Cup was the best option because not only was it the best sailing; it was more than that. It was a concept of a boat, a team, having to find the money and communications to make it all work. All four concepts were as important as each other. And the time was right. With the Cup going to Australia we felt it would be far more interesting to more countries."

Quickly he found a willing supporter in Philippe Briand, a young yacht designer with a string of successes on the fiercely competitive IOR and Ton Cup offshore racing circuit. Briand also had 12-Metre experience. At the age of 19 in 1977 he had worked with Sweden's Pelle Petterson to design that country's first 12-Metre, *Sverige*.

After returning to France to establish his own design company, Briand quickly began to challenge the leading European designers. Three Ton Cups went his way and his maxi design *L'Esprit d'Equipe* tackled the 1981 Whitbread Round the World Race although a broken spar dashed her chances.

In 1984 Briand and Pajot shared a burning ambition to tackle the America's Cup and in Jean Glavany they had a willing ally. Through initial funding supplied by the government they were able to purchase the 1977 Sparkman & Stephens design *Enterprise* and the 1980 defender *Freedom*. Briand was promised government support to research his own 12-Metre design. When Crasnianski finally promised to bankroll the remaining 85 per cent of the $10 million budget in early 1985, it was full steam ahead.

As well as national government support, the syndicate benefited from local backing as well, with the regional government building them a complete training complex at Sete on the Mediterranean coast and providing free accommodation. It was a gesture that would be more than amply rewarded should their yacht return with the Cup.

Briand was given complete access to the Paris military test tanks, but they were designed to test big ships and proved quite unsuitable for 12-Metres. He decided to ignore the tanks and concentrate on computer design instead. To help develop a sophisticated design program he turned to the aerodynamicists at Dassault, the military aircraft design company with the successful Mirage fighter aircraft among its range of products. Like other Cup syndicates, they developed flow and pressure simulation programs using three dimensional studies to even out the flow over the hull and study the winged keel.

For comparison, the computers were fed the lines of *Courageous* and pictures, and as much information as possible about *Australia II*.

Relying on the computers allowed no room for error. Pajot admits it was a testing time as they waited for the results. "I was nervous about the computer and no tank testing, I'm always nervous when something is completely new. We didn't have time to go back and make any changes and with such close competition we knew one mistake could make all the difference. But she is a very aerodynamically designed boat. Long and sleek with a little less sail area. Everything is a question of balance. I don't like the word revolutionary, but it is different, yes."

Computers also played a big role in the design of the sails. Under the leadership of Luc Gellusseau, the design program was developed with the assistance of several government-supported research bodies including CRAIN, the Centre for Architectural Research for the French nautical industry, and CNES, the national centre for space research. As well as using wind tunnels to check shape design, the team used a unique cloth that had been developed for a joint space venture between France and the USSR. In the late 1970s a special space probe was planned, with a French balloon to be sent to the planet Venus, via a Russian rocket. The scientists developed a special composite of Kevlar cloth glued to a polyester film, and while the space probe was abandoned, the material re-emerged in the sails of *French Kiss*.

Pajot meanwhile was building up his crew aboard the two old Twelves on the Mediterranean. As tactician, he recruited 34-year-old Marc Bouet, three times Olympian, World Flying Dutchman champion in 1979 and three times European champion in 470 dinghies. Bouet was also in charge of developing the onboard computer systems.

After 10 years of single-handed sailing, Pajot, with complete control of everything except money, was finding it difficult leading a team again. "It is very, very hard. Sometimes you are the boss, sometimes their friend, sometimes you are somewhere in between. I don't like to mix socially with the crew. We work together, we sail together, I'm with them most of the time. But we all need to get away from each other sometimes."

When *French Kiss* went public late in 1985 it was in style.

Yves Pajot – older brother of the two and fiercely competitive.

Her christening took place as she sat on a semi-trailer beneath the Eiffel Tower in the heart of Paris. One thousand voices sang her praises from a massed choir, 20,000 people looked on as the country's elite admired her grey hull. The name *French Kiss* gleamed from the hull and, in smaller letters beside each steering wheel, was painted Marc Pajot's name. Any cynics in the crowd may have wondered how he would perform if he needed guidance to his position on the yacht.

But after a period of racing against *Freedom*, the new yacht's designer was happy. "She is faster, points higher and tacks quicker than *Freedom*." Then it was off to Australia for the yacht's first real test, the 1986 World 12-Metre championships. At the same time, work had begun on a second Briand design.

In Australia before the *French Kiss* crew had arrived were Yves Pajot, and his team representing the Société Nautique de Marseilles. They had purchased *Challenge 12* and *France III* and were working them up during the Australian summer, while an Andrieu design was built in France. However, they had not found a benefactor like Crasnianski and were struggling for funds. Before the championships began they were forced to dry dock the boats and return to France in an effort to raise more money to continue.

That left the way clear for *French Kiss*, and the team hit town amid a blaze of glory, winning the fashion stakes ashore with a bold range of clothing and promising to perform at sea.

When *French Kiss* lined up against other new Twelves in Fremantle she was obviously different to the rest of the fleet. Her most striking feature was a dramatically swept up sheerline at the bow. With a short waterline at about 44 ft (13.5 m) she still had a smaller sail area at about 1,700 sq ft (157 sq m), but she carried a lot of volume around the keel and paid a penalty in girth measurements. As it turned out she was very fast in strong breezes, despite being less stable with lighter displacement than some other boats. Her long overhangs drooped close to the waterline and, with full stern quarters and a broad stern, her waterline increased significantly when she heeled. She appeared to carry a keel with either a plumb or aft-swept leading edge, with winglets set well aft.

Last minute reprieve for Challenge Francais arriving in Fremantle late September without tuning.

At sea the French not only won admiring looks for their speed; their support tenders gained wolf whistles as well for their names including *Kiss me Tender* and *I'm a French Kiss Too*.

As the 16 yachts battled out the World championships, *French Kiss* discovered an Achilles heel. Her light wind performance was poor and she could only manage to finish mid-fleet. Other troubles dogged her performance: her crew complained that their on-board instruments only worked 30 per cent of the time and in another race they were pushed back in the fleet by seaweed caught around their appendages. But they still managed to win two races (one when they passed a crippled *America II* on the final leg) and gain a second to finish in fifth position overall. Their inconsistent performance was put down to poor light weather sails and lack of racing.

Other syndicates were impressed by their sheer speed in heavy airs, but not by their overall performance. "She is as erratic as a misguided missile," was the comment from Alan Bond's veteran executive director Warren Jones. "The boat is obviously very fast, but the trouble with the French is in their nature," 1983 winner John Bertrand wrote: "They always have 11 individuals on their boats, not teams of eleven."
Briand believed his Twelve had only been sailed to 60 per cent of its potential in the World championships and he said he would be modifying the boat to improve her light weather performance. The second boat, which was already under construction, would be scrapped because he was confident his modifications would improve *French Kiss* considerably. Syndicate backer Serge Crasnianski, who had flown in with 25 French journalists at his expense to make sure the good news reached home, added that there was not enough money available for the second boat, so he was undoubtedly relieved to hear Briand confidently predict that it would be unnecessary.

The partnership between the two self-driven, successful men, Pajot and Crasnianski, was far from made in heaven. Repeatedly they clashed over money during the campaign. While the crew prepared for the racing in Australia, in Paris Crasnianski had told the press that if they did not perform he would scrap the whole project. Crasnianski freely admitted that he did not care about the sailing. "I like sailing but I have no time for it, I am too busy. My involvement is from a marketing point of view and it is working perfectly. It's working in France and overseas. We are using it to thrust into the Australian market which is difficult to crack."

Pajot commented: "There have been clashes with Kis, particularly over the second boat. But that is normal because the sponsor pays the money and he can decide whether or not to give us the money. Then it is our problem to deal with one or two boats. Actually I think we have a very good sponsor because he knows nothing about sailing."

Back in France, *French Kiss* underwent modifications to her keel and afterbody. Just 150 kilometres away, Pajot's brother Yves had finally been forced to admit defeat and his syndicate went into bankruptcy. The boat, *Challenge France,* had been completed but the bills remained unpaid. Several companies were interested in reviving the project at a bargain basement price, but it was not until August, just two months before the elimination series was to begin, that the courts gave the go-ahead for the boat to be given another chance. So it was to everyone's surprise that a second French Twelve arrived in Fremantle just before the challengers' trials began, with Yves Pajot desperately preparing his challenge bid.

Meanwhile his brother Marc was also preparing for his summer of reckoning. "Yes it is the first time I have ever match raced. But all the skippers in such a competition have lots of firsts. All of them are good, the differences are few. When I sailed in the Olympics for the first time I won a medal. When I won the Route de Rhum it was my first single-handed race.

"This is not just important for me, it's important for France also. Sailing is a new sport. Ten years ago there were no boats in France, it has really grown. The Cup will be important for France because I am so popular. If I have something to say I can go to the television networks and talk to the people about the new way I am going. We can show this competition is a technical competition and not a financial one as it was before with people like Baron Bich and Peter de Savary. We are trying to give the competition a new image."

Glossary

ABACK With the wind on the wrong side of the sails (caught aback).

ABEAM At right angles to the centreline of the yacht.

ABOUT To turn the yacht bow-first through the wind so that it is sailing on the opposite tack (go about).

AERODYNAMICS The science of the dynamics of solid bodies in motion in air.

AEROFOIL A curved shape capable of developing life forces in the flow of a fluid medium (also AIRFOIL).

AFT Towards the back or stern.

AMIDSHIPS The middle section of the yacht, between fore and aft.

APPARENT WIND The combination of true wind and the wind developed by boat speed; the wind the yacht feels and, effectively, in which it is sailed.

ASPECT RATIO The relationship between the vertical and horizontal dimensions of the yacht's rig. High aspect ratio rigs have tall masts and short booms; low aspect ratio rigs have the reverse.

ASTERN Behind the yacht; in the direction of the stern.

BACK Reverse a sail; get the wind on the wrong side.

BACKSTAY A wire support from the top of the mast to the stern to prevent the mast toppling foward and to allow sail shapes to be altered by varying tension (see diagram).

BACKWIND Wind deflected from a forward sail onto the sail behind it, e.g. from the jib onto the mainsail.

BALLAST Lead weight placed in the keel and sometimes the bottom of the hull to give the yacht stability.

BATTEN Thin strip of strong but flexible material (timber, fibreglass or a sandwich of exotic materials) placed in a pocket in the leech of a sail to help it hold its shape (see diagram).

BEAM The yacht's width at its widest point.

BEAR AWAY Alter course away from the wind.

BEAT To sail to windward, with the wind first on one side and then on the other. A yacht cannot sail directly into the wind and so must zigzag, sailing as close to the wind as possible on each tack (beating to windward).

BEFORE THE WIND Sailing with the wind blowing from astern.

BILGE Curved part of the yacht's hull beneath the water where it turns towards the keel; the interior of the hull below the floorboards where water collects.

BLOCK Nautical term for a pulley; device with a grooved sheave mounted in a framework which has a point of attachment, and used to gain directional or mechanical advantage on a line.

BOAT SPEED Constantly changing speed at which the yacht moves through the water.

BOLT ROPE Heavy duty line attached along the luff of the mainsail to fit inside the mast track when the sail is hoisted. The mainsail foot may also have some form of bolt rope to fit or zip inside a boom track.

BOOM The spar to which the mainsail foot is attached, usually made of aluminium or sometimes carbon fibre (see diagram).

BOOM VANG A tensioning system - on most 12-Metres hydraulically operated - to prevent the boom rising or skying downwind and to allow alteration of sail shape (see diagram).

BOSUN'S CHAIR Sling chair suspended from a halyard and used to raise someone when work must be done aloft.

BOW The forwardmost part of the yacht (see diagram).

BOWMAN Member of the crew responsible for work on the foredeck, e.g. attaching the jib to the forestay for hoisting, pulling the jib onto the foredeck when it is lowered; managing the spinnaker pole during spinnaker work; calling the distances between the bow and rival yachts during manoeuvres,etc.

BRACE A line used to trim the position of the spinnaker pole (also GUY).

BROACH To go out of control when running before the wind and sea, usually resulting in the boat being turned sideways and laid over. Severe broaches often result in damage, particularly when the yacht spins to leeward through a gybe (Chinese gybe or all-standing gybe). In severe conditions the spinnaker may have to be dropped before the boat can be brought back to an even keel and steering control regained.

BROAD REACH Sailing with the wind just abaft (behind) abeam.

BULB Torpedo-shaped section of lead attached to the bottom of the keel to provide additional stability.

BULKHEAD Structural component inside the yacht's hull, running across the yacht to give strength and rigidity.

BUOY ROOM Rule for buoy rounding, allowing an inside yacht which holds an overlap on an outside yacht to claim ample room to round closest to the buoy when the outside yacht reaches two boat lengths from the buoy.

BUSTLE Area of the hull between the keel and the rudder (see diagram).

BY THE LEE Sailing downwind at an angle greater than 180 degrees to true wind; usually resulting in a gybe.

CAMBER Concavity of a sail (also DRAFT).

CLEAT A fitting in which a line under strain can be secured.

CLEW The lower after corner of a sail, where the leech meets the foot (see diagram).

CLOSE HAULE Sailing to windward with the sails sheeted in hard; holding a course as close as practicable towards the wind.

CLOSE WINDED Describes a yacht capable of sailing very close to the wind.

COAMING Raised ledges on the foredeck to prevent as much water as possible flowing back along the decks when the yacht takes waves over the bow.

COCKPIT Sunken wells in the deck where the crew are situated.

COFFEE GRINDERS Large winching devices which provide great mechanical advantage when pulling on lines under load, e.g. sheets and halyards.

DACRON Synthetic sail material used in working sails.

DISPLACEMENT The weight of water displaced by a yacht.

DOWNHAUL A tensioning system attached to the mainsail tack and used to pull the luff downwards for sail shape alteration.

DRAFT The depth of the keel in the water; also, the depth of fullness of the sail.

DRAG Resistance caused by a shape in a fluid medium.

DRIFTER A very light weight spinnaker or genoa.

EASE To slacken the sails, using the sheets or halyards.

EASE AWAY To bear away from the wind.

FAIRLEAD A fitting used to alter the direction of a line to give it the best angle from a sail or block to a cleat or winch.

FETCH When a yacht sailing to windward can reach her objective without making another tack.

FITTING An item of marine hardware.

FLAT A sail with minimum draft (opposite of FULL).

FOOT The bottom part of the sail.

FOOTING Moving through the water to windward with good boat speed.

FORE AND AFT From bow to stern, in the direction of the keel.

FOREDECK Area of the deck between the bow and the mast (see diagram).

FOREFOOT Underwater area of the hull between the bow and the keel (see diagram).

FORESTAY Wire support which runs from the mast to the bow (see diagram).

FORETRIANGLE The triangle formed by the deck, the front of the mast and

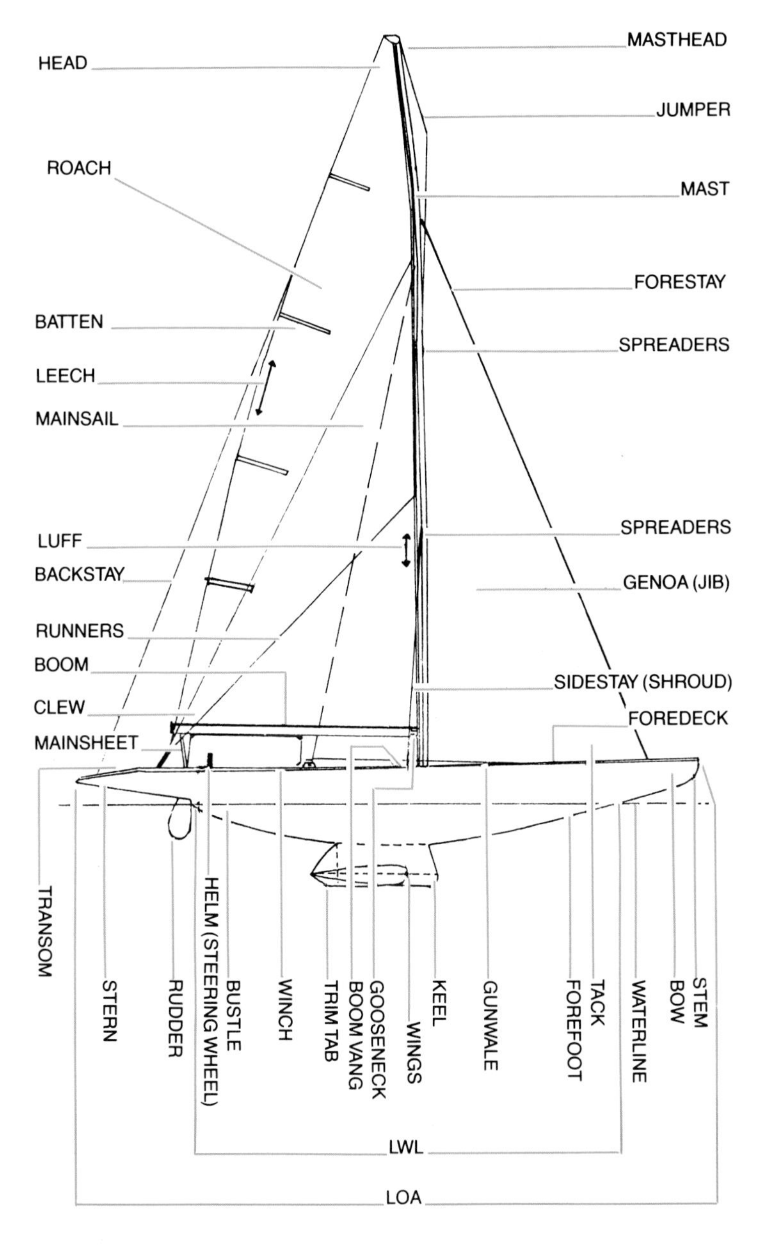

the forestay.

FREEBOARD The distance from the gunwale to the waterline of the yacht.

FULL A sail with a large amount of draft (opposite of FLAT).

GENOA Any headsail which overlaps the mainsail; also called a JIB (see diagram).

GIRTH The fullness of the hull, measured from the deck down to the keel.

GO ABOUT Tack.

GOOSENECK Where the boom attaches to the mast (see diagram).

GRINDERS Members of the crew who operate the coffee grinders to tension the sheets or halyards under heavy load.

GUNWALE The outer edge or rail of the yacht at deck level (see diagram).

GUY A line used to trim the position of the spinnaker pole (also BRACE).

GYBE Change tack with the wind astern; putting the stern of the yacht through the eye of the wind rather than the bow, as in tacking.

HALYARD A line used to haul sails up and down the mast.

HATCH An opening in the deck giving access below.

HEAD The top of the sail (see diagram).

HEADER Shift of the wind which narrows its angle to the yacht's centreline, forcing the yacht to bear away when sailing to windward (opposite of LIFT).

HEADING UP Turning the yacht's bow towards the wind.

HEADSAIL Any sail used forward of the mast; usually refers to the genoa or jib (see diagram).

HEAD TO WIND When the bow is pointed into the eye of the wind. Yachts cannot sail in this direction and will stop with sails shaking (see also IRONS).

HEADWAY Forward motion.

HEEL To lean over.

HELM The steering wheel (see diagram).

HELMSMAN The person who steers at the helm.

HOBBYHORSING Aggravated pitching movement of the yacht, up and down fore and aft, when sailing through waves.

HULL SPEED The limit of speed imposed on a displacement hull by the resistance of its own wave systems. If it can break free of these systems and exceed its hull speed it is said to be planing.

HYDRAULICS Tensioning system using pressurised fluid; on 12-Metres used for a variety of purposes including tensioning of mast support stays, boom vang and boom outhaul, and maststep positioning.

HYDRODYNAMICS The science of forces exerted by or acted on liquids.

INBOARD Towards the centreline of the yacht.

IOR International Offshore Rule, in accordance with which yachts are measured and handicapped for offshore racing events.

IRONS A yacht is in irons when it has gone head to wind, has lost all headway and cannot be sailed off on either tack by steering alone. Co-ordination of sail trim and steering will be necessary to regain forward motion. JIB Headsail which may or may not overlap the mainsail (also GENOA) (see diagram).

JIBE See GYBE.

JUMPER A stay on the upper forward part of the mast (see diagram).

JURY RIG A makeshift rig used after equipment failure.

KEVLAR "Stronger than steel" synthetic fibre, gold in colour with excellent strength to weight, used in the cloth of modern working sails, particularly in high load areas such as the leech. Also used in ropes under high load.

KICKER See BOOM VANG.

KITE See SPINNAKER.

KNOCK See HEADER.

KNOT A nautical unit of speed; one nautical mile per hour equals 1.85 km/h.

LAY LINE Imaginary line marking the position from which a yacht can reach a buoy or objective on a close hauled course. If it approaches the buoy from a point to leeward of the line it will have to tack to reach the buoy, and will be said to have understood; if it approaches the buoy from a point to windward of the layline it will have to bear away and free sheets to reach the mark, and will be said to have overstood. As the wind shifts, so too do the laylines.

LEE The side away from the wind. May be the side sheltered from the wind or the side onto which will drive drifting objects.

LEE-BOW Tactical manoeuvre during close quarters racing, in which the disturbed air blowing aft and to windward from a yacht's sails is used to slow a rival yacht. To lee-bow a rival, the yacht positions itself on the leeward side with its bow ahead.

LEECH The back edge of a sail, running from the head to the clew (see diagram).

LEE HELM The amount of helm required to prevent a yacht pulling away from the wind (opposite to WEATHER HELM).

LEEWARD Away from the wind.

LEEWAY Distance the yacht slides to leeward (sideways) while sailing.

LENGTH The greatest length of the yacht is called length overall (LOA). The waterline (LWL) of the yacht is usually measured at the designed waterline, excluding overhangs at the bow and stern. Waterline length of 12-Metres is measured slightly above the designed waterline (see diagram).

LIFT A change in the wind direction allowing the yacht to point higher when sailing to windward (opposite of HEADER).

LOA See LENGTH (see diagram).

LUFF The forward edge of the sail running from the head to the tack. Also, the manoeuvre of altering course towards the wind until the boat is head to wind (see diagram).

LWL See LENGTH (see diagram).

MAINSAIL The sail set behind the mast, with its luff attached vertically to the aft section of the mast and its foot attached to the boom (see diagram).

MAINSHEET The line used to control the mainsail (see diagram).

MAST Aluminium spar stepped on the structural keel and held upright by stays to support the sails (see diagram).

MASTMAN Member of the crew positioned near the base of the mast and responsible for all duties in that area, particularly correct feeding of all halyards into and out of the mast.

MAST TRACK Groove on or in the mast in which the mainsail slides up when hoisted.

METRE RULE See INTRODUCTION and 12-METRE RULE.

MYLAR Very light, transparent synthetic film used in composite cloths for modern sails; often used in combination with Kevlar in working sails and increasingly employed in spinnaker cloths.

NYLON Material commonly used in the construction of spinnakers.

OFF THE WIND Sailing away from the wind.

ON THE WIND Sailing towards the wind as closely as possible (also CLOSE HAULED).

OUTBOARD Away from the centreline of the yacht.

OVERLAP The extension of a foresail (genoa or jib) aft of the mainsail luff. Also, term used when yachts are sailing beside each other, with neither clear ahead or astern.

OVERSTAND To sail past the layline to a mark (also OVERLAY).

PINCH To point the yacht's bow closer to the wind on a close hauled course than will provide optimum VMG. Often yachts will pinch to round a mark when they are slightly below the layline.

POINT To sail on a course close to the wind. "Out point" means to sail on a course closer to the wind than a rival yacht.

PORT The left side of the yacht when looking forward.

PORT TACK Tack the yacht is on when the wind is blowing over the port side and the sails are to starboard. A port tack yacht must give way to a starboard tack yacht.

QUARTER Either side of the yacht behind the beam.

RAKE The angle of the mast from the vertical.

RATCHET BLOCK A spring-loaded block in which sheet tension engages a pawl that allows the sheave to move only in the "trim" direction, taking up tension.

REACH To sail with the wind coming from abeam; course of sailing between close hauled and running downwind. SHY or CLOSE REACHING is with the wind forward of the beam; BROAD REACHING is with the wind aft of the beam.

REACHER See STAYSAIL.

RHUMB LINE Imaginary straight line between marks.

RIG A general description of the yacht's gear above the deck level; also the act of setting up the rigging and sails.

ROACH The curve of the leech (aft edge of the sail) (see diagram).

RUN Point of sailing where the wind is blowing from astern.

RUNNERS Stays which run from the aft section of the yacht to the upper section of the mast to provide support to and allow control of the rig (see diagram).

RUNNING RIGGING All lines used to hoist, control and trim the sails.

SET The direction of the tide or current, or the leeway of the yacht.

SEWER Below decks area, connected to the foredeck by a hatch, in which spinnakers and genoas are stored.

SEWERMAN Member of the crew responsible for the handling of sails in and out of the sewer.

SHEAVE The wheel of a block over which a rope or wire passes.

SHEER The curve of the yacht's rail from bow to stern.

SHEET The line used to control a sail's trim.

SHOOT THE MARK Manoeuvre employed when approaching the windward mark from below the layline; the helmsman may luff the yacht sharply to carry way around the mark rather than tacking twice for a safer but slower rounding.

SHROUD A wire which holds the mast upright at the sides, supporting the mast laterally (see diagram).

SHY REACH Sailing with the wind just ahead of the beam.

SKEG Continuation of the keel aft.

SLACK To ease or pay out a line.

SLOT The area between the aft portion of the genoa or jib and the leeward side of the mainsail.

SPAR The general term for any pole used to carry and give shape to the sails.

SPINNAKER The balloon-like sail used on the downwind legs (also KITE).

SPREADER Projections from the mast that spread the shrouds to provide more favourable angles between the shrouds and the mast (see diagram).

SQUARE To bring the spinnaker pole or boom more perpendicular to the centreline of the yacht, when bearing away before the wind.

STANDING RIGGING Rigging which is permanently attached and not movable.

STARBOARD The right side of the yacht when looking forward.

STARBOARD TACK Tack the yacht is on when the wind is blowing over the starboard side and the sails are to port. A starboard tack yacht has right of way over a port tack yacht.

STAYS Wires supporting the mast in a fore and aft direction.

STAYSAIL A triangular sail used between the mast and the spinnaker or reaching legs.

STEM The forwardmost section of the bow, running down to the waterline (see diagram).

STERN The aft section of the yacht (see diagram).

STIFF A yacht which tends to resist heeling forces and stands up relatively straight.

TACK The lower forward part of the sail where the luff meets the foot. Also, the side from which the wind is blowing (STARBOARD TACK) or the act of changing from one tack to another (see diagram).

TACKING Sailing to windward by a series of zigzags, passing from tack to tack through the eye of the wind.

TELLTALES Ribbons in the rigging or on the sails to indicate wind direction or the efficiency of sail trim.

TENDER A boat that heels excessively in average winds. Also, the support boat used by syndicates to tow, observe, monitor, assist and protect their 12-Metres.

TOE RAIL Raised outer edge of the deck; on 12-Metres confined to grabrails along the foredeck rails.

TOPPING LIFT A line which prevents the spinnaker pole from falling downwards.

TRACK A metal strip which accommodates a slide or carriage supporting a block.

TRANSOM The aftermost section of the stern (see diagram).

TRAVELLER A track running across the boat, in which runs a traveller car which supports the mainsheet. This allows the boom to be kept in the same plane as it is moved in and out.

TRIM To adjust the set of the sails or the way in which the yacht sits in the

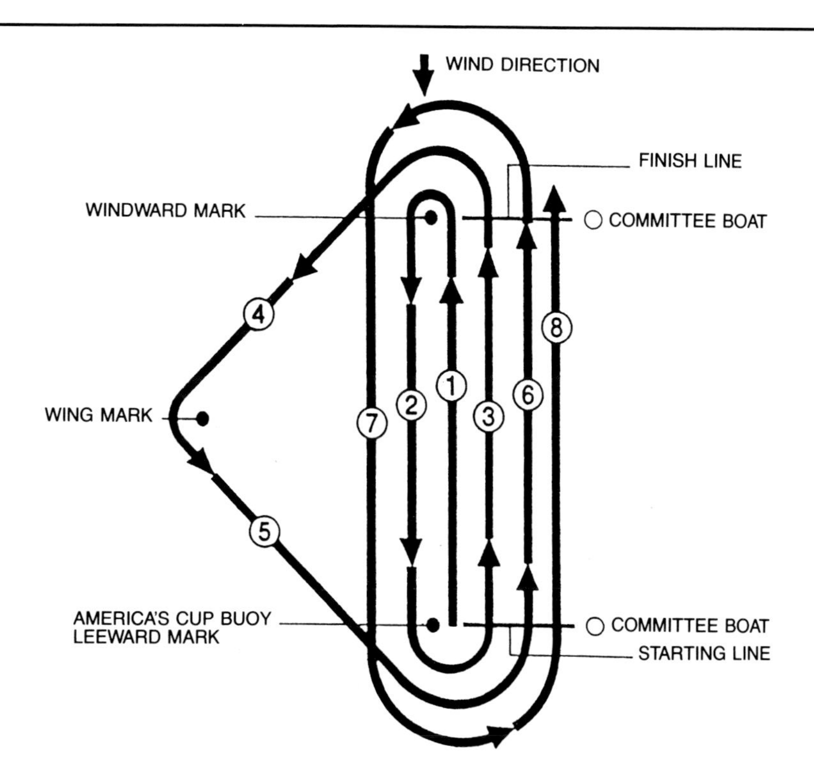

1987 AMERICA'S CUP COURSE

The course for the 1987 America's Cup is not only being sailed for the first time away from the Eastern seaboard of the United States with its predominately light winds, it is being sailed in weather and sea conditions that are totally different, with strong winds and rough seas prevailing. In addition, a new America's Cup Course which places greater emphasis on crew skills and tactics has been devised for 1987.

Gage Roads is a 10 nautical mile stretch of water between the mouth of the Swan River at Fremantle and the beach suburbs of Perth to the north, and the low and rather rugged islands of Rottnest and Garden Islands which, with a series of reefs, form a breakwater against the south-westerly swell of the Indian Ocean.

Over the years the actual type of course for the America's Cup has varied, but since 1970 it's been a standard Olympic course of 24.3 nautical miles, comprising a triangle with a windward leg of 4.5 miles, two reaching legs, another windward leg of 4.5 miles, a square run, and a final windward leg to the finish, also both of 4.5 miles distance.

For the 1987 America's Cup the defending Royal Perth Yacht Club and the Challenger of Record, Italy's Yacht Club Costa Smeralda, have agreed on a more compact course of 24.5 nautical miles.

The windward and leeward legs have been reduced to 3.25 nautical miles between marks, the reaching legs to 2.3 miles each, and to make up the full distance an extra windward and leeward leg have been introduced. The yachts will have to sail eight legs and round seven marks during the Race.

The courses will be centred on the Fairway Landfall Buoy situated 7.12 nautical miles on a true bearing of 327 degrees form the North Mole at Fremantle. This is almost midway between Rottnest Island and City Beach.

For the Challenger and Defender Trials between October and mid-January, several races will be sailed each day and up to three courses will be used. In south-westerly winds these will be centred around the Fairway Landfall Buoy and the No.1 Deepwater Buoy, while in easterly breezes the courses will have to be laid in the Outer Harbour further north. Not all these races will be over the complete 24 nautical mile course.

water.

TRIMMER Member of the crew responsible for the trim of a sail.

TRIM TAB A secondary rudder on the trailing edge of the keel (see diagram).

TRUE WIND The actual wind blowing, before it is modified by a yacht's apparent wind.

TUNING The delicate adjustment of a yacht's rigging sails and hull to achieve the balance which ensures the best sailing performance.

VANG See BOOM VANG.

VEER Change of direction, as in the wind, or a yacht's course.

VMG Velocity made good. The actual distance gained towards a mark or objective, taking into account all aspects, e.g. current, leeway speed and course sailed.

WAKE The waves created and left behind by a yacht.

WATERLINE An imaginary line around the hull at the water surface when the yacht is on an even keel (see diagram).

WEATHER HELM The amount of helm adjustment required to prevent a yacht bearing up into the wind (opposite of LEE HELM).

WEATHER SIDE The side towards the wind.

WETTED SURFACE The immersed area of a yacht's hull.

WINCH Device which provides mechanical advantage when pulling on lines under load, e.g. sheets (see diagram).

WINDWARD Towards the wind (opposite of LEEWARD).

WINGLETS Angled appendages on the bottom of the keel, intended to generate lift and reduce leeway.

WORKING SAIL Sails set on a course to windward, i.e. mainsail and genoa or jib.

12-Metre Rule

Unlike most classes the name 12-Metre does not designate a specific measurement of the yacht, in length or otherwise. Rather, the term 12-Metre refers to the figure obtained by applying a particular mathematical formula to specific dimensions of the yacht.

The formula is: $\frac{L + 2d - F + \sqrt{S}}{2.37} = 12$

In basic translation, this means that the yacht's length plus two times the girth difference minus the freeboard plus the square root of the sail area, divided by 2.37, must equal 12.

The symbols may be briefly explained as follows:

L = The yacht's length, measured at a height of 180 mm above the waterline (load waterline or LWL). Corrections for girth measurements made at the bow and stern are applied to this measurement.

d = The difference between the length of the skin girth and the length of the chain girth, measured down from the deck to a point on the keel 1500 mm below the waterline, about midships (55 per cent back along the waterline from the bow). Skin girth is measured on the surface of the hull, while chain girth is measured by stretching a line taut between the same two points. The latter is then deducted from the former to give the d measurement.

F = Freeboard, or height of the deck above the waterline. Three freeboard measurements are taken: at the bow; at the 0.55 station where girth is measured for d; and at the stern. F is then calculated as one-half of the sum of these three measurements, minus 600 mm. The freeboard at the bow must be at least 20 per cent greater than the freeboard at the midships station. The freeboard at the stern may not be rated as more than 82.5 per cent of the bow freeboard. F shall not be taken as more than 1.21 m in the formula.

S = The rated area of the mainsail and foretriangle in square metres. Rated area of the mainsail is $\frac{(A \times B)}{2}$ where A is the luff length and B is the foot length. Rated area of the foretriangle is $(0.85)\left[\frac{(I \times J)}{2}\right]$, with I the distance above the yacht's covering board sheerline at the front of the mast to the height where the forestay joins the mast, and J the distance from the front of the mast to the aft edge of the forestay at deck level.

2.37 = The mathematical constant.

These are the basic parameters of the 12-Metre formula, but there are other restrictions. Hollows are not allowed in the hull surface between the LWL and the sheerline, except in a section of the stern. Maximum draft is restricted to 16 per cent of the LWL plus 500 mm – if it is greater than this,

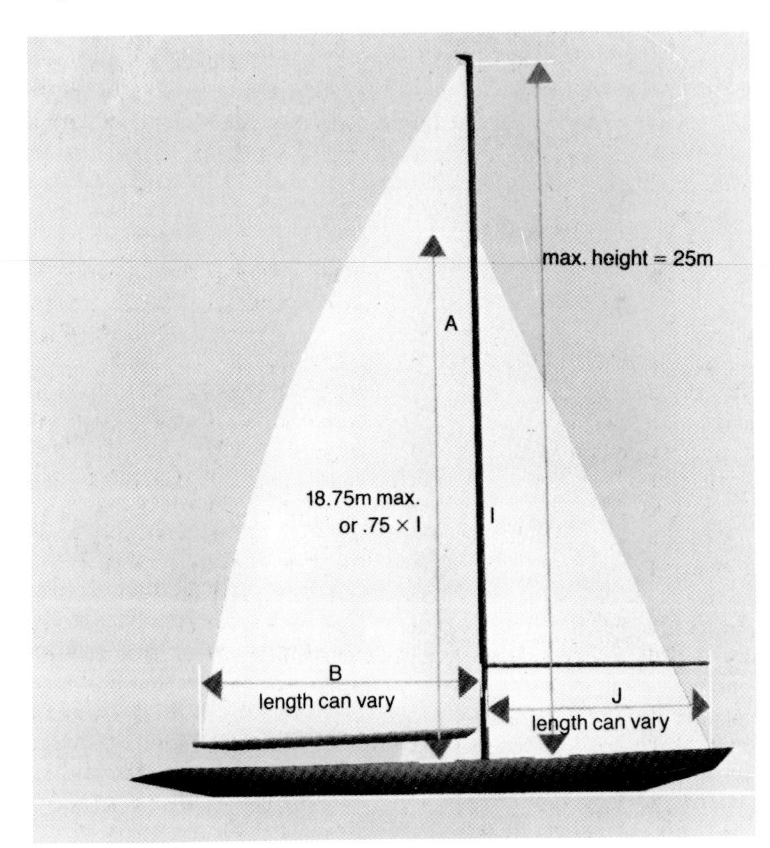

three times the excess must be added to the rating. Beam below 1.7 m of the LWL must not exceed 3.6 m.

Sheer must be a fair and continuous concave curve. Tumblehome (curvature of the yacht's topsides) will be penalised if it is more than two per cent of the extreme beam, by adding three times the excess to the rating.

Displacement in cubic metres shall not be less than $[0.2 \text{ LWL (in metres)} + 0.15]^3$, or a penalty will be incurred in the L measurement. Minimum beam, measured at one-third of the girth station freeboard, is 3.6 m or a penalty will also be incurred in the L measurement.

Maximum sail plan height above the yacht's covering board must not exceed 25.18 m. Spinnakers are restricted by the formula $0.8\sqrt{I^2 + J^2} + 2.5$ m = maximum length of luff and leech, where I is the height of the foretriangle and J is the base of the foretriangle. Foot length of spinnakers must not exceed 250 per cent of J. Spinnaker luffs and leeches must be equal in length.

Other rules govern spar specifications, the amount and type of equipment allowed to be carried, the number of deck openings and the number of crew (no more than 11 during races). In an attempt to put the brake on excessive cost, equipment other than sails must be only of materials which are easily available; metals such as tungsten, berylium and titanium are prohibited except as alloyed increments, or where they are included in standard items on sale to the general public. The use of carbon fibres in rigging is allowed, but composite materials which include fibres such as boron are prohibited. And so on.

All of the above requirements are specified by the Rating Rule and Measurement Instructions of the International Yacht Racing Union. Yachts competing for the America's Cup must also comply with requirements contained in the Deed of Gift of the America's Cup and the Interpretive Resolutions applying to national origins of design and building, and also the eligibility of crews. For example, 12-Metres competing in the Cup must be designed by nationals of the country in which the club the yacht is representing is located (this includes the yacht's hull, rig and sails), and it must be built in that country. The entire crew must also be nationals of the country of the representing club. The term "national" is interpreted as a person who has been domiciled in, or has a principal place of residence in, or has a valid passport of that country for no less than two years before the first race of the America's Cup match racing series.

In a recent interpretation, it has been deemed that designers may be permitted to use towing tank facilities in countries other than their own, but only if adequate facilities do not exist in their own countries.

America's Cup 1851-1983

Year	Winner	Loser	Country of Owner	Score
1851	AMERICA John C. Stevens Syn.	15 British yachts	England	1-0
1870	MAGIC Franklin Osgood	CAMBRIA James Ashbury	England	1-0
1871	COLUMBIA, SAPPHO Franklin Osgood & Wm. P. Douglass	LIVONIA James Ashbury	England	4-1
1876	MADELEINE John S. Dickerson	COUNTESS OF DUFFERIN Maj. Charles Gifford Syn.	Canada	2-0
1881	MISCHIEF Joseph R. Busk	ATALANTA Capt. Alex Cuthbert	Canada	2-0
1885	PURITAN J. Malcolm Forbes Syn.	GENESTA Sir Richard Sutton	England	2-0
1886	MAYFLOWER Gen. Charles J. Paine	GALATEA Lt. Wm. Henn RN	England	2-0
1887	VOLUNTEER Gen. Charles J. Paine	THISTLE James Bell Syn.	Scotland	2-0
1893	VIGILANT C. Oliver Iselin Syn.	VALKYRIE II Earl of Dunraven	England	3-0
1895	DEFENDER C. Oliver Iselin Syn.	VALKYRIE III Earl of Dunraven	England	3-0
1899	COLUMBIA J.P. Morgan Syn.	SHAMROCK I Sir Thomas Lipton	North Ireland	3-0
1901	COLUMBIA J.P. Morgan Syn.	SHAMROCK II Sir Thomas Lipton	North Ireland	3-0
1903	RELIANCE C. Oliver Iselin Syn.	SHAMROCK III Sir Thomas Lipton	North Ireland	3-0
1920	RESOLUTE Henry Walters Syn.	SHAMROCK IV Sir Thomas Lipton	North Ireland	3-2
1930	ENTERPRISE Winthrop Aldrich Syn.	SHAMROCK V Sir Thomas Lipton	North Ireland	4-0
1934	RAINBOW H.S. Vanderbilt Syn.	ENDEAVOUR T.O.M. Sopwith	England	4-2
1937	RANGER H.S. Vanderbilt Syn.	ENDEAVOUR II T.O.M. Sopwith	England	4-0
1958	COLUMBIA Henry Sears Syn.	SCEPTRE Hugh L. Goodson	England	4-0
1962	WEATHERLY Henry D. Merce	GRETEL Frank Packer Syn.	Australia	4-1
1964	CONSTELLATION W.S. Gubelman & Eric Ritter Syn.	SOVEREIGN James A.J. Boyden	England	4-0
1967	INTREPID W.J. Strawbridge Syn.	DAME PATTIE Emil Christensen	Australia	4-0
1970	INTREPID W.J. Strawbridge Syn.	GRETEL II Frank Packer Syn.	Australia	4-1
1974	COURAGEOUS R. McCullough Syn.	SOUTHERN CROSS Alan Bond	Australia	4-0
1977	COURAGEOUS King's Point Fund Inc. Syn.	AUSTRALIA Alan Bond	Australia	4-0
1980	FREEDOM Maritime College at Fort Schuyler Foundation, Inc.	AUSTRALIA Royal Perth Yacht Club	Australia	4-1
1983	AUSTRALIA II Alan Bond	LIBERTY Maritime College at Fort Schuyler Foundation, Inc.	USA	4-3